By Calvin Trillin

Jackson, 1964

RANDOM HOUSE / NEW YORK

Jackson, 1964

And Other Dispatches
from Fifty Years of Reporting
on Race in America

Calvin Trillin

Published in the United States by Random House, an imprint and division of
Penguin Random House LLC, New York.

Random House and the House colophon are registered trademarks of Penguin
Random House LLC.

All of the essays in this collection were originally published in *The New Yorker*.

LIBRARY OF CONGRESS CATALOGING-IN-PUBLICATION DATA

Names: Trillin, Calvin, author.
Title: Jackson, 1964 : and other dispatches from fifty years
of reporting on race in America / Calvin Trillin.
Description: First edition. | New York : Random House, [2016]
Identifiers: LCCN 2015045274 | ISBN 9780399588242 |
ISBN 9780399588259 (ebook)
Subjects: LCSH: United States—Race relations—History—20th century. |
Racism—United States—History—20th century. | Minorities—United
States—Social conditions—20th century. | African Americans—
Social conditions—20th century.
Classification: LCC E185.615 T76 2016 | DDC 305.80097309/04—dc23
LC record available at lccn.loc.gov/2015045274

Printed in the United States of America on acid-free paper

randomhousebooks.com

9 8 7 6 5 4 3 2 1

First Edition

Book design by Susan Turner

Once again, to Abigail and Sarah—my girls.

CONTENTS

AUTHOR'S NOTE

I'm grateful to Professor Robert Cohen of New York University, who suggested this book, and to the editors and fact-checkers at *The New Yorker,* where all of these articles and parts of the introduction first appeared. Three or four of the articles have been shortened for inclusion here, and a few repetitions have been deleted. Otherwise, the articles here appear as they did originally in *The New Yorker.* That includes whatever racial or ethnic or gender terms were in common usage at the time and place.

INTRODUCTION

I WAS ONCE THE CITY AUDITOR OF KANSAS CITY, MISSOURI.
Only for a day. It was High School Day in City Hall. The mayor for the day was Melba Zachery, who went to Lincoln—
what we would have called then, a year before the Supreme
Court's *Brown v. Board of Education* decision, a colored
school. (Lincoln was also the name of the movie theater that
Negroes went to, as well as of a couple of other retail establishments in the black neighborhood. I sometimes wonder if there were children in Kansas City who weren't aware
that Lincoln was the name of a president and not simply a
word that meant "colored people allowed.") I didn't realize
then that Missouri schools were segregated by law. There
were no WHITE ONLY signs or separate drinking fountains
in Kansas City; I never heard any speeches extolling segregation as God's will. It was taken for granted that Negroes
had their own schools in their own neighborhoods and that
white-run restaurants and white-run hotels and white-run
theaters were for white people. It was taken for granted that,
after spending a day learning about how democracy worked,
Melba Zachery would go back to her school and I would go

back to mine. At least, it was taken for granted by me. I can't speak for Melba.

At the time, a lot about race was taken for granted. Much of America was, like Kansas City, segregated without segregationist rhetoric—or segregated even though the dominant rhetoric celebrated the sort of tolerance that could enable a mostly white high school population to elect Melba Zachery mayor for a day. Among white Americans, segregation was widely thought of as a problem of the South. Racial views were assumed to be governed by geography, and a belief in white supremacy was widely considered to be a regrettable but essentially immutable regional characteristic of white Southerners, almost like bragging among Texans. It was not considered disabling.

Even after the Montgomery bus boycott and the sit-in movements—even after, that is, it was apparent that black people had taken matters into their own hands—white Southerners tended to believe that any racial strife in their part of the country was caused by meddling outsiders, probably operating on instructions from some wily, foreign-looking man in New York. "Where you from?" was likely to be the first question asked of a reporter whose dead stop at a stop sign had not lasted long enough to satisfy the deputy sheriff who pulled him over. "I work out of the Atlanta bureau" was not considered an adequate response.

I worked out of the Atlanta bureau of *Time* from the fall of 1960 to the fall of 1961, in the days when race and the South were thought of as basically the same story by national magazines. It happened to be a busy year on what local reporters sometimes called the seg beat: the sit-in movements, the desegregation of public schools in New Orleans and Atlanta, the desegregation of the University of Georgia, the Freedom Rides. In the midst of these, I watched ordinary people make momentous personal decisions—a black college student trying to decide if he'd volunteer to be on the first Freedom Ride bus into Jackson, for instance, or a Greek-immigrant diner owner with tears in his eyes telling black sit-in students in Atlanta that, as much as he sympathized with their cause, serving them would mean the end of his business.

Because Atlanta itself was going through sit-ins, boycotts, and impending school desegregation, even my weekends were spent on the seg beat. I heard so many sermons in black churches that I began holding what I called the Martin Luther King, Jr., Extended Metaphor Contest (King himself was ineligible, since he would have won in a walk every week). I knew all of the verses to "We Shall Overcome." My expense account included items like "trousers torn in racial dispute" and "after-prayer-meeting snack, Tuskegee, $3.75." I could calibrate a white Southerner's racial views by the way he pronounced the word "Negro." I'd been exposed to enough Ku Klux Klan terminology to know a kleagle from a klaxon from a klavern. In the mob scene outside Charlayne Hunter's dormitory during the turmoil that accompanied the enrollment of her and another black student, Hamilton Holmes, at the University of Georgia, I'd heard fraternity boys refer to the Ku Klux Klan, whose arrival was rumored to be imminent, as Tri Kappa.

I was aware that I was expected to keep a certain reportorial distance. I couldn't pretend that we were covering a struggle in which all sides—the side that thought, for instance, that all American citizens had the right to vote and the side that thought that people acting on such a belief should have their houses burned down—had an equally compelling case to make. It wasn't like trying to remain objective while covering the Michigan–Ohio State game. But at mass meetings I would have never put any money in the collection cup. When, at the end of the meeting, people in the congregation locked arms to sing "We Shall Overcome," I always edged away toward the exit.

In questions about when a reporter would be crossing the line from reporting on to participating in the civil rights struggle, I tended to take my cues from the late Claude Sitton, then the Southern correspondent for *The New York Times,* whose sympathy was expressed in the fairness and scrupulousness of his reporting. As the first Freedom Ride bus was about to pull out of Montgomery for Jackson, Claude and I were still standing in the Trailways station, discussing whether being on the bus would make us participants rather than reporters. Finally, we decided that it was a public bus and we had a right to buy tickets. Also, other reporters were buying tickets. We got on the bus.

Fifty years later, at a Freedom Rides commemoration in Chicago, some of those in attendance were carrying around a large book called *Breach of Peace: Portraits of the 1961 Mississippi Freedom Riders,* by Eric Etheridge. They were trying to get as many signatures of Freedom Riders as they could. Occasionally, one of them would approach me and say, "Were you a Freedom Rider?"

"No, I was just a reporter who was on the bus," I'd say.

Some of them insisted that I sign anyway, and eventually I decided that they were probably right in assuming that, after fifty years, the line between reporter and participant was not as bright as I thought it was when I worked in the South. In Chicago, I greeted John Lewis, a sharecropper's son who had grown up to be a congressman, more like an old comrade-in-arms than like someone I'd mentioned in a couple of articles. We had both been at the bus station in Montgomery when men with clubs attacked first the press and then the Freedom Riders.

I'm no longer as certain as I once was about how bright the line was even back then. During Charlayne Hunter's first semester at the University of Georgia, she was isolated in a dorm full of hostile co-eds, and we spoke on the telephone from time to time. We remain friends to this day. During one of our phone conversations, she talked about an uncomfortable train ride she'd just had from Savannah to Atlanta, and I said I'd always heard that the train she'd been on—a well-known train called the *Nancy Hanks*— was particularly luxurious. "Not where we have to sit," she said. What flashed through my mind had nothing to do with all of the knowledge I had acquired on the subject of segregation in transportation from the *Plessy v. Ferguson* decision onward. What flashed through my mind was: "They can't make *her* sit back there!" It was a moment that brought home what black people in the South in those days understood from childhood: This wasn't theoretical, it was personal.

When a session at that Freedom Ride commemoration ended with people linking arms and singing "We Shall Overcome," I made my usual quiet move toward the door. Suddenly, I felt someone link arms with me. Instinctively, I started to pull away while looking around to see who it was. It was an older woman in a wheelchair. Was I really going to wrest my arm away from an older woman in a wheelchair? I stayed. Then I joined in. It turns out that I still know most of the verses.

IN THE LATE-NIGHT COLLEGE DORM discussions I was involved in when the *Brown* decision was handed down, a year after my stint in the City Hall of Kansas City, nobody, including me, thought to wonder why our class of more than a thousand freshmen in a university located in New England included only four or five African Americans. Not long after I left Atlanta, though, it had become apparent, even to those white Americans most intent on taking things for granted, that racism was not simply a regrettable regional peculiarity. In the ensuing years, I have reported stories about race for *The New Yorker* not just in the South but also in places like Seattle and Long Island and Utah and Boston. I was still engaged by the subject when planning began for half-century commemorations of some of the events I'd covered during that year on the seg beat. At the University of Georgia, where I'd watched Charlayne Hunter and Hamilton Holmes walk through crowds of jeering undergraduates, the fiftieth-anniversary celebration, called "Celebrating Courage," went on for several weeks on a campus that now includes an edifice called the Holmes-Hunter Academic Building. There were actually two commemorations of the Freedom Ride, which I had covered from Birmingham to Montgomery to Jackson. Some former Freedom Riders attended both anniversary events, but, described in the broadest terms, the event in Jackson was a celebration of the progress made in race relations in the past fifty years, and the event in Chicago was a reminder that the dream Martin Luther King, Jr., spoke of has not arrived.

There was plenty of evidence presented for each point of view. In Chicago, alluding to some dismal statistics on living standards and education and criminal justice, the Reverend James Lawson, who had been on that first bus into Jackson, said, "We did not desegregate America. We did not dismantle the system." Lawson and some of the other leading figures in the Chicago event were still in the movement. In Jackson, where the Governor welcomed the returning Freedom Riders, it was pointed out that both the mayor and the police chief were African Americans. The Jackson *Clarion-Ledger*, so virulently racist in the early sixties that I was wary about entering the newsroom, had in later years won awards for articles that helped bring civil rights–era criminals to justice—including Byron De La Beckwith, Jr., for the murder of Medgar Evers. The Jackson airport is named for Evers. In Jackson, the Governor spoke enthusiastically of a scheme called the Freedom Trail, which would lead visitors to the sites of historic events, even atrocious historic events, in the struggle for civil rights ("We have to put our past in front of us if we're going to put our past behind us"). In Chicago, some attendees signed a statement charging that Mississippi was "stealing the legacy of the civil rights movement so they can profit from tourism."

The stories in this book can be taken as more conflicting evidence. From the vantage point of fifty years out, of course, the changes can indeed seem astonishing. Reminiscing at one of the Freedom Ride commemorations, someone said to me, "Who could have imagined, when we were in Mississippi in 1961, that we would someday have a black president?" And

I said, "When we were in Mississippi in 1961, I would have settled for a black policeman." A black citizen in Mississippi is no longer taking his life in his hands by trying to register to vote, as he might have been during the Freedom Summer of 1964. But a number of states—not just Southern states but states like Pennsylvania—have recently passed what Justice Ruth Bader Ginsburg has called "second-generation barriers," laws that are meant to suppress the non-white vote as surely as physical intimidation was in the sixties. In 1961, I watched a fraternity at the University of Georgia raise the Confederate flag in celebration of the fact that Charlayne Hunter had been suspended "for her own safety" after a mob scene that included throwing bricks at her dormitory room (Tri Kappa hadn't shown up; the fraternity boys were left to throw the bricks themselves). The Confederate flag that was installed at the South Carolina capitol around that time, presumably to symbolize defiance in the face of the *Brown* decision, was finally removed in 2015, after nine African Americans were murdered in a Charleston church. Progress? Slow progress?

Partly because of the advent of cell-phone and dashboard cameras, the killing of a black man by a white policeman is probably a more common item on the nightly news now than it was when I wrote about such an incident in Seattle in 1975. I haven't heard recently of someone being sentenced to thirty years for giving away a marijuana cigarette, as Lee Otis Johnson, a black radical in Houston, was in 1968. Lately, though, even conservatives have begun to question whether the mass incarceration of black males, often with severe sentences for nonviolent crimes, is not only unjust but counterproductive. Legally sanctioned school segregation has been gone for decades, but a 2013 report by the Economic Policy Institute said, "Today, African American students are more isolated than they were 40 years ago, while most education policymakers and reformers have abandoned integration as a cause." In other words, the presence of what we would have called colored schools is taken for granted. A lot, in fact, is still taken for granted, just as it was when I was the city auditor of Kansas City, Missouri, and Melba Zachery was the mayor.

Jackson, 1964

JACKSON, 1964

Jackson, Mississippi
1964

TO PEOPLE WHO HAPPEN TO BE ADMIRERS OF SPANISH CIVIL
War literature, Jackson as the headquarters of the Mississippi Summer Project is likely to conjure up visions of
Madrid as the capital of the Spanish Loyalists. Physically,
Jackson could hardly look less like Madrid, but the Summer Project—a statewide program of voter registration and
other civil rights activities being carried out by some six hundred volunteers and some one hundred paid workers—is so
thoroughly caught up in a tangle of frenetic planning and
propagandizing that a reader of George Orwell and Ernest
Hemingway half expects to come across military strategists
mapping out campaigns against mountain villages or to see
clusters of ideologists arguing and plotting in small, dark
bars, their conversations occasionally interrupted by a stray
bomb. One difference, of course, is that the Council of Federated Organizations, or COFO—the amalgam of civil rights
groups that runs the Summer Project—does not actually con-

trol even the part of Jackson where it is permitted to exist, and there are constant reminders of who does. A number of editorialists and columnists on the Jackson daily newspapers are not merely segregationists but segregationists of the type who are inclined to indicate their position by referring to Martin Luther King, Jr., as "the Rev. Dr. Extremist Agitator Martin Luther King, Jr.," or by suggesting that President Johnson's theme song should be "The High Yellow Rose of Texas," or by telling cannibal jokes; the community bulletin board of a local radio station occasionally includes, among reports of rummage sales and church suppers, the announcement that Americans for the Preservation of the White Race will hold its weekly meeting that evening and "all interested white people are invited to attend"; the chatty gray-haired lady in charge of a local bookstore, whose inventory appears to begin with the writings of the John Birch Society and move to the right, is available for political arguments with the civil rights workers she refers to amiably as "those COFO things"; one can telephone Dial for Truth, a recorded announcement by the Jackson Citizens' Council of the evils that race-mixing has brought upon the world during the previous week; and the Mississippi Numismatic Exchange, Inc., has a sign in its window reading, KENNEDY HALF DOLLARS 25¢. THAT'S ALL WE THINK THEY'RE WORTH! (The sign says in smaller letters that the case that goes along with one costs fifty cents.)

Still, Jackson, which prides itself on maintaining law and order, has been relatively careful about protecting civil rights workers, and there has not been enough civil rights action within the city limits to provide what COFO people tend to call a confrontation; all in all, the city is more of a communications-and-planning center than a scene of battle. At the COFO headquarters, a storefront office on Lynch Street, in the Negro business district, efficient white girls in cotton print dresses decorate the walls daily with fresh "incident reports" listing arrests or beatings of COFO workers in other parts of the state, but whenever the stray bomb lands—as on the second day of my visit, when two workers were beaten, though not seriously, just a few blocks from the COFO office—the first reaction is that somebody must have broken a truce or wandered out of a demilitarized zone by mistake. At the office, COFO workers in overalls and work shirts who have come into Jackson on errands from small towns in the Delta stroll in and out, and members of the office staff shuttle back and forth incessantly between a row of typewriters and a row of telephones. On Farish Street, in another part of the Negro business district, two groups of lawyers use offices across the street from one another—each on the top floor of a drab two-story building—to deal with the litigation brought on by the constant civil rights arrests. In an office nearby, the National Council of Churches, which has provided ministers, lawyers, and the training facilities for the Summer Project, regularly holds orientation sessions for new arrivals, and a group of respectable-looking clergymen regularly watch quietly as a COFO worker demonstrates how to protect one's kidneys when knocked down. ("Is it considered permissible to get in a punch or two and then run?" a young minister asked the day I was there. "How good a runner are you?" the COFO demonstrator asked in reply.) Over in the white business district, workmen are installing an interior staircase in the expanded FBI office, which now occupies one floor and part of another of the new First Federal Savings & Loan Building, and is still in the unpackaging stage, with crates on the floor and pictures of J. Edgar Hoover leaning against the wall. At the state capitol, a few blocks to the north, where a statue of Governor (and Senator) Theodore Bilbo, the late racist, dominates the ground floor, and vividly tinted portraits of Mississippi's two Miss Americas are enshrined in the rotunda, investigators for the State Sovereignty Commission, the agency charged with preserving segregation, go through Negro newspapers, civil rights literature, and the *Worker* in order to keep track of which left-wingers are where. All in all, there are so many visitors in town that it is practically impossible to rent a car, and the provision of restaurant and hotel accommodations for the visitors has become a minor industry. Under these circumstances, a conversation about the Catalan separatists or the anarchists of the POUM might not sound out of place, but instead the visitors talk about SNCC (called "Snick" and standing for the Student Nonviolent Coordinating Committee), or the National Council (of Churches), or the LCDC (Lawyers Constitutional Defense Committee), or the (National) Lawyers Guild, or the APWR (Americans for the Preservation of the White Race), or the Citizens' Council, or the Klan.

JACKSON HAS NEVER STOOD APART from the rest of Mississippi the way Atlanta has stood apart from Georgia, say, or New Orleans from Louisiana. Traditionally, it has merely been a larger town than the other towns in the state, and not until after World War II was it very much larger. In 1940, it had a population of sixty-two thousand. Now, however, with a population of a hundred and fifty thousand and with ambitions for further expansion, Jackson is the logical place to expect to see any significant indications of moderation on the race issue in Mississippi—simply because it now has the most to lose through the chaos that total defiance of federal desegregation provisions could bring. Such indications appeared recently when it began to look as though the city might comply peacefully with a federal court order that schools start desegregating this fall, and when the board of directors of the Chamber of Commerce made a surprise statement advising businessmen to comply with the public accommodations section of the new civil rights law. After the fact, it is not difficult to find a number of good reasons for the Chamber's statement. This summer marks the first time Jackson businessmen have ever been faced with anything approaching the power of a federal law. Previously, it was possible to see the conflict as one between the state and a group of Negroes; the civil rights law expanded it, potentially, into one between each individual businessman and the federal government. (There is a theory in Jackson that Mississippi fell victim to its own propaganda; that is, there was so much publicity about how a civil rights law could result in a decent American businessman's being hauled off to court or to jail by the federal dictator for choosing his own customers that the local businessmen were psychologically prepared for an early surrender.) It is said that business in Jackson was damaged somewhat by the demonstrations and boycotts of last summer, and that businessmen—particularly those directly affected by the law—were happy to be able to make the inevitable transition peacefully by blaming it on the federal government, especially since many of them apparently believed (erroneously) that all those COFO things in town were likely to stage an impressive demonstration for all the FBI people in town on the Fourth of July. Although the national headquarters of the Citizens' Councils of America is in Jackson, the local Council has never embraced all the important businessmen, as it does in some smaller Mississippi towns, and the suggestion has been made that its point of view seemed to be dominant only because a segregation issue of vital importance to business had not come up. According to one person who was close to those who drafted the Chamber's statement, "Folks didn't realize the number of people here who are able to recognize the inevitable when it arrives." Those people, who had remained silent while the inevitable was approaching, acted with a suddenness that caught the Citizens' Council element by surprise. There is reason to believe that their action will result in preserving almost complete segregation while avoiding public disturbance—since the facilities, if made available without challenge, are not likely to be used by a great many Jackson Negroes—but in the past, even that argument was not enough to justify a public statement in favor of desegregation. So while people familiar with Jackson are able to explain why such a statement was wise, they admit surprise that it was issued. The Chamber's statement, according to one member of its board, was "a calculated risk," and once it had succeeded—of the fourteen hundred firms affiliated with the Chamber, only four resigned—there was bound to be less pressure against those willing to recognize the possibility of change in Mississippi.

A few days after the Chamber advised compliance, the mayor of Jackson supported its stand, and a week or so after that, when Mississippians for Public Education, a group composed mainly of housewives, announced its existence and its intention of opposing any scheme that might damage the public schools—such as the establishment of private segregated schools supported by state tuition grants—its members, to their amazement, met with practically no abuse. Four days after the group's announcement, its president had received only two letters criticizing her position (one of them asked, among other things, if she realized that "academic standards have fell in any place that has had integration"), and none of the officers in Jackson had received a single unsigned hate letter or late-night phone call.

Still, much of Jackson's inclination toward compliance can be explained not by any decrease in segregationist feeling in Jackson but by an increase in pressure from the outside. Desegregating restaurants in compliance with a federal law is quite a different thing from desegregating them through negotiations with local Negroes, and now that ten years have passed since the original Supreme Court decision, federal courts have eliminated practically every alternative to obeying a school desegregation order. All the fund cutoffs, school closings, and various postures for standing in the schoolhouse door have lost most of their force even as ritual. It is clear to most people in Jackson that the public schools will be desegregated no matter what opposition is put up— something that was apparently not clear to many of them before the University of Mississippi desegregation—and about all that the last session of the legislature could think of to do about it was to provide tuition grants for those who wanted to attend private segregated schools. The immediate effect on the rest of the state of the Jackson Chamber's statement is expected to be limited. The important long-range effect of both the Chamber's statement and the appearance of Mississippians for Public Education is that, in the words of a Jackson lawyer, "some crack has been made in that wall of Never."

The wall of Never was built on the proposition that in Mississippi complete segregation could be maintained without violence by means of rigid control—some say police-state control—within the state and a united front against outside pressure. As the outside pressure becomes greater and more firmly supported by law, there is often no way to oppose it except by lawlessness. Many of this summer's incidents—the burning of Negro churches unconnected with civil rights activity, for instance—are typical not of the systematic intimidation associated with the Citizens' Councils but of the irrational violence indulged in by terrorist groups of a sort that cannot be controlled by strategists in Jackson. Organizations such as the Klan and the APWR hardly existed in Mississippi a year or two ago, and although the administration of Governor Paul Johnson has not condemned them out of hand, it has discouraged people from joining them. Although Governor Johnson did advise businessmen not to comply with the Civil Rights Act until it had been tested in the courts, he is still considered quite a bit less extreme than former governor Ross Barnett, and there are certainly indications that the state has tried to avoid trouble that might bring federal intervention on a large scale. When Martin Luther King, Jr., visited the state recently in support of the Freedom Democratic Party (a predominantly Negro political party that is attempting to unseat the regular Mississippi delegation at the Democratic Convention, on the theory that the regular party cannot represent people it prevents from voting), he was carefully, if unobtrusively, protected by the state as well as by the FBI. Outright violence against COFO workers has been officially discouraged, and despite the murder of the three civil rights workers in Philadelphia during the Summer Project's first week, there has been less of it than many people expected. Those in control of the state would much prefer to deal with COFO by calling its workers Communists and beatniks and by arresting them for some crime such as distributing leaflets.

I HAPPENED TO FLY FROM Atlanta to Jackson on the same plane as Martin Luther King, Jr., who was about to begin his tour of Mississippi with some speeches and meetings in Greenwood. He was accompanied by four of his aides in the Southern Christian Leadership Conference—Andrew Young, C. T. Vivian, Bernard Lee, and Dorothy Cotton—and except that all of them are Negroes and that the men were wearing buttons in their lapels that said S.C.L.C. FREEDOM NOW, the group might have been thought to consist of a corporation executive off to make a sales-conference speech accompanied by efficient, neatly dressed young assistants brought along to handle arrangements and take care of the paperwork. As the plane left Atlanta, Young began going through a number of file folders, making notes on a legal-size yellow pad and occasionally passing them up to King, who paused in his reading of the *Times* and the news magazines now and then to consult with Young or Mrs. Cotton. Lee opened *The Souls of Black Folk*, by W.E.B. Du Bois, and Mrs. Cotton brought out a copy of *Southern Politics in State and Nation*, by V. O. Key, Jr., which she read when she wasn't talking with King. Across the aisle from King, there happened to be sitting a stocky, nice-looking young white man with a short haircut and wearing Ivy League clothes. He looked as if he might have been a responsible member of a highly regarded college fraternity six or eight years ago and was now an equally responsible member of the Junior Chamber of Commerce of a Southern city that prided itself on its progress. About halfway between Atlanta and Montgomery, the plane's first stop, he leaned across the aisle and politely said to King, in a thick drawl, "Excuse me. I heard them calling you Dr. King. Are you Martin Luther King?"

"Yes, I am," said King, just as politely.

"I wonder if I could ask you two questions," the young man said, and Young, Vivian, and Lee, all of whom were sitting behind King, leaned forward to hear the conversation. "I happen to be a Southerner, but I also happen to consider myself a Christian. I wonder, do you feel you're teaching Christian love?"

"Yes, that's my basic approach," King said. "I think love is the most durable element in the world, and my whole approach is based on that."

"Do you think the people you preach to have a feeling of love?" the young man asked.

"Well, I'm not talking about weak love," King explained. "I'm talking about love with justice. Weak love can be sentimental and empty. I'm talking about the love that is strong, so that you love your fellow men enough to lead them to justice."

"Do you think that's the same love Jesus taught?" the young man asked.

"Yes, I do."

"Even though you incite one man against another?"

"You have to remember that Christ was crucified by people who were against him," said King, still in a polite, careful tone. "Do you think there's love in the South now? Do you think white people in the South love Negroes?"

"I anticipated that," said the young man. "There hasn't always been love. I admit we've made some mistakes."

"Uh-huh. Well, let me tell you some of the things that have happened to us. We were slaves for two hundred and fifty years. We endured one hundred years of segregation. We have been brutalized and lynched. Can't you understand that the Negro is bound to have some resentment? But I preach that despite this resentment, we should organize militantly but nonviolently. If we organize nonviolently, we can show the injustice. I don't think you'd be talking to me now if we hadn't had some success in making people face the issue."

"I happen to be a Christian," the young man repeated.

"Do you think segregation is Christian?" asked King.

"I was anticipating that," the young man said. "I don't have any flat answer. I'm questioning your methods as causing more harm than good."

"Uh-huh. Well, what do you suggest we need?" King was able to say "uh-huh" in a way that implied he had registered a remark for what it was worth and decided not to bring up its more obvious weaknesses, but he and the young man did seem genuinely interested in each other's views.

"I think we need respect and goodwill," said the young man.

"How do you propose to get that?" King asked.

The young man hesitated for a moment and then said, "I don't know. I just don't agree that it does any good to incite people. I know there's resentment, and you're able to capitalize on this resentment and create friction and incite discord. And you know this."

"I don't think we're inciting discord but exposing discord," King said.

"Well, let me ask you this," said the young man. "Are you concerned that certain people—well, let's come out with political labels—that this plays into the hands of the Communists?"

"I think segregation and discrimination play into the hands of the Communists much more than the efforts to end them," said King.

"But it's certainly been playing into the Communists' hands since you and the others—as you put it—started exposing what was there. There's certainly more attention given to it."

"Don't you think that if we don't solve this the Communists will have more to gain?"

"I think much more progress was made between the two races before the last few years, when you and other people started inciting trouble between the two races."

"What is this progress?" asked King. "Where was the lunch-counter desegregation? Where was the civil rights law?"

"In good relations," the young man answered.

"Good white relations," interrupted Vivian, who apparently felt unable to keep out of the argument any longer.

"Well, I just wanted to ask those questions," said the young man. He seemed ready to end the discussion.

"Uh-huh," said King. "Well, I'd like to be loved by everyone, but we can't always wait for love. Maybe you ought to read my writings. I've done quite a bit of writing on nonviolence."

"Well, I think you are causing violence," the young man said.

"Would you condemn the robbed man for possessing the money to be robbed?" asked King. "Would you condemn Christ for having a commitment to truth that drove men to crucify him? Would you condemn Socrates for having the views that forced the hemlock on him? Society must condemn the robber, not the man he robs."

"I don't want to discuss our philosophical differences," said the young man. "I just wanted to ask you those questions."

"Uh-huh. Well, I'm sorry you don't think I'm a Christian."

"I didn't say that."

"Well, I'm sorry that you don't think that what I preach is Christian, and I'm sorry you don't think segregation is unchristian."

King turned back to his paper for a few moments, as if the conversation had ended—without progress but with no animosity—and then he looked up and said to the young man, "What do you think of the new civil rights law? Do you think that's a good law?"

"Well, I haven't read it, but I think parts of it just carry on the trend toward federal dictatorship."

"You sound like a good Goldwaterite," said King with a slight smile. "Are you going to vote for Goldwater?"

"Yes, I expect I will," the young man said.

"It's too bad you're going to back a loser, because I'm afraid we're going to hand him a decisive defeat in November." King's tone was light; he might have been joking with a longtime neighbor who had always been a member of the opposing political party.

"I've voted for losers before," said the young man.

King turned back to his reading, and Vivian said, "What do you mean by federal dictatorship?"

The white man didn't seem anxious to take on a fresh adversary, but he replied, "I think everything should be done at the lowest level of government."

"How about all the federal hospitals? The roads?" said Vivian. "You say you want the federal government to stay out of everything unless it has to do it. That's why you have those hospitals and roads in Georgia, because Georgia was too poor to pay for them. Do you know how much more Mississippi takes from the federal government per person than it puts in? You didn't start talking about federal dictatorship until it came to race—"

"Are you asking me a question or making a speech?" said the young man.

"Both," Vivian said.

King looked up from his paper and smiled across at the young man. "We're all preachers, you see," he explained, and then turned to discuss something with Mrs. Cotton as the young man was making a point to Vivian.

"You must be talking about Toynbee's book," said Vivian, and he launched into a rapid-fire series of questions about Toynbee's theories on race.

"There's no need to debate this," the young man said finally, and he began to look out the window. At Montgomery, he walked off the plane.

"What do you think of that?" King asked, shaking his head as the white man left. "Such a young man, too. Those are the people who are rallying to Goldwater. You can't get to him. His mind has been cold so long, there's nothing that can get to him."

The young man returned to the plane before it left Montgomery, but with a quick, embarrassed smile, he walked past King and the others and settled in a rear seat.

Lunch was served between Montgomery and Meridian, and afterward Lee went to sleep and Young crossed the aisle to talk with Vivian about arrangements for that night. "I called the Justice Department today, and they said they think we should go back to Jackson after the meeting," he said.

"I don't like to have Dr. King on the road at night," Vivian replied.

"Apparently, Greenwood is the kind of place now where a mob might form," said Young. "They came right into the Negro neighborhood a few months ago to get the kids at the SNCC office."

"I never know if the Justice Department knows something it's not telling us," said Vivian. "But I hate to be on the road."

"Even with a state patrol escort?"

"That state patrol isn't a patrol," Vivian said.

"I hear they were pretty good with the congressmen who went down there," said Young.

"Well, maybe so."

"Well, let's see what the mood is when we get there," Young said in conclusion. He walked across the aisle, lowered the back of his seat, and soon went to sleep. In front of him, King was engrossed in a newsmagazine.

* * *

A NUMBER OF THE WHITE Mississippians who do not consider COFO workers Communists or beatniks—and they are clearly in the minority—believe that the presence of people who *look* like Communists or beatniks is enough to alarm the residents of a small, churchbound, isolated Mississippi town, even if it is not the sort of town whose sheriff ordinarily shows his alarm by beating up strangers. Mississippians have given a good deal of attention to the appearance of the COFO workers—who favor overalls, old shirts, and, in some cases, beards—and particularly to the appearance of the white volunteers. Although it is true that the people attracted to the Summer Project include some who would qualify as beatniks in Mississippi, where the word is defined broadly, the great majority of the volunteers are white college students who tend to dress the way their hosts dress. As it happens, COFO is, for all practical purposes, a project of the Student Nonviolent Coordinating Committee (the participation of the other national civil rights organizations involved—the Congress of Racial Equality, the National Association for the Advancement of Colored People, and the Southern Christian Leadership Conference—ranges from limited to nominal), so the style-setters are the staff members of SNCC, which may once have been a coat-and-tie organization but is no longer. With their overalls, SNCC field-workers often wear the flat-topped, broad-brimmed straw hats that are popular among rural Negroes in Mississippi; James Forman, the Negro executive secretary of SNCC, who has set up headquarters in Greenwood for the summer, is usually seen in blue jeans; and the founder and director of the Summer Project, a twenty-nine-year-old Negro SNCC worker named Robert Moses, who has been in Mississippi for three years, wears work pants and a T-shirt even when he is in New York trying to raise money. What has been obscured by all the talk about the volunteers being beatniks is that the dress of the COFO workers is really quite significant as an indication of how deeply the protest movement has changed in the few years since Negro students—some of them the same ones who are now involved in COFO—sat at dingy dime-store lunch counters dressed in freshly pressed three-button suits. Moses has remarked, "This movement is pointed in a different direction—not toward the downtown white but toward the rural Negro, not toward acceptance by the white community but toward the organization of political and other kinds of expression in the Negro community; or really toward the organization of a Negro society. And the dress is a symbol of that."

"Basically, we're dealing with poor people, and these are the people we identify with," Forman has explained. "It even affects our salary scale. One reason it's so low is just lack of money, but another reason is that we think you can't come out from a nice hotel every day to work with these people and then go back at night. Besides, in Mississippi, as a practical matter, you have to look like a rural Negro in order to get to talk to a rural Negro. And then we have to move a lot, and there's no use wearing a coat and tie if you're likely to end up sleeping on the floor. Another thing that's operating here, too, consciously or unconsciously, is: Why should we have to comb our hair and put on a coat and tie to get what are basically our rights? The student movement was positive, and without it we couldn't have had this, but it was also defensive—to show people we were clean. This is a different game. Also, there's a certain mystique about the dress, a certain morale factor. Maybe we've overdone it; it's almost a uniform now. A lot of this summer's volunteers went out and bought blue denim shirts and overalls. They thought they had to have them."

The attitude toward clothing has its counterpart in other phases of the Summer Project. In 1960, the Atlanta sit-in movement—which, admittedly, was even more middle-class than the movements in most cities—avoided association with CORE, partly because of a belief that it was too far left politically. COFO, against the advice of many of its Northern-liberal supporters, and after a good deal of internal debate, decided to accept help from the National Lawyers Guild—which is sometimes accused of being pro-Communist—because its leaders believed that the need for competent lawyers was desperate enough to make the loss of Northern-liberal support worth risking in order to get them. (It was partly in response that the Northern liberals sent lawyers of their own, whose help COFO was also happy to accept.) The Freedom Houses that COFO has established in a number of communities throughout the state to lodge its workers, and the other accommodations it has arranged in private homes, are usually interracial and unchaperoned. The COFO answer to suggestions that this might be bad strategy is that Mississippi does not have a renters' market in Freedom Houses and it is more important to send as many workers as possible to whatever houses are available than to worry about antagonizing local whites, who are likely to be antagonistic anyway. "When I first came down here, I walked down the street to the courthouse with two local Negroes, and some people tried to beat my brains out," Moses says. "If you get the most extreme reaction to the most innocent move, you might as well do what you want. This isn't an army. We can't call up people in the field one day and say now the Communist issue will be imposed, and call up another day and say now the dress-up-and-clean-up issue will be imposed, or now the white-girl issue will be imposed. These people are risking their lives. They have to make their own decisions, and they tend to emphasize their involvement rather than disguise it. We really look upon all these things—the political arguments of the thirties and the forties, the impressions of the whites— as impositions from the outside."

At the heart of SNCC's lack of concern with the impressions that its people make is the fact that its interest is not in having Negroes accepted into Mississippi society but in changing Mississippi society; its approach is—in the pure sense of the word, rather than in the sense more common here this summer—radical. The decision to begin with the most impenetrable state, Mississippi, was itself radical. The SNCC approach since 1961—when the organization, then almost dormant, decided to hire full-time field-workers rather than merely to coordinate the activities of college students— has been split between direct action and voter registration, sometimes combined to produce what Forman calls "community mobilization." SNCC was convinced from the outset that Mississippi had to be cracked, but soon discovered that direct action, which ran into a stone wall of high bails and severe jail sentences, was not the right method of cracking it. (Today, Jackson businessmen need have no fear of COFO demonstrating in restaurants. As a matter of strategy, SNCC leaders prefer to keep the Mississippi conflict based on the most fundamental constitutional right—the right to vote—and as a matter of philosophy, they do not consider restaurant integration particularly relevant in Mississippi; in fact, they do not even patronize the restaurants that have desegregated under the civil rights law. "Sure we could go to the desegregated restaurants," Moses says. "But could the Jackson Negro who might get fired for it go there? And how about the Negro who makes fifteen dollars a week?") It was also in 1961 that Moses—an intense, soft-spoken, and self-effacing young man who graduated from Hamilton College, got a master's degree in philosophy from Harvard, and had been teaching mathematics at the Horace Mann School in New York—went South to see what he could do to help. Working as a SNCC field secretary, Moses moved from one city to the next until he found a place where there was no established Negro leadership to resent him as an outsider: That turned out to be rural southwest Mississippi. At that time, some SNCC leaders believed that the Justice Department was advising concentration on voter registration to divert civil rights groups from the more explosive field of direct action, but Moses discovered that, as he later said, "in Mississippi voter registration was itself an act of confrontation," and one that could eventually result in the most fundamental changes.

So far, in Mississippi, the confrontation has continued to be more significant than the registration. The simplest way to misunderstand the Mississippi Summer Project is to think of it as a project whose primary aim is to achieve a gradual increase in the Negro vote. Because of Mississippi's complicated literacy tests, the fear and apathy of its Negroes, and the range of intimidation available to its whites, COFO, at its current pace, will never register enough Negroes in the state to make any difference. In his speeches throughout Mississippi, Martin Luther King, Jr., in calling for federally appointed marshals to register voters in some counties, pointed out that for all the extraordinary efforts of the past three years, even at slightly better than the present rate, it would take a hundred and thirty-five years to register half the state's eligible Negro voters. The Voter Education Project—a coordinated voter-registration effort supported by foundation grants and administered by the respected Southern Regional Council—supported SNCC's Mississippi registration drive for two years and then withdrew, on the ground that an organization committed to registering Negro voters would never be able to justify the expenditure of any money in Mississippi. The organization's second annual report declared, "V.E.P. has only been able to add 3,871 voters to the rolls in Mississippi during the past two years, a figure lower than the results from a single small city like Brunswick or Decatur, Georgia, or Winston-Salem, North Carolina. . . . We only hope that the situation improves before V.E.P. goes out of existence, but it will not change appreciably without massive federal action."

Not only is it difficult to get Negroes registered in Mississippi, but it is almost impossible even to find out how many Negroes have been registered; information is so skimpy that the figure usually quoted for Negro registration—twenty-eight thousand, which many people believe is an overestimate—has as its original source a 1955 University of Mississippi master's thesis.

Moses is interested in registering Negroes, and still more interested in breaking through their fear enough to convince them that they should try to register. Most of all, though, having found that in almost any town a small group of Negroes could be built around voting, he sees voter registration as a means of organizing a society. Arguing that "you can't have a political revolution in a vacuum," he maintains that without organizing themselves and creating leaders of their own, Negroes in Mississippi will not be able to use the vote effectively when it comes, and will also never be able to help themselves socially and economically. Almost everything that COFO does has two or three purposes, in addition to the basic idea that there is value in organizing Mississippi Negroes and "shaking up the state" no matter what the purpose. The Freedom Schools set up by COFO in some thirty Mississippi communities may teach Negro teenagers enough civics and English to help them pass the voting test someday, but they also provide a means of improving the teenagers' pitiful education, of permitting them, for the first time, some freedom of inquiry, and of developing leaders who are not afraid to lead. (A large percentage of SNCC's Mississippi staff is composed of young people who have been recruited over the past three years by Moses and others during the organizing of Mississippi communities.) The Freedom Democratic Party is partly a means of demonstrating how many Negroes would vote if they were permitted to, partly a means of inspiring Negroes to vote, partly a means of teaching them the rudiments of political structure, and, inevitably, partly a means of just organizing. This constant organizing of lower-class Negroes means that the civil rights movement, which, until the past two or three years, was largely a middle-class movement in the South, is now much more deeply concerned with social and economic problems. COFO has established community centers that are basically social-work centers, and it has a branch, called Federal Programs, that investigates discrimination in the distribution of federal funds and also tries to show Negroes how to get the federal aid that they are entitled to. Among SNCC workers, "bourgeois" is widely used as a term of insult.

The concern with social and economic problems reflects the views of Moses, who describes himself as merely an organizer and seems to have no interest in being a "civil rights leader." Many of those who work with him consider him, quite simply, a saint. "You should hear him talk to some of these people," one of them told me. "I heard him in Ruleville once talking to a church full of farm laborers. He said, 'This spring, you're going to see a plane overhead and something is going to come out of the back, and that will be weed-killer, and it will kill all the weeds in the cotton field. That means that nobody will be chopping cotton this spring. Then, this fall, you're going to see a machine go up and down the rows of cotton, and that will be an automatic cotton-picker. And that means there will be nobody picking cotton this fall. That airplane and that cotton-picker together are automation. Now, everybody say "automation." "Automation" means that a lot of people won't be eating this winter. But don't go to Chicago, because you won't be eating there, either. So we'll set up a food program to hold you for a while, and we'll organize and see what we can do.'"

After three years of such efforts, Moses does not have to be told that any significant improvement in either the economic or the political lot of Mississippi Negroes is going to require changes from the outside. The Summer Project was set up as one way to go about getting them. In the eyes of some of the SNCC leaders, the Project, which grew out of the participation of Yale and Stanford students in a mock election last fall, had certain drawbacks. There were fears of efficient, well-educated Northern whites taking over the movement, of undermining the painfully built self-confidence of Mississippi Negroes through receiving help from whites, and of a strong backlash when the volunteers left. Countering these fears was a realization not only of all the work that five or six hundred volunteers could do but of the remarkable opportunity that the Summer Project presented for drawing the rest of the country into some involvement with Mississippi rather than a casual dismissal of the state as hopeless. Over the past year or two, SNCC leaders have found that the personal involvement of Northern whites—and particularly of well-educated, well-connected Northern whites—creates a pressure that otherwise would be missing. "We've operated in the past three years on the theory that the two things the local segregationists don't want are more federal involvement in any way at all and more public focus," Forman says. "Our problem is how to get the government to do what it's supposed to do. How can you get the Justice Department to press certain suits, for instance? One way is to make a lot of noise about the fact that they're not doing it, create a public consensus, get people to call in about it, and make it easier for the government to act. It's a question of balancing opposing forces."

Federal involvement—or federal intervention, or federal presence—is a much-discussed subject in Jackson, and most people close to COFO believe that what its leaders are divided over is not whether federal involvement is desirable but simply what form it should take and what should be done to get it. Almost everybody in COFO denies any desire to see federal military occupation, and it is often pointed out that having a hundred and fifty FBI agents in the state this summer, instead of a mere fifteen or so, even if they keep insisting that they are not there to protect anybody, is a huge increase in federal presence. The theory advanced by some Northern columnists and editorialists after the disappearance of the three murdered civil rights workers in Philadelphia that the summer volunteers are being used as unwitting martyrs to provoke federal intervention infuriates even Moses, whose composure is ordinarily awesome. Having been in Mississippi for three years, virtually by himself and almost completely ignored, Moses is understandably irritated at the implication that he is a Machiavellian who sits in an office somewhere, coldly sending innocents to the slaughter. COFO leaders point out that the Summer Project volunteers were repeatedly warned ahead of time of the dangers they would be facing, that they are not sent to places where violence is considered to be what Moses calls "repeatable" (the southwest area of the state, around Natchez, is such an area), and that a good deal of time is spent in setting up elaborate security arrangements. Still, they acknowledge that protection for Negroes in Mississippi is likely to be provided only when whites are involved and that ordinary pressures, such as publicizing incidents and writing to congressmen, probably would not have brought in the FBI if the murders had not occurred. No sophisticated study of public opinion is needed to establish the fact that in the United States, North or South, a white life is considered to be of more value than a Negro life. In the mimeographed newspaper published by the COFO Freedom School in Holly Springs, a local girl wrote,

"When we heard about the three freedom workers missing we were hurt but not shocked because many of our people have come up missing and nothing was said or done about it. Ever since I can remember I have been told of such cases from my people. But never have I heard it said on the news or over the T.V. or radio."

In discussing federal involvement, SNCC people tend to go no further with specific suggestions than Forman's statement that the government ought to do "what it's supposed to do." Moses says, "It's not our function to decide what form federal pressure should take; it's our function to holler loud, and that's what we do. It's a matter of whether Americans have the right to vote. I don't see how the country can come out with a negative answer—unless Goldwater gets in. We want to demonstrate to the Negro community, the country, the federal government. The presence of the FBI in Mississippi is a big step. If they're not able to maintain control, the symbolic presence of marshals may be needed in the worst counties. The point is that the fact of the terror is out in the open, and the country has to do something about that." Moses believes that a breakthrough could come through litigation that would eventually result in a court ruling supporting SNCC's thesis of "One Man, One Vote." He has particular faith in a favorable decision on the case of *U.S. v. Mississippi,* a suit that has been instituted by the Justice Department and that would result in the elimination of most of the legal obstacles to Negro registration. Moses has also been heartened by a recent decision in Panola County, where a federal judge invoked what is known as "the freeze theory" for the first time, ordering the county registrar to ignore the prescribed voting tests for Negroes for a period of a year, on the ground that the tests had been ignored for a number of years in the registration of whites. Favorable action on *U.S. v. Mississippi* would take at least a year—it is now on appeal to the Supreme Court after being dismissed by a three-judge federal court in Mississippi—and freeze-theory rulings would have to be based on evidence in eighty-two separate suits, one for each of Mississippi's eighty-two counties. Moses seems prepared to wait—despite the idealism implied by his presence in Mississippi, he gives the impression of being a remarkably realistic man—but even his patience has limits. Upon being asked what he would do if a favorable ruling on *U.S. v. Mississippi* did not serve to stop the subterfuge and intimidation, he said, "We'd set up our own election, call in observers, and ask that we be recognized as the true government of Mississippi."

Other members of COFO are still less patient, and many people who are basically sympathetic to the Summer Project believe that some of those involved in it welcome the antagonism of Mississippi whites as the best way to get large-scale federal intervention—or occupation. "I think some of them would do just about anything to get massive federal intervention," one such observer said not long ago. "That's what they want, consciously or unconsciously. They have some fancy words for it—showing the nation the evil, bringing the hostility to the surface—and they won't go outside the bounds of the voting drive to achieve it, but basically, it amounts to provoking Mississippi into doing something that the federal government won't take. Why?

Maybe they're just tired. Maybe they just want to bring everything to a head after all this. Sometimes I can't blame them."

WHATEVER THE REASON, THE EMPHASIS on violence and arrests is so great at the COFO office in Jackson that a stranger could spend hours there without being aware that a voter-registration drive was being carried on throughout Mississippi, that nearly fifty Freedom Schools are operating in the state, or that a new political party is being organized. About the time of King's visit, voter-registration workers began to concentrate on the mock registration for the Freedom Democratic Party, so that its delegates could demonstrate to the Democratic Convention how many people they represented, but a chart on the rear wall of the office that was supposed to show the registration results by counties was never used, and until a small notice went up on the bulletin board a few days after King left the state, there was no indication at all of how the campaign was faring. The Party was being organized from the precinct level up, and several COFO workers who attended a county meeting near Canton, north of Jackson, the day after King left returned bubbling with enthusiasm. But the next day the blackboard on the front wall of the COFO headquarters said nothing of the fact that three hundred Negroes had attended a meeting of the Freedom Democratic Party, instead offering the usual reports of violence: "Batesville 1:00 A.M. Freedom House had tear gas grenade thrown into it. . . . Occupants vacated house. McComb 1:30 A.M. House of NAACP prex had two packages of dynamite thrown at it. . . . No injuries . . . Damage slight. Tchula

3:00 A.M. SNCC automobile set afire. 2/3 burned . . . Interior gutted."

Both the internal and the external communications handled by the Jackson office are dominated by incidents. Most of the material that is provided for visiting reporters—or residents who stroll by the office, for that matter—concerns violence or security. The Jackson office has two WATS (Wide Area Telephone Service) lines operating at a flat rate for unlimited calls anywhere in Mississippi, so that workers can constantly be kept track of by phone; the SNCC office in Greenwood has a WATS line for Mississippi and one on which calls can be made throughout the country; and the SNCC office in Atlanta has one for the Eastern United States. Checking goes on incessantly—by means of sign-out sheets, perpetual telephoning, and, lately, even shortwave radio— and any indication of trouble is immediately reported to the North. On the first day of my visit, two Northern lawyers who were traveling from Jackson to Natchez to try to make contact with some Natchez lawyers neglected to phone the COFO office to report their safe arrival. According to those in charge of their project, by the time the two were tracked down a few hours later, the Attorney General of the United States was about to call the President out of a meeting to inform him of their disappearance.

One reason for emphasizing violence to the press, apparently, is that, in the unceasing effort to draw the nation's attention to Mississippi, violence has proved to be about all that the nation responds to. Another reason is that one of Moses's immediate goals is merely to enable integration groups to exist in some parts of Mississippi in relative safety. SNCC leaders are not always specific about their goals—

beyond, of course, "shaking up" the state and drawing the nation's attention to it—and the goals often appear to be idealistic and practical at the same time. In one sentence, a SNCC worker may be speculating on what long-range psychological effect organization for voter registration will have on the Negro community, and in the next sentence, he may be speculating on what effect a large Negro vote in Mississippi might have in the 1967 gubernatorial election if a breakthrough should come by then. Some of the SNCC people call the "One Man, One Vote" campaign a means of assuring a large enough Negro vote to soften the racial policies of the state's politicians, and then say that if the principle is established that even an ignorant man has a right to decide who rules him, the next step has to be the acceptance of some responsibility for seeing to it that he is not ignorant. Defeating a Mississippi senator may be spoken of as a way to help end the congressional bottleneck that is holding up progressive welfare legislation, as well as a way to get better representation for Mississippi Negroes. "Different people have different goals," I was told by a white SNCC staff worker who has been in Mississippi for several months. "Some are practical: to get one sheriff to stop hitting us over the head, say. Some are subjective—like the satisfaction of seeing a Mississippi Negro woman like Fannie Lou Hamer emerge as a leader, or that meeting in Canton yesterday. I think if we did nothing else, the summer would be worth it for that one meeting. Or seeing the people come to sing after the bombing of the Freedom House in McComb, or five hundred people go to the courthouse to register in Hattiesburg, or seeing people realize that they don't have to dress up to come to a meeting. Some are specific: to get the vote and get some base of power, to get people to talk to their congressmen and get people involved, to show the social problem that Mississippi is."

SNCC leaders believe that they can see some progress in Mississippi when it is compared with the monolith of segregation Moses found in 1961. "All other civil rights groups considered Mississippi hopeless," Forman says. "Now at least a beachhead has been established. We've got organizations all over the state. We've been forming a basis all the time for the Justice Department's voting suits. We've changed the atmosphere in the Negro community. And we're getting more resources, more people, and a consensus that something is wrong. By plugging away, you get the National Council of Churches involved, you get people building community centers, you get things like the Harvard summer teaching project at Tougaloo College, you get white Northern lawyers talking to some of these people for the first time."

The success of COFO depends partly on how consistently its projects are carried on after the summer is over—some of the volunteers are expected to stay on, and Moses, who sees his commitment in terms of "three-year hitches," plans to remain in Mississippi until 1967—but even if the projects thrive, and even if some breakthroughs in litigation are made, it is likely to be a long time before a COFO worker can see that his efforts have had any substantial effect on the state. "I think that concern over civil rights moves by plateaus, and we had to make sure Mississippi got in on this move," Moses says. "But this commitment has to be for the long haul. People say, 'Why are you doing this?' or 'Why are you starting with this aspect?' or 'Where can this approach ever get you?' And we say, 'What else would you have us do?' "

. . .

A year after the Mississippi Summer Project, Lyndon B. Johnson signed into law the Voting Rights Act of 1965. The act was extended with bipartisan support until 2013, when the Supreme Court struck down one of its key provisions— the requirement that states that had a historical pattern of discrimination obtain Justice Department approval for any change in their voting laws. In maintaining that the provision was no longer necessary, Chief Justice John Roberts mentioned that the black registration rate in Mississippi had increased to seventy-six percent. Once the decision was handed down, the secretary of state of Mississippi announced that the state's voter-ID law, which had been awaiting federal preclearance, would be implemented.

Robert Moses became an anti–Vietnam War activist and, for a time, a separatist. After several years of working in education in Tanzania, he returned to Harvard in 1976 to continue his graduate studies while teaching math at a local high school. Eventually, he founded the Algebra Project, a national program that aims to improve the math of students in poor communities. In 1982, he was awarded a MacArthur Fellowship.

THE ZULUS

New Orleans, Louisiana
1964

EVERY YEAR, IN NEW ORLEANS, THE FIRST IMPORTANT MARDI Gras ceremony on Shrove Tuesday is the landing of the Zulus, a group of Negroes who parade in blackface makeup. King Zulu, their leader, traditionally docks his "royal yacht" at the Poydras Street Wharf on the Mississippi at about nine in the morning—although the Zulus have never been finicky about punctuality, and their fans would not be at all surprised to see them arrive at a different hour or, considering some past Zulu vagaries, even at a different wharf. The Zulus' arrival is scheduled to precede by an hour the parade of the Krewe of Rex, which everybody except the Zulus considers the most important parade of the Mardi Gras season. Rex always includes fifteen or twenty magnificently decorated floats, at least a dozen marching bands, scores of lavishly costumed maskers tossing strings of beads from the floats to the clamoring onlookers, and, on a float of his own, Rex, the King of Carnival, a prominent civic leader who is dressed in a costume that might have been inspired by a deck of playing cards and who magnanimously waves his scepter down toward his subjects. King Zulu matches the regal grandeur of this display only in his attitude, which is every bit as imperious as that of Rex, but he has always attracted a large crowd. By nine o'clock on Shrove Tuesday morning this year, several hundred spectators, almost all of them white, had gathered at the Poydras Street Wharf. Some of the spectators were in Mardi Gras costumes of their own—dressed as clowns, say, or pirates—but most of them were in informal street clothes. As an incessant blast of foghorns heralded the approach of the royal yacht—which on less ceremonial occasions is the tugboat *Bisso*—many of them got cameras ready. A loud cheer went up when the King, accompanied by four of his Warriors, stepped ashore. "Make way for the King," someone shouted. The crowd parted.

King Zulu was a corpulent man of average height. Jet-black theatrical makeup covered his face—except for the rims of his eyes and mouth, which had been painted a contrasting white, in minstrel-show fashion—and the color theme was repeated in black tights, black gloves, and a wig of black moss. The King's costume, however, was hardly limited to black. He was wearing gold boots, a yellow grass skirt, a jacket that was a combination of purple silk, green silk, green velvet, and gold sequins—arranged in a way that produced seemingly endless juxtapositions of color—and a crown of green silk with a rim of gold fleurs-de-lis. The King's jewelry included earrings studded with ersatz diamonds, a dozen strings of beads, and a bright silver nose ring. As he walked onto the dock, he blessed the crowd with a two-handed gesture—as if constantly parting and then tightly closing a curtain high above him—while continuing to hold a fat cigar in one hand and, in the other, a scepter weighted at the upper end with a silver coconut.

Included in the party assembled to meet the King were his Queen, a middle-aged Negro woman in a white organdy dress and a fur stole, and half a dozen of his Warriors, all of them, like the four who had accompanied him on the royal yacht, wearing some variety of what the Zulus sometimes call "authentic jungle costumes"—a style that can vary as to capes or jackets but always includes blackface makeup, black tights, and a grass skirt. The remaining elements of the Zulu parade—four floats pulled by old pickup trucks, a supply of painted coconuts, which the Zulus traditionally ration out to the begging crowd, and a Negro brass band—were also on hand. King Zulu, like Rex, had a float of his own—it was labeled KING ZULU 50TH—which would lead the parade. Another float was for the Queen and her court. A third float, decorated in purple, green, and gold foil and featuring a collection of shrunken heads and a small menagerie of papier-mâché jungle beasts, was for the Big Shot from Africa, a traditional participant almost as important (and easily as haughty) as the King. The final float was to have been named "The Royal Prognosticator," for a new Zulu character, but, through one of a series of spelling errors that have plagued the parade over the years, it was entitled "The Royal Proganistor" instead. Next to "The Royal Proganistor" stood three hired flag-carriers, one of them carrying the Zulus' official banner. It was blue on one side and black on the other, and on both sides it bore the words THE ZULU SOCIAL AID & PLEASURE CLUB. FOUNDED MAY 4, 1916. INCORPORATED SEPTEMBER 26, 1916.

At a time when white marchers have been enjoined from wearing blackface in the Philadelphia Mummers Parade and when a wave of protest is likely to descend upon any television station that decides to broadcast reruns of *Amos 'n Andy,* the Zulu Social Aid & Pleasure Club has not been without its critics. At one point, in fact, pressure to end the parade seemed about to succeed. The 1961 Mardi Gras occurred about three months after the city was torn apart by a token start at court-ordered school desegregation, and many Negroes believed that a pre-Lenten celebration proclaiming New Orleans to be "The City That Care Forgot" was hardly appropriate at that time. In what was generally conceded to be the only united action in its history, the Negro community boycotted the 1961 Mardi Gras; the Mardi Gras balls given by Negro clubs were canceled, and few Negroes watched the parades or joined the street maskers on the climactic day of the season—Mardi Gras itself, or Shrove Tuesday. As the only Negro Mardi Gras parade, King Zulu's progress through the streets was the event that Negro leaders were most eager to have called off—many of them had been opposed to it for years, in any case—and an impressive campaign was mounted against it. An advertisement in *The Louisiana Weekly,* the New Orleans Negro newspaper, presented a petition, signed by some twenty-seven thousand people, that read, "We, the Negroes of New Orleans, are in the midst of a fight for our rights and for a recognition of our human dignity which underlies those rights. Therefore we resent and repudiate the Zulu parade, in which Negroes are paid by white merchants to wander through the city drinking to excess, dressed as uncivilized savages and throwing coconuts like monkeys. This caricature does not represent

us. Rather, it represents a warped picture against us. Therefore, we petition all citizens of New Orleans to boycott the
Zulu parade. If we want respect from others, we must first
demand it of ourselves."

Members of the Zulu Social Aid & Pleasure Club could
hardly have been encouraged by those harsh words, and
since they possessed the ability to see their yearly parade in
both ideological and financial terms, they must have been
troubled by some of the organizations listed as sponsors of
the advertisement. The appearance on the list of the Cres-
cent City Funeral Directors and the New Orleans Embalm-
ers Association represented a considerable defection, because
funeral homes once provided the principal Negro financial
support for the parade; in fact, year after year, the King had
toasted the Queen on a grandstand in front of the Geddes &
Moss Undertaking & Embalming Co., Ltd. In the same issue
of *The Louisiana Weekly*, it was reported that the Tavern
Owners of Greater New Orleans Association, Inc.—a Negro organization whose members had customarily purchased
the privilege of having King Zulu and his followers make
"stops" for rest and refreshment in the course of their long
march—had agreed that the King would no longer be welcome.

Under this pressure, the Zulus voted to cancel their parade. Immediately afterward, however, the mayor of New
Orleans and the superintendent of police dropped in on a
meeting of the club and managed to convince the members
both that it would be in their best interests to parade and
that they would be fully protected from hostile elements in
either the Negro or the white community. The decision of the
Zulus to go along with the mayor—and thereby help counter

any notion that Mardi Gras might not be held or that tourists attending it might become involved in some sort of race trouble, or, for that matter, that the city had any race trouble to be involved in—further enraged a great many New Orleans Negroes. A *Louisiana Weekly* editorial charged that the Zulus had "turned their backs on the Negro community by completely ignoring hundreds of requests not to parade in the same disgraceful, disorderly and despicable way just for a few dollars and laughs from the white folks. . . . The fact that twenty-six African nations have gained their freedom in the past few years and hold seats in the U.N. with respect and honor [and] would not look kindly on . . . making mockery of a proud and honorable African tribe did not reach the Zulus. All they could see was the white face and green money."

The Zulu parade that year was a hurried, joyless event, watched over by a police detail that sometimes seemed as large as the crowd of onlookers. Both the King and the Queen originally selected for the 1961 parade had publicly resigned under threats of business boycotts—the King's resignation causing particular sadness among Zulu fans, because he worked in a produce house and it had been rumored that his supply of coconuts would be limitless. There was a substitute King Zulu in the parade, but whoever was under the makeup chose not to reveal his name—a departure from custom equivalent to a film actor asking that his designation for the Academy Award be kept secret—and nobody came forward to play the Queen, who has to parade undisguised. The New Orleans *Times-Picayune*, a newspaper that seems to prize discretion above all other virtues, managed to cover the parade without once referring to the pre-parade difficulties, but its account did mention that "an air of calmness kept the frenzy of the usual madcap merrymakers at a low pitch," and in the fifteenth paragraph, it noted without further explanation that "by-standers were not allowed to parade too closely along the King's float, as two police dogs belonging to the police department's canine corps marched along the route."

Writing in a pamphlet a year later, Harrison Baker, who was then President of the Zulu Social Aid & Pleasure Club, defended the club's decision in rather typical Zulu prose. "During the 1960–61 Carnival Season the Zulu King Carnival Club and its President were improperly and severely criticized, boycotted, and ostracized—even defamed," Baker wrote. "Fortunately, the almost jealous 'better than thou' attitude against our Carnival Revelry is only a mere accusation against our dignity." The 1961 Zulu parade had needed to be held, Baker maintained, because of "a commitment directly and indirectly with the City and citizens of New Orleans"—the indirect commitment being that "for forty-six years the Zulus have been the main Carnival attraction," and the direct one being that the club had received "financial contributions voluntarily and by solicitation [and] it's dishonest and illegal to spend such money without delivering as promised." Considering the vehemence of the anti-Zulu campaign in 1961 and the lackluster parades in 1962 and 1963, plus the growing militancy of Negroes throughout the country, there was reason to believe that the validity of these commitments would be questioned with increasing energy by the New Orleans Negro community, and as this year's Carnival season approached, there was some talk in New Orleans that the 1964 Mardi Gras might have either the last parade of the Zulus or no Zulu parade at all.

Nevertheless, several weeks before Shrove Tuesday, the Zulus had applied for and received their usual parade permit and had sent out their usual fund-raising form letter to white businessmen. The letter was headed "King Zulu Carnival Club—Organized 1916," with the words "50th Anniversary" on each side, and said that "because of the unusual makeup of 'King Zulu' and his Warriors, quite a few people come to our fair city to see the King do his stuff." The form letter seemed to constitute final proof that King Zulu, Queen Zulu, the Big Shot from Africa, and the Zulu Warriors would parade once again, and that anybody who doubted whether a group of Negroes would march for five or six hours through the streets of an American city in 1964 wearing blackface, dressed as burlesque savages, and handing out coconuts need only show up at the Poydras Street Wharf at nine o'clock to be convinced.

THE MAN WHO USUALLY SPEAKS for the Zulu Social Aid & Pleasure Club in matters having to do with Mardi Gras is the parade chairman, Alex Rapheal, Jr. The exact nature of Rapheal's workaday occupation is obscure—a state of affairs that is endemic among the Zulus, and often results in newspaper accounts that identify the same Zulu with a different occupation at each mention. It is not unusual to see one man referred to in successive stories as, say, a businessman, the operator of a candy store, a law clerk, and a bail bondsman—and to hear the same man described succinctly by a Negro lawyer as "a hustler around the courthouse." Rapheal definitely works in the stockroom of a New Orleans bank from four in the afternoon until midnight, and in the

morning and the early afternoon, he works at home by telephone at his daytime business, which has been selling insurance, according to one account and, according to Rapheal's
own fond recollection, was at one time publishing a religious
magazine. Rapheal's business assets include a phone number that is easy to remember (the last four digits are 4040)
and a unique greeting. He always answers the phone with
"Hello and good morning"—unless it happens to be between
noon and the time he leaves for the bank, when, since this
period falls into what is called "evening" in New Orleans, he
says "Hello and good evening." Two weeks before the 1964
Mardi Gras, upon phoning Rapheal to express interest in
learning about the Zulu Social Aid & Pleasure Club, I soon
discovered that "Hello and good morning" is the most cheer-
ful part of his conversation. If he is pressed for a description of his business activities, he describes himself as "an old
hunk of failure," and he tends to speak pessimistically of the
obstacles placed in the path of such a man by the imposing
forces that always seem to be aligned against him. Rapheal
told me he was doing his best to get the Zulu parade on the
street for Mardi Gras, despite every kind of bad luck, conspiracy, and act of God working against it, and added that
if he could free himself from a staggering load of work, he
would meet me at the home of former President Baker the
following afternoon.

Baker, like thousands of other New Orleans residents,
white or Negro, lives in a "shotgun" house—a remarkably
narrow one-story white duplex whose apartments face the
street across a common porch and extend straight back, one
room behind another, like a New York railroad flat. A large,
shambling man in his sixties, who turned out to be Rapheal,

met me at the door and, wearing a troubled expression that matched his telephone voice, introduced me to the current President of the Zulus, a saloonkeeper named Joseph Hayes, and to Baker, a very dark, soft-spoken old man who had also been a saloonkeeper before his retirement. Baker's living room was almost filled by three pieces of a sectional couch and two small coffee tables. The only light was coming from a gas heater in front of the fireplace, but I could read a triangular tin plaque on the mantel. It proclaimed, U CAN'T FOOL GOD SO DON'T TRY TO BLUFF HIS SON.

When I had taken a seat on a section of couch, Rapheal handed me a booklet published by the Zulus in 1941, and said, "As you can see, the Zulus were officially organized in 1916, although they paraded many years before that. When they saw it was going pretty well, they organized the Tramps. They went on with that for a number of years, and then they saw the Smarter Set, a show that had a King Zulu vaudeville skit in it, and presto, that's it—the Zulus. The first Zulu King masked with a lard can for a crown. The reason for that lard can is that they used to use those cans to get beer for five cents, so it was really a beer can. The first scepter was a banana stalk, and the first King had a sack suit pasted all over with pictures that came out of tobacco cans and cigarette packs. The first float, after a while, was a furniture wagon—what year we really don't know."

"It was 1917," said Baker.

"They first came up the Old Basin Canal," Rapheal went on.

"New Basin Canal," Baker interjected quietly.

"Yeah, the New Basin Canal," Rapheal said. "They were rowing a skiff. Later, they used an outboard motor, and then some businessmen loaned boats, and now King Zulu comes in from the river in a tugboat that the salvage company loans us. I think there you have the complete and authentic history up to the present day. What do you think, Brother Baker?"

"There's not much more you can tell him, I don't think," Baker said.

Having absorbed the history of the Zulus, I turned the conversation to the problems that had reached their peak in 1961 and asked Rapheal if he saw any merit in the argument that the Zulus should end their parade.

"King Zulu's costume is a grass skirt, black-and-white face, and coconuts," Rapheal said. "That's why some of our folks beat their chests and say the Zulus oughtn't to parade, and they beat their chests when they see King Zulu and they say, 'That's me! That's me!' Well, we don't go along with that. The grass skirt is from Hawaii, the coconuts are from South America, the moss wig is from Louisiana, and the man is from Louisiana. So you can see that's an original creation there. We got Hawaii represented, South America represented, and Louisiana. We had good public relationship until 1961, and then a certain group of our folks told us not to parade, for various reasons. We, the Zulus, thought we should parade, for more than one reason. First, we thought it was an infringement of our constitutional rights. They're always running around talking about constitutional rights, and we have a constitutional right to parade. We're in harmony with what they're doing, because we're Negroes, and what they're doing helps us. But we had our back to the wall. We had spent money for floats and bands; there was no way to give it back. But when we said this, they said it didn't make any difference, we weren't going to parade. Well, naturally, we wouldn't want anybody else to tell us what to do, and President Baker told me, he said, 'Brother Rapheal, you have nothing to fear but fear itself.' So I took this as my instructions and I went on and planned the parade. Brother Baker said, 'If the Russian Army is there, we are going to parade.' Well, maybe you saw it that year. It was spotted with peace officers and what all, and it wasn't so good. We were forced to parade, but it left a bad taste in a lot of people's mouths."

Rapheal paused and then went on as if it had never occurred to him that the Zulus had to parade because their backs were to the wall. "It's our civic duty to parade," he said. "New Orleans is the capital Carnival city of this country, and the Zulus are the only Negro club that marches, and King Zulu is a great attraction."

"You see, the merchants want this parade on the street," Baker said. "The Carnival would go on if there was no Zulu, but the life would be took out of Carnival. The thing of it is, we're the main attraction. People don't care anything about Rex and those parades."

Despite this, Rapheal complained, the white merchants had been much slower with their contributions since the trouble in 1961, and the Negro funeral parlors had stayed with the enemy. Rapheal said he had sent out only three hundred fund-appeal letters this year, compared with as many as seven hundred in the past, and that he was having difficulty "selling stops" to bars. Although the Tavern Owners of Greater New Orleans Association, Inc., had apparently forgotten that the Zulus were banished in 1961, the business of selling stops had been affected, it appeared, not only by the feeling of some Negroes against merchants who supported the Zulus but also by the diminishment of the Zulus' Second Line. The crowd following any New Orleans parade that has a brass band is called the Second Line, whether it's following a founders' day parade or a funeral, and the Zulu parade once attracted a Second Line of legendary enthusiasm. Added to the neighborhood people who would gather at a bar stop to await the parade, it could cause a significant boom in liquor sales. It is difficult for anybody following a New Orleans brass band not to walk with some bounce, and eventually, most people are happy to find themselves doing a kind of jitterbug step that is sometimes know as Second Lining. Normally, active Second Liners are not able to keep on the sidewalks, their proper area, but tend to dance in the street, and most of the Zulus' Second Liners found this pastime much less enjoyable when police dogs were added to the parade.

Rapheal told me that part of the cost of the parade would be defrayed by the King, the Queen, and the Big Shot from Africa, all of whom are roughly responsible for their own floats. "In June, we elect the King," Rapheal said. "Everybody who wants to be King puts up the money, and the one who's elected, his money stays up."

Recalling that Louis Armstrong had been King in 1949— an event that is remembered in New Orleans both because he was given the key to the city by the mayor and because the Second Line, inspired by superior music and a desire for souvenirs, destroyed the royal float—I asked Rapheal whether the King of the Zulus, like Rex, had to be a member of the club.

"We make him an honorary paying member," Rapheal

said. "Being a paying member is the very first consideration. You must pay your dues. We can't just go around and elect nonmembers King."

The Zulus, according to Rapheal and Baker, have about twenty-five regular paying members. Although founded as a Carnival organization, it has more in common with the old-fashioned New Orleans burial societies than with the more modern Carnival clubs, whose activities are dominated by an annual Mardi Gras ball. "The club is chiefly to be a help in the community and to help the members," Rapheal explained. "We have a room to meet in, and we have a plan on foot to get another place. If a member is sick, we pay him so much a week. When he dies, he gets a band of music at his funeral. We have socials during the year. Carnival is just one project. You might say it's the major project."

With Mardi Gras only two weeks away, the major project was not going well enough to suit Baker and Rapheal, both of whom, I came to realize, invariably took on an aura of resigned gloom when they were discussing the parade in the presence of anybody who might be remotely considered a contributor. "This is the fiftieth parade coming up, and it's not living up to expectations," Baker said, shaking his head sadly. "Three or four floats for the fiftieth year! It looks like you're shrinkin' up in place of stretchin' out."

THE NATIONAL ASSOCIATION FOR THE Advancement of Colored People is the pressure group most often mentioned by New Orleans whites who, in discussing the Zulus' possible demise, express either a hostility toward any sign of Negro race consciousness or a simple sadness at the thought that an old tradition might end. I was therefore surprised to discover that Ernest Morial, the president of the New Orleans branch of the NAACP, did not feel particularly strongly about the Zulus or about a proposed Negro boycott of all balls and parades surrounding the 1964 Mardi Gras. He didn't think that there was branch support for a boycott.

Morial said that some whites who were normally sympathetic to Negro progress were fond of the Zulu parade. "The white liberals love Zulu," he said. "The jazz buffs and all see it as part of a culture, something artistic. They like all the street parades. I don't have any real quarrel with Zulu myself. Sure, I would like to have no Zulu parade and see the Negro community integrated into the regular parades—allowed in the Krewe of Orleanians, the line of trucks that follows the Rex parade, for instance. But that might not happen until a long time from now. I think it's a matter of priorities, and there are a lot of things more important. If we accelerate our efforts in the areas that present real problems—voting, jobs, school dropouts, getting more people to use the facilities we've desegregated—the Zulu parade will become passé. Sure, it's undignified, but so are a lot of things that Negroes do all year long. This is only one day. And the Zulus themselves just love it. It's a real thrill. They say that unless you've been on one of those floats, sitting up there and having people look up and say, 'Throw me something,' you don't realize what it's like."

The next day, Dr. Leonard Burns, a Negro chiropodist who, as the energetic president of a loose federation of Carnival clubs, had led the 1961 boycott, corroborated Morial's statement that, since 1961, attempts to end the Zulu parade had not been able to work up much steam. Some negotiations were held about how to make the parade more dig-nified, but they broke down over the Zulus' insistence on keeping the blackface King. (I later learned that when the 1955 Zulu King, Nathan King, who was by way of an early reformer, showed up without blackface, that deviation was corrected on the tugboat *Bisso* by three Zulu traditionalists bearing greasepaint.) "I really don't see any way of ending the Zulu parade as long as the Zulus are getting the money from white businessmen," Burns told me. "To tell you the truth, we've just about given up on them; we voice a protest, but not much else. I was talking with a doctor in town today about the possibility of some respectable Negroes joining the Zulus and changing the thing with their votes. Maybe that would work."

RAPHEAL AND BAKER SEEMED TO agree more or less with Burns's estimate of their intransigence, but they disagreed em-phatically with the widely held belief that this intransigence stemmed from an eagerness for personal profit. I brought up this subject with Rapheal one day while I was accompanying him on some of the errands he had assured me he could not possibly complete in time for the parade.

"The consensus among my enemies is that I make a lot of money off the parade," Rapheal said. "It is a public secret, but a public secret is not always a public fact. This work is strictly volunteer. For me, it's the inward satisfaction to get the parade on the street. It's a satisfaction especially when it appears that everybody is against it—although I don't think the people are really against it. And it's a satisfaction when people are trying to keep you down and you come up some way—especially if it's the bigwigs trying to keep you down, the lawyers and all against me, a poor little old porter. We got nothing against those fellows, but it seems like they got everything against us."

Rapheal had promised to introduce me to the 1964 Big Shot from Africa, Milton Bienamee. We found him at the city courthouse, where he runs a patrol service that specializes in finding people who have jumped bail. Bienamee turned out to be a cheerful-looking, dark-complexioned Negro with graying hair and a graying mustache.

"Whaddaya say, Brother Rapheal?" Bienamee said, getting into our car to chat.

"Oh, not so good," Rapheal replied. "I'm getting old, and I have a lot of work to do, a lot of work."

"I know what you mean," Bienamee said. "I got all troubles but domestic. If I didn't have such a wonderful wife, I'd have committed suicide by now. She's always a bright cloud."

Bienamee then turned to me and said that while he had been on other Zulu floats, this would be his first appearance as the Big Shot from Africa. "And the last time, the way it looks," he continued. "I already spent about six hundred dollars. I didn't know what it would cost."

"Well, you're the *Big* Shot," Rapheal said. "What do you expect? You want to be the Little Shot?"

"The material for my costume cost forty-six dollars just for the cape," the Big Shot said. "I'm having it made by one of the most fabulous tailors in town. It's leopard skin with gold on the inside and diamonds on the outside. I'm wearing one of those expensive beaver hats with a diamond lining. I told you I'm going to *be* out there, and I'm going to *be* out there. Why, I've spent a hundred and seventy-five dollars on presents. I'm the only one who has to hand out gifts. I got monkeys that cost seventy-five cents apiece, and I got coconuts and those Zulu dolls—pickaninnies. The CORE won't like that."

"The what?" Rapheal asked.

"The Congress of Racial Equality," said Bienamee.

Rapheal dismissed the Congress of Racial Equality with one contemptuous look, but Bienamee, I gathered, still had the subject in mind as he went on to explain to me why he had decided to become the Big Shot from Africa. "I feel this way—I'm putting my whole heart and soul into this," he said. "Our organization is being attacked, and I want to make it impressive, and maybe that will knock out that ill wind that propaganda has been sending around. Maybe this bad public sentiment can be thrown off by something impressive."

"Regardless of what kind of parade we put on, or how much trouble and expense we go to, there's one thing they won't overlook," Rapheal said. "That's the facial disguises. And that's the original idea. As long as we have that, they'll be against us. They do want us to parade, but without the facial disguises. But if ever we did away with them, we'd have done away with the parade."

"There'd be no more Zulus then," Bienamee agreed.

"We'd let them help us," said Rapheal. "We don't care. We've done this for fifty years; let them do whatever they want for fifty years. There are only two conditions. One, they have to keep the name, and two, the King must be dark-complected. No mulatto man can be King."

"He's a Zulu King, and he should be a dark man," Bien-amee said. "He has to be dark."

"Well, if they didn't do it three years ago, there's not a powerful chance they can do it now," Rapheal said, winding up the discussion.

BEFORE THE INJUNCTION AGAINST BLACKFACE in the Philadelphia Mummers Parade this year was granted, the Congress of Racial Equality had threatened to block the parade with "a human barricade." New Orleans has a CORE branch, but when I called on its president, a chatty young lady named Oretha Castle, a few days later, she seemed in no mood to organize any human barricades or even to picket the Big Shot's use of pickaninny dolls. For one thing, while Mrs. Castle is not a fan of the Zulu parade, she also suspects the alternative. "I think Zulu is a disgrace," she told me. "But some of the fight is out of me about it this year. Zulu is just a big mess, that's all. Many people feel we should get rid of Zulu because the white people think that's the way we are, and then they want to have a parade that imitates the white people. Well, that's not us, any more than the grass skirts and the coconuts are. I don't think Zulu will be with us forever, but there's so much internal fighting that the people who are against it are just left to say to themselves, 'What *are* we going to do about Zulu?' This is simply not a militant community, and besides, we're split in so many different ways. We don't have just Negroes. We have our Catholic Negroes and our Protestant

Negroes, our downtown Negroes and our uptown Negroes, our light Negroes and our dark Negroes. And we have too many Negroes who don't think they're Negroes."

In New Orleans, "downtown" means downriver from Canal Street—which used to constitute a dividing line between the French and the American settlements—and many of the Negroes who live there are Catholic and light-skinned. At one time, some of them set themselves off from darker Negroes so completely that New Orleans was generally thought of as having three races rather than two. Even now, downtown Negroes occasionally refer to their opposite numbers living above Canal Street as "American Negroes," and they can talk about a club being "integrated" without intending any reference to whites. One theory given for the current lack of militant opposition to the Zulu parade is that some New Orleans Negroes do not really consider themselves and the Zulus to be of the same race, and therefore do not feel affected by the Zulus' behavior. In the words of one downtown Negro, "Folks on this side of Canal Street just don't carry on that way." I'd heard the other side of that from Milton Bienamee: "These Negroes who are fighting us just recently started admitting dark-skinned Negroes like me to their clubs. The ones who fight us are more prejudiced than the whites. . . . We're degrading the race by having black faces? I've been having a black face three hundred and sixty-five days a year for forty-eight years."

In the past decade, New Orleans Negroes have become increasingly race-conscious, but a resident sociologist—Daniel Thompson, a professor at Dillard University—told me, "Despite the fact that the Negro community has never resented anything as much as Zulu, it doesn't have the leverage to end it; we have no real political pressure; we can't even get ourselves heard." Thompson is originally from Atlanta, and he acknowledges that any parade deeply resented by *that* Negro community—with its relatively tight organization, its powerful vote, and its militant student movement—would not survive long; but the New Orleans Negro community, he has written, "is to a large extent isolated from the mainstream of the protest movement." One historical reason consistently given for the relative absence of protest is that in New Orleans—a port town, with partly European traditions—segregation has not customarily been accompanied by the systematic oppression found in some parts of the South. In discussing the division among New Orleans Negroes, Thompson also stresses that a third of them are Catholic—a fact that accounts not only for the presence of such phenomena as the Holy Ghost Baptist Church but also for the absence of the Southern Negroes' traditional leader in racial matters, the Negro Protestant minister. Whatever the reasons for the lack of a united protest movement, the direct result has been that New Orleans Negroes, who used to look on such cities as Atlanta as crude fortresses of segregation, now find, ironically, that Negroes in these cities have much more power and much more freedom of movement than they have in their own.

Some of the characteristics that Thompson has attributed to the New Orleans Negroes—such as a lack of economic vitality, a tendency to identify themselves by neighborhood, a strong class consciousness, and a fondness for tradition—resemble those often attributed to New Orleans whites, and Thompson agrees that the city's strongest traditions are biracial. "Clubs like the Zulus are a case in point," he told me. "In other places, social aid and benevolent societies existed because, for a long time, white insurance companies wouldn't write policies for Negroes. They were essentially a form of insurance. And in other cities they passed out of existence when the economic need was gone. Here this form of insurance was fragmented—Catholic burial societies, upper-class Protestant burial societies, lower-class Protestant burial societies—and it developed a social function. So the societies still exist here to some extent, and you can see the Carnival motif. In New Orleans, whenever you find anything happening, from a funeral on out, you can see the Carnival motif. There's always some kind of show. Church services, funerals, social functions, wakes—anything."

ON THE DAY OF RAPHEAL'S deadline for notifying the float-makers if there was enough money for a fourth float, which he had decided to devote to a character called the Voodoo Doctor, I called him up to see if the money had been raised.

"Hello and good evening," Rapheal said.

I asked him if the Voodoo Doctor would be appearing on Mardi Gras.

"I thought you were in knowledge of that," Rapheal said. "We're going to have the fourth float, but I've decided to call it 'The Royal Prognosticator.' "

"You must be selling a few stops, then," I said.

"It's not easy," Rapheal replied.

I had read that the Zulus had not marched below Canal Street the previous year because of a possibility of trouble downtown, where feeling against them was thought to be fairly strong, and I asked Rapheal if his route would take the Zulus downtown.

"We have never missed going downtown," he said, and pointed out that the parade had gone as far as Bienville Street, which is two blocks below Canal Street, the previous year. It would go several blocks farther this year, he assured me, and continued, "The route depends on my selling ability. It depends on where I sell stops. There had been some interracial trouble, and after that I discontinued pushing, because I didn't want to stop the business harmony between the businesses and the people. When all this trouble came up, all the Negroes thought they could kick us around. It's just become my luck in life to have to defend this thing in this unpopular position you find it in. But I have something to sell. I'm not begging and I'm not giving anything away; I have a good business deal for them. Now they're feeling the pinch downtown, and they call me and say, 'Mr. Rapheal, we want to talk with you.' What determines how far we go across Canal Street depends on who wants to donate to the cause. It's not because we're afraid. If they don't want me, I don't want them. We don't depend on the Negro public. We depend on the merchants. We have had as high as twenty-six, eighteen, fifteen stops at one time. Now we only have four or five. We're not up to par, but we are still out there, and a lot of what they're saying about us is not true."

A NOSTALGIC VIEW OF THE old days is taken by many of the Zulus, for many of the Zulus are elderly. There was a stronger African theme in the old days—the royal yacht usually had a name like *Addis Ababa;* there were tales of real Zulu warriors like Cetewayo—and the parade was much grander. On one occasion, I was told of the past glories of the Zulu parade by William Boykins, the club's treasurer, who has been King Zulu twice. "We had the Dukes," Boykin told me. "Thirty or forty Dukes. They all rode mules, not horses—the oldest and deadest mules they could find. Warriors with spears—we had thirty or forty of them. The President rode in a buggy alone by himself—a Boston buggy—and then there was a buggy for the Bride and Groom and one for the Kingfish. We were something in them days. The Zulus were something to look at then."

The simplest historical view of an old-fashioned Zulu parade is that, however it may have been to look at, it was merely a daylong drunk. Accounts of the parades of the twenties and thirties tend to dwell on the drunkenness of the Warriors; the sometimes disgraceful behavior of the Baby Dolls, bands of Negro prostitutes dressed as little girls, who used to follow the Zulu parade, the uptown and downtown bands occasionally breaking into armed combat; and the necessary halts—sometimes for hours—in the parade's haphazard progress when the King or one of its other officials had disappeared into a barroom. In those days, it would often take the New Orleans papers five paragraphs to approximate the route of the parade. Kid Thomas Valentine, an elderly jazz trumpet player from across the river in Algiers, used to play for Zulu parades, and he once described an old-fashioned one to me in the present tense. "They talk about cutting it out now," Kid Thomas said. "They carry on so much, and drink, and get drunk. They drink liquor and all that stuff, you know. They fall off the wagons and get crippled up. They raise a lot of sand." Being a traditional-ist, Kid Thomas finds this kind of performance preferable to the modern white parades, which he describes as "the same old soup bone over and over again," but he acknowledges that some reform had to come. "In those days and times, it's dangerous—you know what I mean?" he told me. "Some-body might throw a brick at you."

In 1949, the Zulus found not only their one nationally known King but also their best historian in Louis Arm-strong. Armstrong writes what might be called interjective prose—he frequently interrupts himself for digressions or for experiments with punctuation—but manages to sound very direct nonetheless. Replying to a letter from a New Orleans editor who had asked about his memories of being King Zulu, Armstrong devoted a paragraph or two to his boy-hood, when he dreamed of being King Zulu, then described how a Zulu invaded his hotel room in the early hours of the morning to apply makeup "everywhere he could swirve a brush," and finally turned to the parade itself:

> We had a real time, all over the city, throwing coconuts to the people, and saying hello and waving to the old friends, etc. Just think—twenty thousand coconuts which each member on my float threw to the crowd. . . . I hap-pened to look up on a porch where a young man was just yelling to me, "Come on Satchmo (meaning me) throw one of those fine coconuts up here." . . . And I taken a real good aim and threw one at him, with all of my might. . . . The guy waited until the coconut reached him and the coconut hit the tip of his finger, and fell down on a bran new Cadillac. . . . Geee . . . I just turned by head to

the direction in front of me, just as nothin happened. . . .
Wow . . . Close shave, huh? . . . I shall never forget the
incident when our float reach Dumaine and Claiborne
Streets, and as I was sitting, I see straight down Claiborne Street for miles, seemingly, and the whole street
were blocked with people waiting for the parade to come
down their way. . . . But instead—the float turned the
other direction. . . . And—all of those people made one
grand charge at once, towards the float . . .

The rushing crowd—together with the extra people he
had on the float—resulted in an accident a few blocks later.
It is described in what must be the most expressive sentence
ever written about the Zulu parade. "Just then," Armstrong
noted, "my float commenced to crumbling down to pieces."

THE ZULU PARADE CAN BE taken as a parody of any white
Mardi Gras parade—there are about twenty-five of them
in the ten days leading up to Shrove Tuesday, and although
they vary both in splendor and in social status, a strong case
could be made for Kid Thomas Valentine's theory that they
are "the same old soup bone over and over again"—but it is
more specifically a parody of the Rex parade. While almost
every club that parades has a king, Rex, since he is King
of Carnival, is the logical model for anybody who wants
to be "ruler of the Negro Mardi Gras." Even the arrival of
King Zulu from Africa on a royal yacht is a mimicry of Rex,
though in this case, the mimicry has outlived the original.
Before World War I, Rex used to arrive from some make-
believe land on a real yacht the day before Mardi Gras, to

receive the key to the city from the mayor. King Zulu has also borrowed Rex's imperious tone. "There never was and there never will be a King like me" is a traditional King Zulu arrival statement, though in the confusion at the Poydras Street Wharf, the King often forgets to make it. Both Rex and Zulu are given to issuing proclamations. This year's Proclamation of Rex, an elaborately designed scroll displayed in store windows during the week before Mardi Gras, ordered, in part, that "Our Devoted People, young and old of all degrees, ages and sexes, embrace Laughter and Joy and Camaraderie." The Zulu custom of handing out painted coconuts is an instance of a burlesque that has become costlier than the original. A coconut, even before it is decorated, costs more than the white paraders' gift of a string of beads from Japan (or, lately, Czechoslovakia), and, to judge from a speech by Rapheal on paint and labor costs, a decorated coconut is more expensive than a string of real pearls from Fifth Avenue. The thrill of being King Zulu and Rex also appears to be closer than the relative social positions would at first indicate. Unlike King Zulu, Rex is, by definition, a man who has received recognition in other ways, but he has never received a badge of unquestioned primacy that equals being Rex, and it will remain part of his identification as long as he lives in New Orleans. He plays his role with a seriousness and enthusiasm that seem remarkably close to the attitude of King Zulu, and those in New Orleans who are not enthusiasts of Mardi Gras often remark, "You can't understand Carnival until you realize that those people who are Kings really believe they are Kings."

The most important officer in each Carnival Krewe is the Captain, who is in charge of organizing the parade and usually leads it himself, riding out in front of the first float on a handsome horse. Four or five days before this year's Mardi Gras, I had a chat with a prominent businessman who is the Captain of Rex. (After our talk, he explained that the identity of a Krewe's Captain is traditionally a secret, though it was an open one in his case, and that therefore he should not be further identified.) He was accompanied by Scoop Kennedy, who works for the public relations department of City Hall but who, I was assured by the Captain, had come along only because he happened to be a member of Rex. People such as the Captain and Kennedy like to emphasize that Mardi Gras is the product of spontaneous enthusiasm on the part of private clubs, with no organization or financial support from the city. Among such people it would be considered bad manners to talk about the promotions of the tourist bureau, the overseeing of parades by the mayor's executive assistant, the erection of stands and decorations by the city, and the typing of Rex's proclamations in the public relations department of City Hall.

"The real Mardi Gras is a series of private parties, and the parades are just for tradition and to share with the public," the Captain had told me on the phone. Tourists were welcome, he had added, but were merely a by-product of the Carnival.

The Captain, who has the reputation in New Orleans of being a relatively progressive man, explained to me that the Zulu parade was "a petty little part of Mardi Gras" and a part he himself did not like. "I think it would be fine if we had a real Negro parade," he said. "The Zulu parade does not represent Mardi Gras. It's not a reflection of what the Negroes could do."

"If it was a white parade, we wouldn't allow it," Kennedy said.

I asked the Captain why he didn't try to stop the Zulu parade, since he disapproved of it. He said that because the Zulu parade was traditional, there was no possibility of discouraging white businessmen from supporting it.

"Some people think it's necessary as a comic relief to Rex," I told the Captain.

"I don't see where comic relief comes into it," he said in a slightly offended tone. "Rex is the King of Merriment. People come to see Rex to have fun."

THE CAPTAIN'S DISAPPROVAL OF THE Zulu parade was not characteristic of the white businessmen of New Orleans, who, I found, usually spoke of their contribution to the Zulus as an act of goodwill.

"The New Orleans Hotel Association sends a check to Zulu every year," I was told by Seymour Weiss, president of the Hotel Roosevelt. "It's an interesting, funny adjunct to Carnival, and the colored people don't have much money. Also, somebody might write me a letter and say, 'Mr. Weiss, I want to get some throwaways,' or 'Mr. Weiss, I'd like to have an especially good costume.' The King this year is one of my waiters, for example, and I might send him a little check. I'm always happy to contribute, and so is everybody else, I believe. There's no one I can think of in the city of New Orleans who isn't a beneficiary, directly or indirectly, of Mardi Gras. For instance, the Negro bands are given jobs, and the Negroes who carry the torches are well paid. Everybody benefits, and we do everything to encourage the Zulu and other parades. I wouldn't be surprised if the merchant association sent a check."

Despite this atmosphere of largesse, I was assured by Nathan King, the would-be reformer, that Rapheal's "poor-mouthin'" was not totally unwarranted. King, who represents Old Crow whiskey in the Negro community, said, "My company paid the expenses when I was King. My company decided that the more popular I was, the more whiskey they might sell. But there wasn't the bitter sentiment then. If the Zulus had seen the handwriting on the wall and changed the parade then, they might have been okay. Some of the middle-class people from Dillard and all were always against them, but that one year when the Zulus didn't back out, they lost everybody else, too. Integration has had a lot to do with the way the Zulus have gone down. For instance, my company wouldn't give them a toothpick to throw away now. They're afraid of a boycott."

Why the Greater New Orleans Tourist & Convention Commission doesn't end these difficulties with a check is sadly puzzling to Baker and Rapheal. "Oh yeah, the city likes it so much that if we're a little slowful about getting a permit, they call us and write us and I don't know what all," Rapheal said to me one day. "But that's all. No money."

The Zulu parade is mentioned only briefly in the Commission's literature—"The Negro population has its own Mardi Gras celebration, including a parade on Shrove Tuesday led by King Zulu," one leaflet says—and Glen Douthit, the Commission's executive director, told me, "The Zulu parade is a fair tourist attraction, but we don't hang a peg on it. And if Zulu stopped parading, it wouldn't make that much difference. You see, Mardi Gras is so big that even if two or three organizations didn't parade, it wouldn't make that much difference. We would feel very bad if Zulu didn't parade, because it's something traditional, but it wouldn't be the end of Mardi Gras—just one less parade. Anybody would have to go out of his way to get a race angle on this Zulu thing."

The idea that Zulu might be just one more Mardi Gras parade brings a patient smile to the face of Daniel Thompson. He has no difficulty finding a race angle in it. "As long as the race factor is the main factor in this society, I don't know how Mardi Gras could exist without Zulu," he told me one day when I visited him at Dillard. "Zulu has the same psychological function as a clown at the circus. A man going up on a high wire is more effective if two clowns fall off first, and Rex is more beautiful because Zulu is ridiculous. The clown doesn't have to be a Negro—I think the white community could do it quite well—but in this area, where we think in terms of black and white, it's logical that it should be a Negro. This ludicrous individual, to make himself really ludicrous, has to be black. It's no accident that Zulu and Rex are on the same day. There's nothing in the South as important as being white or Negro, and you can't have an all-white Carnival or the whiteness wouldn't show. I don't mean that there has been a conscious effort on the part of whites and Negroes to perpetuate the tradition, but over the years, Zulu has become an integral part of Carnival. People are conscious of Zulu only to the extent to which Zulu dies out. It's like the theme music in a movie: You don't miss it until it stops."

* * *

THE DAY BEFORE MARDI GRAS, I phoned Rapheal and, after receiving the usual greeting, asked him how he was getting along with his final preparations.

"Oh, not so good," he said.

"What's the matter?" I asked.

"Everything's the matter," said Rapheal. "I'm at my deadlines. I got to get some work done."

I asked him about the story for the parade.

"Up until this time, I haven't had the time to write a story," Rapheal said. "I've been trying to write something around this new float, 'The Royal Prognosticator,' but I haven't had time to work it up, and of course, it's too late now. The next course I use is to adopt a snappy song or a snappy saying. I haven't thought of one."

Proud though Rapheal had seemed of the elegance of the floats a few days before, he now told me that he was worried for fear the parade was becoming too fancy, and that he disapproved of the efforts of the Big Shot from Africa and the King to out-look each other. "This is not a parade of beauty," he said. "This is a comical parade. That's what made it internationally known. The beautiful float will not fit in. This is for fun. We're not supposed to portray those things of beauty. We leave that to Rex."

I suggested that Rapheal might agree with the theory that Zulu's role in Mardi Gras was to make fun of Rex.

"There's no making fun in it," he said. "*Now* they're trying to ape after Rex. Before that, we had something original. Before, you'd look at that King, with moss on his head, then horns like a cow, and a body like a rabbit, and as you went down his body, it would change animals. Man, that was a terrible-looking sight. Maybe public opinion is forcing them to ape after Rex. That's completely out of harmony with the original idea. Either the public is doing it or these fellows don't understand, but it's easing us out of our comical role. If public opinion is doing it, then they're letting public opinion do it."

Rapheal went on to tell me that he was sending out news releases about the King and Queen and was trying to sell some more stops. "I'm just one of these fellows who try to get things together under the direction of the other fellows," he said. "We go along and do what we have to do—put on our parade. Did you hear about the boycott?"

"What boycott?" I asked.

"I think they're trying to boycott us," he said. "One of our chief aims in life seems to be making enemies as we go along."

As far as I was able to determine, Rapheal was the only person in New Orleans who could detect an attempt to boycott the Zulus. *The Louisiana Weekly*—apparently having forgotten its stand in 1961 that the Zulu parade was "disgraceful, disorderly and despicable"—had gone back to covering it as if nothing had happened.

AT ABOUT EIGHT O'CLOCK ON Mardi Gras morning, an hour before the Zulus were scheduled to land at the Poydras Street Wharf, I drove over to the tugboat *Bisso*, which was tied up about a mile down the Mississippi, and found the King, a Warrior or two, and the Big Shot from Africa preparing for the parade. According to Zulu lore, the Big Shot represents the wealth of Africa. "Those coconuts of his are not coconuts—they're from his diamond mine in Africa," Rapheal had told me. "He comes over and brings gold to you poor fellows here."

Bienamee's costume lived up to his advance claims. "This is imported fur skin. The material for this cost me seventy-five dollars," he said, spinning around to give everybody a good look at his leopard-skin cape, which was trimmed with gold and had three or four large ersatz diamonds sewn on it. More diamonds served as buttons on the Big Shot's leopard-skin jacket, and he had large diamond rings on both hands. His hat was the expensive top hat he had promised, his grass skirt was thick, and his jewelry included gold earrings and a large pendant. The Big Shot was, of course, in blackface, and his identity was further obscured by large sunglasses. He carried a huge sequined coconut in one hand and a gold cane in the other, and he was smoking a cigar even bigger than the cigar being smoked by King Zulu.

A bit later, when the Big Shot's makeup was being touched up in the tugboat's galley by one of the Warriors, Joseph Hayes, the Zulu president, came in, wearing street clothes but carrying a gavel decorated with ribbons.

"Do I look like the Big Shot, Prez?" Bienamee asked him.

"You look *big* enough to have you and your wife in there, too, Brother Bienamee," Hayes replied.

Bienamee's leopard-skin jacket did make him look rather bulky, but he seemed saddened by Hayes's remark. Then Hayes relented and said, "Milton, you look like the Big Shot."

After the *Bisso* had pulled out, I drove over to the Poydras Street Wharf, meeting a station wagon full of burlesque savages who were heading for the boat but had missed the sailing. Everybody got together at the wharf, and the Warriors accompanied Melvin Greene—who, as the Captain of the Zulu parade, was resplendent in a green silk costume and a plumed hat—as he jitterbugged with the King and Queen from the dock to the floats, which were waiting on the other side of the loading sheds. The Big Shot's float was particularly impressive—outfitted not only with papier-mâché wild animals but also with the Big Shot's collection of shrunken heads. Sunny Jim Poole, an immense man in a tentlike yellow costume and a top hat, shared the Big Shot's float, standing in the front like a burlesque figurehead, with one hand resting on a lion and the other on a zebra. As the participants climbed aboard their floats, the crowd was already pressing in to beg for coconuts, shouting, "Hey, Zulu, give me a coconut!" and "Hey, Your Highness, how about a coconut!" Baker was moving up and down the line of floats, selling fiftieth-anniversary medallions and an occasional souvenir coconut to the onlookers. There was a large police detail at the wharf—plus some special police from Bienamee's patrol agency—and it was dominated by four specially built three-wheeled motorcycles, each with a flat wooden bed behind the driver that held a barking, snapping police dog.

After a few minutes, Hayes shouted, "Is the King on? Is the Queen on? Is the Big Shot on?"

Everybody was on, and the floats began to move. The band and the flag-carriers had already moved out a block or two, in the first of many separations, and as the King's float caught up with the band, the motorcycle policemen began what was to be their procedure throughout the day. Whenever a Second Line formed between the band and the first float, or a number of people gathered close to a float to beg for coconuts, the motorcycles would swoop in and weave in and out, scattering the crowd. The parade moved quickly out of the business district. A thin crowd, almost all white, watched from the sidewalk, and every time the parade slowed down and people gathered around the floats, the motorcycles chased them back. There were six or eight Warriors sitting around a pot on the "Royal Proganistor" float, and they occasionally tossed coconuts out to the crowd. The Queen and her court appeared sedate and a bit chilly in the morning air, but King Zulu was clearly in fine spirits. He bowed his head magnanimously at the crowd, never ceasing to bless his subjects with his two-handed gesture. Baker and Hayes rode in the old pickup trucks that pulled the floats. Emile Ware, dressed in a uniform left from the days when the Zulu parade had a burlesque police rank of its own, helped Rapheal keep things moving, although nobody seemed to be in charge. As the parade got into the uptown Negro district, a friendly crowd, one or two deep, lined the street to watch the floats pass. The cries for coconuts now took the form of phrases like "All right, throw me a coconut, man." At one corner, the parade was almost stopped by the presence of dancing Second Liners between the band and the King's float. The Second Liners were quickly broken up by the motorcycles and the snapping dogs. The parade was moving remarkably fast—the floats jerked away from the first stop, Alex's Lounge & Bar, so quickly that Sunny Jim Poole almost lost his balance—and I asked Rapheal about the haste.

"We have to move fast," he said. "All this is by the

hour—the special police, the flag-toters, the band. It's all by the hour." And he hurried off to investigate a tie-up.

Only an hour or so after leaving the Poydras Street Wharf, the parade reached the Geddes funeral home, on Jackson Avenue. Describing the traditional meeting of the King and Queen there during the 1940 parade, the book *Gumbo Ya-Ya* began, "Thousands waited to see the Queen greet her lord. The King posed for cameramen, and bowed to everybody graciously. He leaned over and accepted flowers and a ribbon key of welcome from Doctor W. A. Willis, whose wife sponsors this use of the funeral parlors every year." The description went on to talk about champagne and "a thousand fancy sandwiches."

Some twenty years later, the Zulu parade moved past a new brick building housing the Gertrude Geddes Willis Life Insurance Co. & Funeral Home without even slowing down. Two or three women were standing in the doorway, but there were few other spectators on the street.

Despite its atmosphere of haste, the parade kept being slowed down by mishaps. The floats regularly got separated. At each stop, the owner of the bar came out to pour drinks for the King and Queen, usually standing on a makeshift platform bearing a sign that read, KING ZULU WILL STOP HERE. The crowds at the stops were enthusiastic, but any suggestion of a Second Line was swiftly discouraged by the police. At one point, as the parade passed under a long viaduct, a Second Line of about a hundred people formed—the largest of the day. As the four motorcycles swooped in and broke it up, the noises of the band, the barking dogs, the motorcycles, and the screams of the scattering Second Liners blended in a weird echo from the viaduct.

* * *

EVENTUALLY, A TREE BRANCH KNOCKED down the oversize crown that had been shading the throne on the King's float. There were several other holdups, and finally, two blocks from the downtown bar where the parade was to disband, the truck pulling the King's float ran out of gas.

One motorcycle policeman went back to see if he could get the float moving again. The three other policemen, after six hours with the Zulus, were in no mood to bother about breaking up some dancing that had started in the street outside the final stop.

"There might be a riot," one of the policemen said wearily. "You bring those uptown niggers downtown and you never can tell what'll happen. But all I want to do is get out of here."

Yet if the policemen were feeling harried after their chore, they were also proud of their effectiveness. "These four dogs did more than a hundred men could have done," one of the policemen said. "Although a few people were bitten."

"Without that band, we could really have moved this parade," another said.

Two blocks away, the King of the Zulus could be seen surrounded by a crowd that had accompanied the band back down the street to his stranded float. The King's float was far from what it had been. Somebody had gotten close enough to tear the bright foil off one side, leaving the cardboard base exposed, and the crown that had been shading the king's throne was lying incongruously on the top of one of the pickup trucks. The King, however, was still smiling down at the crowd and making his gesture of blessing, as if opening and closing a curtain.

THE DAY AFTER MARDI GRAS, I phoned Rapheal to say goodbye.

"Hello and good morning," he said, and asked if the parade had lived up to my expectations.

I told him I had found the police dogs somewhat disturbing.

"I requested the police dogs," Rapheal said. "They don't keep people from enjoying themselves on the sidewalk, but they keep them out of the line of march—keep them from knocking into the musicians and all. The Second Line is important to me; I sell that Second Line to merchants. The dogs were first used in 1961—or whenever that trouble was—and I think it was a blessing in disguise. When it happened, I saw how necessary the dogs were."

I asked Rapheal whether he thought it possible that the Zulu parade had come to an end after all—whether a parade that had been known for its rowdiness and spontaneity was no longer the same parade if it now had to be hurried along its way, with the crowds kept in line by police dogs.

"Oh, no," Rapheal said. "I think it creates a more orderly group of onlookers is all. I think the Zulu parade will always go on. All the club has to do is to find some new material to promote the thing. I'm too old. I'm just an old hunk of failure. I told them it depends on the tenacity and the courage of the people who take over. If they have the tenacity to sell and the courage to hold on, there will always be a

Zulu parade. Of course, I can't see into the future. I'm not the Royal Prognosticator."

· · ·

In the seventies, the strategy mentioned by Dr. Leonard Burns in 1964—the infiltration of the Zulu Social Aid & Pleasure Club by respectable members of the community—was implemented. The parade grew more substantial and more orderly. The ranks of the club swelled. The many prominent new members included Ernest Morial, the NAACP president who, in 1977, became the first African American mayor of New Orleans. In 2009, a decorated Zulu coconut was presented to President Barack Obama at the White House, where Desirée Glapion Rogers, a former Zulu Queen, was serving as social secretary. But on the parade floats, the King and the Big Shot and the King's retainers and many others (some of them white) continued to wear blackface makeup. What had been criticized as a despicable mockery of African Americans became regarded as a treasured New Orleans tradition—a fact that seems to support those literary critics who maintain that it's not so much the text that is important but what the reader brings to it.

DURING THE THIRTY-THIRD WEEK OF NATIONAL GUARD PATROLS

Wilmington, Delaware
1968

THE RAT PATROL

ON THURSDAY NIGHT, LETHA'S BEAUTY SHOP, ON NEW CASTLE Avenue, on the southeast edge of Wilmington, was held up by two men wearing ski masks. The call came over the police radio about nine. The two robbers—colored males, armed—had fled from the scene on foot. I was riding in a Delaware state police car Thursday night, jammed in the backseat between two National Guard sergeants who wore helmet liners and carried M-1 rifles. Three jeeps full of Guardsmen followed the state police car, forming a menacing-looking convoy that traveled slowly up and down the narrow streets of a Negro neighborhood just west of the downtown business district—a neighborhood that has become known as the Valley. It was one of the regular National Guard convoys that have routinely patrolled the Negro neighborhoods of Wilmington since last April. The state trooper who was driving had stopped at the beginning of the evening to pick up one of the Wilmington Police Department's mobile radios, and when he heard the robbery report, he headed for the southeast part of town, the jeeps trailing him. As the convoy drove through a public-housing project, the sergeant on my right put a clip of ammunition in his M-1. When the driver came to a bridge that covered a wooded culvert—what seemed to him a good hiding place—he stopped the car, reached for his flashlight, and got out. The sergeant with the loaded rifle also got out, and the two of them walked into the culvert to look for the robbery suspects—fruitlessly, as it turned out. The search seemed like a natural part of the evening's routine, but then it occurred to me that the people who robbed Letha's Beauty Shop were the only stickup men in the country being hunted by the National Guard.

The National Guard is officially patrolling Wilmington's streets to prevent civil disorder, rather than to help with ordinary police work, but the nights have dragged since the cold weather set in, and the state troopers in charge of the convoys often don't limit themselves to police calls that indicate the possibility of a crowd forming. The streets are no longer lined with people, as they were during the hot summer evenings; when one of the Guard caravans slows down at an intersection, someone may shout, "Hello, Rat Patrol!," but the side curtains have been put on the jeeps to protect the troops from the cold, so there is no longer much conversation between the National Guard and the citizens. A lot of people hurrying along the streets don't seem to notice the caravans, and those who do may just stare for a moment and continue on their way. "As you ride through, it doesn't seem like they have a feeling of resentment," a state trooper told me. "It's more like pure hate." With the cold weather, the Guardsmen seem to spend more of their duty tour at the Hollywood Diner, where the NCOs who ride in the state police cars carefully stow their rifles in the trunk before going in to eat hamburgers and joke with the waitresses, or at a lot near the Purina Chows plant, where a sudden flicking on of headlights will expose dozens of rats scampering along a pile of refuse. The first time local papers carried a story about Guardsmen being bored with duty in Wilmington was on April 11, a couple of days after the disorder in the Valley that had led the Governor to mobilize the Guard. Compared with some other reactions to the assassination of Martin Luther King, Jr., the disorder was rather mild; there were no deaths or serious injuries. Seven months later, the federal funds available for Guard training having run out, the last of the troops stationed at the Wilmington Armory were released, but the street patrols continue, manned by local Guardsmen—some of them reluctant designates of whichever battery has drawn the night's duty, some of them steady volunteers who can use the extra pay. The jeeps continue to cruise slowly past the redbrick row houses of the Valley—past burned-out or boarded-up storefronts, past storefronts with signs that provide some defiance even when everyone is off the street. The United Brotherhood of Black People has a picture of a black arm ending in a clenched black fist. The Black Library and Coffee House, sponsored by the Blackettes, is next door to a corner store that is considered by some people to be the former headquarters of the Black Liberation Army—it is considered that by everyone who believes that there ever was such a thing as a Black Liberation Army in Wilmington—and that is generally acknowledged to be the former headquarters of the Blackie Blacks (also known as Blackie's Blacks), a group with a reputation almost as fearsome among people who believe in the existence of the Black Liberation Army. In the police cars leading the convoys, the NCOs and the state troopers sometimes talk about livelier times—the time a bottle broke the car's windshield, or the time a riot seemed imminent after "a bunch of 'em" had gathered when Guardsmen stopped to arrest someone who had shouted an obscenity at the jeeps. Last spring, Guardsmen were present while city police were arresting some robbery suspects, and in circumstances that have never been made completely clear, a specialist fourth class who ordinarily works as a clerk in a construction company shot and killed one of the suspects. As far as is known, that was the only shot fired by a Guardsman on the streets of Wilmington since the Guard was mobilized last April.

THE GOVERNOR

"I didn't put them in for political reasons, and I won't take them off for political reasons," Governor Charles Terry, a heavyset man of sixty-eight, was telling a television interviewer when I arrived for an appointment at the state capitol, in Dover. The Governor, a Democrat, lost the November election to a moderate Republican, but in the opinion of people who follow Delaware elections, if he was keeping the Guard in Wilmington for political reasons, it was pretty good politics. The Governor led the Democratic ticket, and a lot of people—including the Governor—believe he would have won easily if he hadn't had a heart attack a month before the election. ("There's no doubt that most voters in the state were in favor of keeping the Guard in Wilmington," I was told by a Wilmington business leader who believes that efforts to have the Guard withdrawn were doomed once the patrols became a political issue. "The point is whether or not calling out the Guard is the kind of thing that should be decided by majority rule.") The Governor told the television interviewer that he intends to maintain patrols in Wilmington throughout the remainder of his term in office, and he was asked what made him think that Wilmington was the one city in the United States that required nightly patrols by the National Guard. Intelligence sources, the Governor said—intelligence sources that would be snuffed out if revealed.

After the television interviewer left, I talked with the Governor about the Guard and the election. He had lost by only a couple of thousand votes, and, in discussing the events of the campaign, he would occasionally pause and shake his head sadly and say, "That could've been the difference right there." The Governor believes that the mayor of Wilmington—John Babiarz, another Democrat who lost to a moderate Republican—cost the ticket votes by first asking that the Guard be removed and then changing his mind twice. (Babiarz even pulled city police off the patrols in the spring, which forced the Governor to assign state troopers, since the Guardsmen, awesome though they are as a symbol of law and order, require the presence of ordinary policemen to perform such tasks as making arrests—more or less the way the Queen's Guards who used to stand outside the Buckingham Palace fence needed ordinary bobbies to protect them from the pawing of American tourists.) "He got off the wagon and on the wagon and off the wagon," the Governor said. "I told him, 'John, you have to make up your mind. Let's keep them there as cheap insurance until this racial thing clears up.'" The Governor shook his head. "That could've been the difference," he said. "I didn't do it for political reasons, but you notice that the two or three who stuck with me—running for council and things—goddammit, they won!"

PETITIONERS FROM CONTINENTAL AMERICAN LIFE INSURANCE COMPANY

In August, some of the secretaries at the Continental American Life Insurance Company, encouraged by a local radio talk-show performer, decided that the side of law and order had to be heard. The Wilmington papers had been running editorials demanding the removal of the Guard, going so far as to compare the patrols to Linus's security blanket; a group of clergymen had signed a letter stating that "the presence of the National Guard has contributed to the increase of . . . destructive emotions rather than to their decrease"; and the Governor had revealed that a couple of the most prominent industrialists in town had made a trip to Dover to try to persuade him to remove the patrols (he told them that secret intelligence reports had warned of trouble brewing). The secretaries began to spend their lunch hours standing on street corners gathering names, and eventually they presented Governor Terry with a petition asking that the Guard remain. I had lunch with several petition organizers one day, and one thing they agreed on was that it was hard to understand why any law-abiding person would object to having the Guard around. "I see the Guard, but I obey the law, and I know they're not going to bother me," one of the secretaries said. "If the state can afford it and it makes people feel safe, why not have them?"

Compared with those who oppose the presence of the Guard, the secretaries at Continental American tend to be pessimistic about the standards of personal safety in Wilmington—perhaps because they have a more acute sense of the ominous. For instance, the arrest of several militant young Negroes who were shooting guns in a place called Cherry Island Marsh in August—an incident that led to the seizure of some stolen ammunition and to an announcement by the mayor that the Guard might be necessary after all—is generally referred to by opponents of the patrols as a few street toughs shooting at rats near the city dump, and is always referred to by the secretaries as "the Black Liberation Army practicing guerrilla-warfare tactics." One secretary—the wife of a city policeman—said, "People are afraid to go out at night. We're lucky, of course. We have three German shepherds."

"A lot of people have tear-gas pistols," another girl said, and she drew one out of her purse and laid it on the table.

THE (WHITE) COALITION

One evening, I went to a meeting of a group called the White Coalition for Justice Without Repression—or, more often, simply the White Coalition. In the opinion of the white liberals who formed it, having the Guard patrol Negro neighborhoods is not only insulting but dangerous; they believe that the Guard could exacerbate tensions to the point where its services would be required. They have found, though, that once the Guard has been established on the streets, its presence can be easily justified no matter what happens; peace can be interpreted as a dissuasion of troublemakers by the Guard, and trouble just goes to show that the Guard is needed after all. The Public Witness Committee of the White Coalition has produced anti-patrol bumper stickers and has expressed its concern at a meeting with the superintendent of the state police (he mentioned secret intelligence reports), but the white liberals seem resigned to having the patrols in Wilmington at least until the new governor takes office. One evening just before the election, about two hundred and fifty white people took part in a candlelight ceremony held by the Public Witness Committee in Rodney Square, the central square of Wilmington, but not many other white people watched the ceremony. Not many white people watch anything in Wilmington at night; most of them live in the suburbs and come in only for work (Wilmington was about fifteen percent Negro in 1950 and is now about forty percent). In fact, a lot of white people who work in Wilmington have never seen the Guard patrols, and suburban members of the White Coalition have occasionally surprised their neighbors by mentioning the fact that the Guard was still around. For ghetto residents, the connection of the suburbanites to Wilmington was best symbolized on the day of the April disturbance, when businesses let their employees out early in the afternoon and everyone got stuck in a vast traffic jam attempting to flee the city.

There were about forty people at the White Coalition meeting I attended, in an Episcopal church in one of the few attractive residential districts within the city limits. Everyone was white except a guest speaker, who told the group that whites should work exclusively with the white community and blacks with the black community. The speech reopened an argument that had come up at previous meetings. A woman at the back of the room said she had been disturbed by a feeling that the White Coalition actually discouraged Negroes from participating. A young man in blue jeans—a student at the University of Delaware who had come to inform the group of some academic-freedom problems there—stood up and explained that if the woman had the kind of experience he had gained while working with a black youth project, she would realize the futility of such efforts. "In working with these black youths, I had a lot of hang-ups," he said, "and what came out was my own inherent racism." When the student had finished, a man in a business suit stood up and said angrily that he wasn't going to attend any more meetings if they consisted of such juvenile confessions of inadequacy, and that anyone who wanted to do no more than argue with white people could talk to his own neighbors. A couple of speakers agreed that it should be possible to work with Negroes, but the director of a Catholic inner-city project said he had learned that whites tended to destroy the unity of the black community and undermine black leadership. By the time the young man in blue jeans got another turn, his attacker had stamped out of the room. "Obviously, this guy has never seen a straight razor coming at his throat," the student said. "He has never faced police dogs. He doesn't know what it's all about. Maybe he should go through a radicalizing experience, like I have." After some more speakers had supported the idea that the White Coalition should restrict its work to white people, an older man wearing a sports shirt stood up and said, "I can't see accomplishing anything by segregation. If this is open to the public, being segregated is almost unconstitutional." He looked puzzled. A woman in the back of the room asked if there was any objection to dropping "white" from the organization's name, since it seemed to offend a good number of those present, and a woman near her said, "Isn't it possible that if somebody hears about this group now, they could think it was the Ku Klux Klan or something?" The man who thought segregation was unconstitutional got up again, to say that the country clubs in the area had struck the word "white" from their bylaws because it was discriminatory. "The word 'white' is always discriminatory," he said. Finally, after about an hour, the chairman appointed a committee to look into changing the name.

THE BLACKS—POLARIZED

I went to the offices of the Wilmington Youth Emergency Action Council (WYEAC) one afternoon to talk with a staff member and a minister who had helped organize Operation Free Streets, an effort by the Negro community to get rid of the Guard patrols. WYEAC was designed as a way for business and the federal government to involve young militants and troublemakers and gang members—the kind of people who might join the Blackie Blacks, or even the Black Liberation Army—in some constructive activities, and it has been attacked constantly for employing a bunch of young militants and troublemakers and gang members. Federal funds have been withdrawn by now, of course, and about all that the WYEAC members have to show for their experience with institutionalized uplift is a tendency to speak in Street Federalese, a language now common in most American cities; when I asked the WYEAC worker about the Guard, he said,

"Man, these cats has polarized everyone, you know what I mean?" These days, the Guard keeps only a few convoys on the streets—and, in the words of one Valley resident, "a neighborhood like this is always under minimal martial law anyway." But many residents of the ghetto find the presence of an armed military force of any size a unique symbol of their helplessness, a reminder that they have neither the physical force nor the political influence to do anything about it. It is generally agreed that a number of ghetto residents—particularly older people—favor the presence of the Guard, but Leonard Williams, a black Municipal Court judge, has said, "Every black man in Wilmington who's worth his salt, when he leaves his job in the evening and sees the convoys, something happens to him."

The minister told me that Operation Free Streets had been organized to gather a petition with twice as many names as the one gathered by the Continental American secretaries—this one demanding the Guard's removal. Eventually, the petition had been burned publicly to symbolize the failure of the authorities to pay any attention to the demands of the black community. There has been some talk of an economic boycott, but ghetto leaders seem resigned to the fact that there is nothing they can do about the Guard except to hope that the next governor removes it. Some of them seem equally troubled by the prospect that young people will treat the Guard as a challenge that must be met with violence and by the prospect that the young people will learn to tolerate the Guard, as their parents have learned to tolerate so many other things. "With the Guards here, there's a loss of dignity and communications and everything, man," the WYEAC worker told me. "How long would a white community allow a black army to patrol their streets?"

. . .

Governor Terry did keep the Guard in Wilmington throughout his term in office. The man who defeated him in the 1968 elections, Russell Peterson, withdrew the Guard in his first act as governor. The Delaware National Guard's presence in Wilmington is sometimes spoken of as the longest military occupation of an American city since the Civil War.

A HEARING: "IN THE MATTER OF DISCIPLINARY ACTION INVOLVING CERTAIN STUDENTS OF WISCONSIN STATE UNIVERSITY OSHKOSH"

Oshkosh, Wisconsin
1968

AFTER THE EVENTS OF NOVEMBER 21, NINETY-FOUR OF THE hundred and fourteen black students enrolled at Wisconsin State University Oshkosh were suspended almost immediately. They were told that a hearing could be requested by filing written notice within ten days. On December 9, Federal District Judge James E. Doyle, finding that the suspensions had been imposed without due process of law, ruled that the university would have to reinstate the students unless it conducted the hearing on a specific charge and announced the results by December 20. The Board of Regents of State Universities, which had assumed jurisdiction over the cases, chose to maintain the suspensions, and a hearing was held. In his opinion, Judge Doyle summarized what had happened at WSUO on November 21, and then wrote, "The events described in these affidavits cannot be recounted without evoking deep sadness; sadness in the memory of decades, even centuries, of injustice, the fruits of which are now so insistently with us; sadness that this legacy seems now to be producing a profound sickness in some of our people, and specifically some of our younger black people; and sadness that some of them appear so unaware that there is a sickness there."

ROGER E. GUILES, PRESIDENT OF THE UNIVERSITY, TESTIFIES TO BEING THE VICTIM OF UNDESIRABLE ACTIONS IN HIS OWN OFFICE:

Guiles *(A distinguished-looking man with a remarkable resemblance to the actor Fredric March, he speaks slowly from the witness stand and twiddles his thumbs slowly as he speaks):* I looked up, somewhat surprised to find students standing in the doorway or moving through the doorway. . . . I looked up and asked if they had an appointment. . . . As I looked again, I noticed that they were in front of a much larger group of persons, who moved in through the office until there seemed to be no more space available. . . . I was presented with an eight-and-a-half-by-eleven-size sheet of paper on which were listed a number of demands, and I was told that I was expected to sign the statement. I was reminded that this was not to be a session for discussion or dialogue, that it was my signature that was being demanded and I'd better sign. . . . The students were crowded very tightly against all sides, and other students were sitting on the desk. . . . I pointed out that, Number One, I could not sign the statement. . . . I also asked the students to consider the fact that they were acting in a very undesirable manner and it was not to their advantage to remain in the room. This, however, was not accepted by them, as evidenced by the fact that they did not move. . . . After some fifteen or twenty minutes—a time during which I was unable to really communicate because my statements were interrupted—someone gave the signal of "Do your thing." . . . At that time, the room exploded. . . . In a relatively few minutes, the interior of the office became a shambles, as did the adjacent offices in rapid succession.

Just about everyone in Oshkosh was outraged by the property damage. It was originally reported, erroneously, at about fifteen thousand dollars. The Oshkosh Chamber of Commerce circulated a petition demanding that the students be expelled and be required to pay for the damage—then recalled the petition when it was pointed out that this uncharacteristic venture into the area of collegiate crime and punishment might be misinterpreted as reflecting some animus toward Negro students. A newspaper reporter who collected public reactions in Oshkosh a couple of days after the event found most citizens so angry and astonished that they could explain the destruction only in terms of outside influence, perhaps Communists. It was Oshkosh's first experience with modern student unrest—unless one counts some springtime trouble a couple of years ago when the legislature was considering raising the legal beer-drinking age.

Even people who considered themselves particularly sympathetic to the black students were shocked. "Nobody could understand why they did it," a local reporter told me. "I'm not sure that they understand why themselves." The university, after all, had consciously recruited Negroes and had established a special committee to assist them—the Advisory Committee for Culturally Distinct Students. The demands given to the president on November 21 were basically the same demands that had been turned over to the committee five weeks earlier—demands for an Afro-American cultural center, and black instructors, and courses on the black experience in America—and the university said later that the committee had actually been making considerable progress toward meeting the demands. An old house, due to be torn down next summer, had been offered as a temporary cultural center but was rejected; a couple of courses concerning black Americans were planned for the spring semester; letters had been sent to predominantly Negro colleges expressing interest in hiring Negro faculty members. Even before the demands were made, the university library had begun to stock *Ebony* and the plays of LeRoi Jones. "I think we did pretty well for five weeks," the committee's chairman told me. "After all, this is a bureaucracy."

PRESIDENT GUILES TESTIFIES TO THE PRESENCE OF BLACK STUDENTS AT THE UNIVERSITY:

Lloyd Barbee *(the lawyer for most of the suspended students—a bearded, frail-looking man who is the only Negro in the Wisconsin state legislature):* President Guiles, when you first came to the university here, it was known as a state college, is that not correct?

Guiles: That's right.

Barbee: And at that time did you have any black students?

Guiles: I believe that we've always had black students. I'm not absolutely sure of that, but as far as I can recall, we've always had black students.

They were Africans. When Guiles arrived in Oshkosh in 1959, after seventeen years at the state college at Platteville, there were about two thousand students enrolled. There may have been a few black African students among them, but until a few years ago, black African students were the only kind of black students who came to Oshkosh. In 1964, the new director of admissions, Donald D. Jorgenson—now the registrar and the chairman of the Culturally Distinct Students committee—mentioned to Guiles that the university ought to have some American Negroes, and was encouraged by the president's response. The following year, some Negro high school seniors in inner-city Milwaukee, ninety miles away, began to receive visits from Jorgenson and even free bus tours of the WSUO campus; Negro high school seniors as far away as Newark, New Jersey, began receiving WSUO applications in the mail. In 1967, a federally supported educational-opportunity center was established in Milwaukee and began channeling dozens of black students toward WSUO. The white enrollment had also been growing at an extraordinary rate. WSUO now has eleven thousand students. About half of them are studying education—the university was called a teachers college before it was called a state college, and was called a normal school before that—but the university has promised a "sustained thrust toward various forms of interdisciplinary studies." Through its interdisciplinary program in international affairs, WSUO made some arrangements with universities in Ghana and Sierra Leone and, this year, began sending students off for a junior year in Africa.

PRESIDENT GUILES TESTIFIES ON THE DIFFICULTY OF ESTIMATING THE BLACK POPULATION OF THE CITY OF OSHKOSH:

Barbee: Doctor, do you know what the black population of the city of Oshkosh is?

Guiles: I haven't exact information. I have some idea. . . .

Barbee: What is that idea in terms of numbers?

Guiles: I do not know exactly, because that's not in my realm of responsibility.

Barbee: Is it large or small?

Guiles: Well, I don't want to get involved here with relative terms—what you mean by small, what you mean by large. I would assume that if you leave off the university population, it would certainly be a very small percentage of the population.

If you leave off the university population, there aren't any black people in Oshkosh. There are very few Negroes in any of the cities along the Fox River Valley, from Oshkosh to Green Bay, but Oshkosh, a city of fifty thousand people, has been known for its singular whiteness. Before a few African students began coming to WSUO, about the only black people Oshkosh citizens ever saw were some who came up from Milwaukee on summer weekends to fish from the bridges. Off the campus, black students have occasionally run into fights and have regularly heard shouts of "Nigger!" from passing cars. In some bars, they have inferred that their patronage wasn't really welcome. More important, they have constantly felt stared at, strange, alone. "In Milwaukee, you go downtown and at least you see some black faces, even behind the counters," one of them told me. "Here everyone looks at you like you're some kind of freak."

Some of the black students didn't feel a lot more comfortable on the campus. The style and experience and dialect of the Milwaukee inner city did not provide an easy bridge for contact with middle-class white students from middle-class white towns in central Wisconsin. "This semester, everything seemed to go wrong," one of the black students told me. WSUO is not a particularly demanding college—admission is automatic for any state resident in the top three quarters of his graduating class; one undergraduate summed up the university as "a high school with ashtrays"—but graduates of black inner-city high schools are likely to have difficulty at any college, and the attrition rate of black students has been high from the start. This fall, a number of them also seemed to be running into administrative problems with the scholarships and loans that had been arranged through state and federal programs. "They should make black students feel at home, just like white students," one of the black students told me. The black students—almost all of them freshmen and sophomores—felt a long way from home. They tended to go around together in groups and to keep their own counsel. (The white liberals on the faculty who denounced their suspension became close to them only after November 21.) Few of them took part in the ordinary student activities. Every Wednesday, they got together for a meeting of the Black Student Union and talked of demands that black students should make. "That cultural center was important to us," one of them told me. "It would be a psychological symbol that we exist."

PRESIDENT GUILES TESTIFIES ON THE COMMITTEE THAT HAD BEEN GIVEN THE DEMANDS IN OCTOBER:

Barbee: Dr. Guiles, what could this . . . committee do in view of the demands that the black students had given it?

Guiles: Well . . . it is true that a large part of their responsibility hinges upon the art of persuasion, but that's not uncommon on a university campus.

"If the university was serious, they would have given the demands to a committee that had some power and money," one of the black students told me. In the opinion of one faculty member sympathetic to them, the black students had a sense of urgency about the demands that the administration never understood—and a need to assert themselves. They found the normal language of academic bureaucrats mad-dening. They considered the committee a stall, and events since November 21 have tended to convince them that they were right. Despite the talk about hiring black professors, for instance, the students have been told by white liberal fac-ulty members that the departments felt no serious pressure to do so, and the one black instructor now at Oshkosh— a Nigerian—has said that when he gave the university some leads, they were ignored; at a university convocation held a couple of days before the hearing, Guiles said, "Here faculty is selected on the basis of background and ability for the position to be filled. Race should have nothing to do with it." At the same convocation, university officials replied to accusations that the then-accepted damage figure of twelve thousand dollars was inflated by perhaps five hundred per-cent. It was explained that the figure had reached the press by mistake—being not the actual damage but the total of an accounting that the university had made, for some reason, to show what the cost would be if every piece of furniture in-volved were replaced, so that a tipped-over desk showed up as a new desk. "They were really thorough about adding up the damage," one of the black students said. "What they're not interested in is what really caused the damage."

PRESIDENT GUILES TESTIFIES TO PROBLEMS OF
IDENTIFICATION IN A LARGE UNIVERSITY:

A State Assistant Attorney General *(Acting as prosecu-tor for the regents):* Now, Dr. Guiles, were these stu-dents all black?

Guiles: All of these students who were in the offices—all the students I observed—happened to be black.

Assistant Attorney General: Now, do you recall any particular student who was in your office on this morning?

Guiles: I think I would have to say, first of all, that with an enrollment of eleven thousand students . . .

It is agreed by the eyewitnesses that only a certain number of the students who were present participated in damaging the president's office, but the eyewitnesses are unable to say which students they were. The damage was what had outraged everybody—that and the idea of students presenting demands rather than requests to the president—but the hearing had to be held on the charge of blocking the use of a university office. All the students had been arrested for refusing to leave the suite of offices, and the police arrest list had provided the names for the mass suspension—even the names, it turned out, of a few students who, perhaps not having been present the previous evening, when the Black Student Union decided to stage the demonstration, had been in class during the time the damage was done and had joined the crowd in the presidential suite only later in the morning. It is agreed by both sides that many students merely stood in the office all morning, and that some stood there only through the pressure of racial solidarity. (The solidarity was eventually carried further: The black students remaining at WSUO presented Guiles with a statement saying that they would not return next semester if any of the suspended students were expelled.) The suspended students say they weren't asking that their demands be met immediately but that the president sign the paper immediately, as an indication of his good faith.

"You know," I was told by a girl who had been present, "we were just praying he would sign that paper."

E. O. THEDINGA, VICE PRESIDENT FOR STUDENT
AFFAIRS, TESTIFIES TO WHAT HE DID UPON
HEARING THAT THE BLACK STUDENTS HAD TAKEN
OVER THE PRESIDENTIAL OFFICE:

Thedinga *(He has been at Oshkosh since 1936 and is as distinguished-looking as President Guiles; the students call him the Silver Fox):* I immediately picked up the phone and dialed for Mr. James McKee. He responded. I said, "Do you know that the black students have taken over the presidential office and the executive suite?"

The plans for attracting black students to WSUO did not establish any office or program to give them special attention once they arrived. Last February, after it was brought to the attention of a WSUO faculty member that a number of the black students were carrying unrealistic class loads, he organized an ad hoc committee that was eventually made into the formal Advisory Committee for Culturally Distinct Students. This fall, the university hired James McKee, a Negro, to coordinate its efforts for the culturally distinct, and hired one of the first Negro graduates of WSUO as his assistant. The committee considered the hiring of McKee a solid accomplishment and considered McKee its link with the students.

Testifying at the hearings, McKee went out of his way to indicate his sympathy for the students, but on November 21, he had been as surprised as E. O. Thedinga to hear that they were occupying the president's office. "The students thought of me as part of the administration," McKee told me. "I hadn't talked to them in weeks."

SERGEANT DISCH, OF THE OSHKOSH POLICE, AND SERGEANT MISCH, OF THE WINNEBAGO COUNTY SHERIFF'S DEPARTMENT, AND OTHERS TESTIFY THAT THEY TOLD THE STUDENTS TO LEAVE, IN THE NAME OF THE STATE OF WISCONSIN, AND LOADED THEM ON TWO HERTZ RENTAL TRUCKS AND TOOK THEM TO JAIL; BARBEE THEN MAKES SOME CLOSING REMARKS:

Barbee: The university administration here is used to operating a certain type of higher-educational institution that it has always run and that has not become flexible enough to meet the realities of the current generation . . . the university attempted to handle the situation in the normal middle-class administrative way of appointing a committee . . . and engaged in the kind of vague semantic language that was no substitute for action.

What a college administrator might expect from black students at a predominantly white Northern university was, of course, quite a bit different in 1964, when the idea of recruiting Negroes came up at WSUO, from what it is today. "I think a lot of people here thought it would be a good idea both for the black students and for the broadening of the white students, a lot of whom come from pretty parochial backgrounds," a faculty member told me. "I think that even after students were being recruited directly from the ghetto, there was some feeling that they would just be black versions of our middle-class white students. It was hard to accept the idea that they had different patterns of behavior, different expectations." Some of the black students I spoke with during the hearings had reached the conclusion that the entire program was cynical—a way to qualify for federal grants. (The university says there is absolutely no federal money in question.) A lot of the black students, though, think the administration wanted to do the right thing. "I think they were sincere," one of them said. "They just didn't know what they were being sincere about."

Robert Silverstein, a Lawyer Representing Several of the Students, Makes Some Closing Remarks:

These students were trying to tell us something . . . obviously the signing of that paper by the president was nothing more than a symbol—a symbol saying, "Yes, we realize we haven't listened. We're listening."

The Assistant Attorney General Makes Some Closing Remarks:

I'm not going to engage in a philosophical or a sociological argument. . . . However, I don't believe that any group of students, whether they be black or white, has the right to present such an ultimatum as was presented to President Guiles on the morning of November 21. No group has that right.

Two days after the hearing ended, the Board of Regents, adhering to the time limit set by Judge Doyle, expelled ninety of the ninety-four suspended students.

• • •

Five of the expelled students later returned to the university and completed their degrees. The events of late November 1969 are now referred to at the university as "Black Thursday." Since 2013, an African American Student Leadership Award has been given annually in commemoration of the "Oshkosh 94." In the fall of 2015, the University of Wisconsin Oshkosh had among its 14,000 students 337 African Americans.

DOING THE RIGHT THING
ISN'T ALWAYS EASY

———

Denver, Colorado
1969

JAMES PERRILL AND FRANK SOUTHWORTH SAID
THE ISSUE WAS FORCED BUSING

WHEN MARTIN LUTHER KING, JR., WAS ASSASSINATED, THE
Denver Board of Education resolved to integrate the schools.
The vote was five to two. The supporters included the only
Negro board member, who had offered the resolution; Edgar Benton, a lawyer in his early forties who had been the
city's most articulate advocate of school integration for half
a dozen years; two relatively conservative board members
whose views on integration had changed during their tenure;
and a state senator named Allegra Saunders, who sometimes
seemed to interpret majority rule to mean that she was obli-
gated to go along with the majority wherever it happened to
be going. In the Denver public schools, the twenty percent of
the students who belong to the Spanish-surname population

usually referred to as Hispanos have, as a group, the lowest academic achievement and the highest dropout rate. But it is the black children—about fifteen percent—whose schooling is most restricted by de facto segregation and whose parents have been the most insistent about the need for change. As a first step toward integration, the school board eventually resolved, by the same five-to-two margin, to adjust the ratio of black to white in the schools of one area next fall by changing some attendance boundaries and transporting some children by bus—devices that are familiar to the white citizens of many Northern cities under the name of Destroying Neighborhood Schools by Forced Busing.

The school board held public hearings on the resolutions. Most of the people who testified—many of them members of an integrationist coalition that had been formed after King's death—expressed approval of the integration plan or criticized it for being too mild. They became known in Denver as A Vocal Minority—the assumption being that most people (at least most white people) would express a contrary opinion if they happened to be the kind of people who testified at school-board hearings.

There was a lot of talk in Denver about how the school board had been pressured by A Vocal Minority into acting contrary to the desires of The Silent Majority. This spring, about a year after King's death, a simple remedy presented itself to The Silent Majority. The seats held by Ed Benton and Allegra Saunders came up for election. Two conservative Republicans named James Perrill and Frank Southworth announced that, in the interests of giving the citizens a clear choice, they were running for the school board as a team committed to combining with the board's two dissenters to form a majority that would rescind the integration resolutions. The integrationists organized behind Benton and Monte Pascoe, a young lawyer with similarly strong views about the necessity of integration, and the Democratic Party officially endorsed the ticket—an endorsement that failed to prevent five more Democrats from running as independents. The clear choice Perrill and Southworth had in mind concerned forced busing. Their campaign advertising started with billboards proclaiming them to be FOR neighborhood schools and AGAINST mandatory busing—a position that also served to sum up the educational philosophy of most of the independent candidates—and it ended with a newspaper advertisement that asked, "Why, Mr. Benton, are you for Forced Busing which will Destroy the Neighborhood Schools?" In their public appearances, Perrill and Southworth managed to elaborate on that limited theme with a kind of creative redundancy. Mandatory busing and forced busing combined to become mandatory forced busing. They also mentioned crosstown busing, massive busing, and massive crosstown busing. By the end of the campaign, Southworth was talking about "forced mandatory crosstown busing on a massive scale."

ALL THE CANDIDATES EXCEPT BENTON AND PASCOE SAID THE ISSUE WAS NOT INTEGRATION

All the candidates said that they personally believed in integration—the general rule in such campaigns being that a nominal commitment to integration is expected from everyone involved except the voters. Perrill said integration would come about when the economic status of Negroes improved and when some changes were made in men's minds—the kind of changes that could not be dictated by laws or resolutions. He and Southworth said that voluntary busing would be fine—another rule being that anytime white people are expected to associate with black people, they ought to have a choice in the matter. All of the candidates who were running against forced busing said they were distressed at the implication that they harbored ill feelings against other men on the basis of race, creed, or color. The implication seemed particularly galling to Nathan Singer, the most entertaining of the independent anti-busing candidates, an aeronautical engineer who read intently from set speeches that included dramatic proclamations and an occasional rhyme ("Be aware, vote with care" or "Some may choose not to accuse, but I shall"). At one of the many PTA meetings addressed by all the candidates, Singer offered as a proof of his tolerance the fact that Sammy Davis, Jr., belongs to his fraternity. "And anyone who wants to check that," he told the McMeen Elementary School PTA, "can call the national headquarters of Tau Delta Phi, in Chicago."

BENTON AND PASCOE SAID THE ISSUE WAS NOT FORCED BUSING

The Benton-Pascoe campaign recognized that there were genuine concerns about the inconveniences or educational disadvantages that busing might bring, and about whether busing was really the best way to provide equality of education, and about integration itself. Benton-Pascoe advertisements did not attempt to explain the board's intricate plans for integration, but in answering questions in smaller groups the candidates explained that the racial composition of each school would reflect the entire school district's population, so that white children would be bused to schools that would become predominantly white, and black children would be bused to schools with a substantial black minority. By the end of the campaign, though, a lot of the Benton-Pascoe canvassers came to believe that most of the questions people raised about the problems inherent in busing were not meant to be answered. Benton repeatedly pointed out that the Denver school board had, for one administrative reason or another, employed forced busing in the schools to some degree for at least forty years—a process that had involved hundreds of thousands of schoolchildren without provoking any citywide controversies about the length of the ride or the provisions made for taking care of a sick child. (Nine thousand children are now bused, about half as many as would have to be bused in the final stage of integration. As it happens, Destroying Neighborhood Schools is an old habit of the Denver school board, which used to manipulate boundaries to avoid having to send white children to predominantly black schools; in fact, some of the children in the area most bitterly opposed to the proposed destruction of neighborhood schools would actually be transferred to schools closer to their homes.) Late one night, a few people were at Pascoe's house talking over the evening's meetings when the phone rang. The caller shouted an obscenity at Pascoe and called him a nigger-lover. Pascoe smiled when he repeated the conversation to his guests. "I've probably met that guy at some meeting," he said. "And he's told me he's all for integration, but what about the effect

busing will have on after-school activities or parent participation?"

BENTON AND PASCOE SAID THE ISSUE WAS DOING THE RIGHT THING

What else could they say? Candidates normally try to appeal to the voter's self-interest, and Benton and Pascoe could
hardly argue that sending children to school out of the neighborhood on a bus was a convenience that every taxpayer had
been looking forward to. White people opposed to busing
didn't have to be racists but merely people who didn't feel a
strong enough commitment to integration to make any personal sacrifices for it. As a minor theme, the Benton-Pascoe
campaign linked the integration plan to the future health of
the city. Compared to other cities of similar size, Denver still
has a small Negro population, and a relatively high percentage of it is middle-class; by chance, the expansion of the Negro neighborhood has been toward solid neighborhoods that
have houses desirable to whites. Benton and Pascoe argued
that Denver still had time to prevent the inner-city decay
and separated societies that are found in Eastern cities—the
first step being the school board's plan to prevent East High
School and Smiley Junior High School, the most important
schools on the edge of the Negro neighborhood, from becoming all black. But nobody in the Benton-Pascoe campaign really believed that the white people who live in, say,
the outlying middle-class residential districts of southeast
Denver actually consider their future linked to the state of
the inner city or that they feel any urgency about prevent-
ing the creation of separate societies. When Pascoe visited a
high school in the area, the complaint expressed about the

Negroes who had come to the school by bus under a small experimental program was that only two of them had joined the Pep Club.

The appeal to white people that Benton and Pascoe were left with was an appeal to do what is right in reversing the inequalities existing in Denver schools. "Doing the Right Thing Isn't Always Easy," their brochure said. "But Doing the Right Thing Is Always Worth Doing." The issue, Benton said in one speech, was whether "there is enough humanity and enough charity among the majority to hold out a helping hand to these children, not to say, 'We believe in holding out a helping hand, but there are many reasons why we can't do it.' "

PEOPLE IN PARK HILL SAID THE ISSUE WAS PARK HILL

A few years ago, the customary housing pattern of Negro expansion and white panic selling may have been reversed in the southern part of an area called Park Hill—an attractive, convenient area once considered the place to live in Denver—mainly because of the efforts of a neighborhood organization called the Park Hill Action Committee. The houses that come up for sale in Park Hill now are bought by white people as well as black people—young people of the type who prefer a solid old house to life in the subdivisions, or liberals who welcome the opportunity to live in an integrated neighborhood, or just people looking for a good buy. East High School and Smiley Junior High School, which would both be given large white majorities by the integration plan, serve Park Hill. Without the plan, East, which is about forty percent black, and Smiley, which is about seventy-two percent black, represent the most serious threat to Park Hill's future as an integrated neighborhood. A number of Park Hill people—black and white—considered the Benton-Pascoe campaign the culmination of a nine-year fight. The campaign presented a rare opportunity, one resident observed during a huge Park Hill fund-raising party for Benton and Pascoe. People could work for their beliefs and their property values at the same time.

MOST OF THE CANDIDATES SAID THE ISSUE WAS THAT THE BOARD HAD FORCED ITS WILL ON THE PEOPLE

In the North, integration is now almost invariably an elitist movement. The more democratic the decision-making process, the smaller the chance any plan for purposeful integration has of being put into effect. There had been no clear-cut integration vote in Denver, but the results in the previous school-board election and the defeat of a school-bond issue a few years ago were both interpreted as being caused partly by anti-integration sentiment. People who serve on a school board in a city like Denver—seeing ghetto schools at first hand, studying the difference in achievement between the average Hispano child and the average Anglo child, reading reports about a national crisis in race, feeling themselves responsible for the future, listening to A Vocal Minority— are bound to take some actions that are difficult to explain to The Silent Majority. The school-board election became partly an argument about the extent to which public officials should represent their constituents—whether, a *Denver Post* article said, the public preferred school-board members who lead or "school-board members who, in effect, follow the wishes and feelings—including prejudices—of the voters who elected them." Perrill often said that "power comes from people, not from ideas," and that the integration resolutions had to be rescinded in order to clear the air and restore the confidence of the people in the board. All the anti-busing candidates emphasized that the people had not been given a choice—that forced busing for forced integration had been forced on them.

In Denver, both school integration and the preservation of neighborhood schools have been white-collar movements; with little heavy industry, Denver has a relatively small working-class population. But the Benton-Pascoe campaign—in its formulation of the issue as something approaching noblesse oblige, and in the backgrounds of its candidates and its staff—had a kind of Ivy League tone. When one independent candidate, a truck driver named Robert Crider, finally lost his temper near the end of the campaign, the first thing he thought to say was that the problem on the school board for the past eight years had been that Ed Benton thought he knew more than anyone else.

SOME NEGRO LEADERS SAID THE ISSUE WAS BASIC SYMPATHY

Black separatists were said to be treating the election as merely the final frivolous delay before serious talk began on who was to control the schools of each neighborhood. But even the integrationist Negroes who supported Benton and Pascoe seemed reluctant to go into details about a program whose premise is that the way to improve the performance of black children is to expose them to white children. About a week before the election, the most influential Negro adviser to Benton and Pascoe suggested that campaigning in the Negro areas should concentrate not on the complicated arguments about busing but on the fact that Benton and Pascoe would be basically sympathetic to minorities. During the last weekend of the campaign, the handbills passed out in the Negro neighborhoods contained a simple statement of why Negroes should vote for Benton and Pascoe: "They're for us."

THE HISPANOS DIDN'T SAY MUCH OF ANYTHING

In Denver, Hispanos are noted for being politically silent. They vote Democratic, but they often don't vote. The most visible and by far the most militant Hispano leader, Rudolfo (Corky) Gonzales, is a separatist who believes that Negro pressure for integration is just a manifestation of the black man's inferiority complex; the few conservative leaders who exist to form a link with the Anglo community would probably agree. In between, there is no equivalent of the usual Negro integration organization—and little organization of any kind. The Hispanos, many of them migrants from the isolated farming villages of northern New Mexico and southern Colorado, are generally worse off economically than Negroes in Denver. But those Hispanos who think about such matters tend to believe that neither the causes nor the cures for the Hispanos' plight have much in common with those usually associated with the problems of the black community. Most Hispanos don't appear to be concerned with such issues one way or the other. The only approach that the Benton-Pascoe forces could think of to make to them was an appeal to party loyalty. One Benton-Pascoe brochure had on the back page a long explanation of busing under the headline TODAY'S SCHOOL IS A WORKING MODEL OF TOMORROW'S SOCIETY. In the version distributed in Hispano neighborhoods, the equivalent space was taken up with block letters saying ENDORSED BY THE DENVER DEMOCRATIC PARTY.

BENTON SAID THE ISSUE WAS EDUCATING THE PUBLIC

From the start, Benton and Pascoe knew they would probably lose, but everyone in their campaign seemed surprised at the magnitude of the defeat. Soon after the polls closed, it became obvious to the people who had gathered in Benton-Pascoe headquarters that Southworth and Perrill would win by a margin of at least two to one. A heavy Perrill-Southworth vote was expected in outlying white neighborhoods, but it also came in some white areas closer to the center of town. One Benton-Pascoe worker pointed out an area in the East High district and said that in that neighborhood, it was logical to expect even pure bigots—at least bigots with some foresight—to vote for Benton and Pascoe on grounds of self-interest; the integration plan would mean increasing the white enrollment of their children's school and probably increasing the value of their property. "That precinct went two to one against us," the worker said. "Reason has nothing to do with this." In a speech at the party for campaign workers that night, the Benton-Pascoe campaign manager said that Ed Benton and Monte Pascoe had had the courage to step out in front of the community and try to lead. Benton was asked by a local radio station what the results indicated. They indicated, he said, that it was difficult to present complicated issues concerning inequality to the public, and that it was difficult to persuade people to change established ways of doing things—ways of doing things that had become convenient for one section of the population and devastating for another. "It's always difficult to educate people," he went on, "whether it's children in the classroom or people in the community."

. . .

In 1976, a federal court ordered Denver Public Schools to adopt a mandatory busing plan—the first such order outside the South. Twenty years later, the court allowed the abandonment of the plan. At that point, largely because of white flight to the suburbs, the schools were, according to The New York Times, *"more racially segregated than ever"— a phrase that could have served as a succinct summary of a report that the school board received twenty years after that, in 2015. That report said that only twenty-nine of Denver's one hundred eighty-eight schools could be considered integrated.*

CATEGORIES

Provo, Utah
1970

> *The position of the Church of Jesus Christ of*
> *Latter-day Saints affecting those of the Negro*
> *race who choose to join the Church falls wholly*
> *within the category of religion. It has no bearing*
> *upon matters of civil rights.*
> —The First Presidency, Church of Jesus Christ
> of Latter-day Saints, December 1969

MOST AMERICANS BELIEVE THAT A MORAL ISSUE CAN BE contained within a category, and they often find themselves astonished or irritated by those Americans who do not. A lot of university trustees can't imagine why students who are receiving a perfectly peaceful liberal education should concern themselves with the fact that some other department of the same institution happens to do research for the Department of Defense. Most Americans do not hold a Rockefeller in

New York accountable for what kind of regime his family's bank helps support in South Africa. But a lot of young people and black people insist on considering everything connected. Because Brigham Young University, which is operated by the Mormon Church, happens to be one of the few places in the country where even the students believe in the sanctity of categories, it is difficult for nearly everyone there to understand how objection to a Mormon religious belief could be translated into rudeness to the BYU basketball team. In reaffirming that priesthood orders, which every male Mormon must hold in order to participate fully in the Church, would remain closed to Negroes, the First Presidency clearly stated not only that the matter was wholly within the category of religion but also that in the civil category, the Church specifically teaches that all of God's children should have equal constitutional rights. Furthermore, the university's president has pointed out, the Church has nothing to do with arranging athletic events; and furthermore, the coaches often say, some of the players are not even Mormons, and the athletic field obviously would not be the place to argue politics or religion even if they were. Yet BYU basketball players can hardly appear anywhere without being hooted at as racists, and Stanford University announced last fall that it would no longer meet BYU in athletic contests. Keeping the argument within its original category, Ernest L. Wilkinson, the president of BYU, called Stanford's action "flagrant religious discrimination."

Since the demonstrators obviously have no interest in joining the Mormon Church, it follows to any strict categorizer that they are insincere troublemakers who have merely chosen BYU athletics as a shortcut to national publicity. BYU distributes an article from the NCAA newspaper in which the editors, in their first venture into political undercover work, report being reliably informed that revolutionaries were laying their plans against BYU last summer. BYU also makes available reprints of an anti-Mormon article from a Communist newspaper—a get-the-Mormons signal to the Communist Conspiracy, according to an accompanying analysis by W. Cleon Skousen, a former Salt Lake City police chief who is a member of the BYU religious-instruction department. It is assumed by nearly everyone at BYU that even if the Communists are not behind the demonstrations, the people who are behind them have chosen an innocent party for their abuse, and the result is often described around BYU as "persecution." Mormons have been persecuted for their religious beliefs before, of course, and some Mormons explain the current difficulties almost completely as more of the same—an unpleasant and unfair but not unexpected attack from the gentiles. What strikes the BYU administration as particularly unjust about dragging the BYU basketball team into the argument from four or five categories away is that BYU students are not merely innocent but demonstrably more innocent than any other students. "The students are hurt and angry," I was told by a university public relations man. "There's probably not a higher-type student body in the United States. Look at that campus! Not a drop of paper on it. No cigarette butts. When the flag goes up, the students come to attention. On other campuses, the students burn the flag. Our students are patriotic and they're well dressed, and these are the people who are being persecuted. The kooks, the hippies, the filthy people—*they're* not persecuted."

If a BYU student acknowledges that any of the black students demonstrating against the basketball team are sincere, he usually explains their actions as a failure to understand. It is said they fail to understand that Mormons have nothing to say about Church doctrine, since a belief central to the religion is that doctrine comes, through a process of continuing revelation, from God to the president of the Church and from the president to the membership. There is a feeling among students and administrators that the press has not fairly presented the university's position that the restriction on Negroes holding the priesthood is purely a religious matter and has no connection with the university's policies on race—the complete whiteness of every basketball team ever fielded by BYU having been explained at length within a separate category. I often asked BYU students about the possibility that a black student at Arizona or Colorado State might not believe that such distinctions were important compared to the presence of yet another institutionalized implication of his inferiority. Most of the BYU students I asked would pause for a few moments, as if they had never considered that possibility, and then acknowledge that a sincere black student might understand everything perfectly well and decide to demonstrate against the BYU basketball team anyway—even though the result would be persecution of an innocent party.

THE MORMON CHURCH LEAVES LITTLE room for loyal dissent, and Brigham Young University leaves practically no room at all. Mormonism has not only a strong belief in revelation as the only source of doctrinal change but also an authoritarian structure and a tight sense of community and a history of outside pressure that sometimes makes disagreement seem the equivalent of ammunition for the gentile enemy. Yet there are Mormons who manage to express disagreement about the denial of priesthood to Negroes—to argue about its origins and point out its contradictions—and still stay within the Church. At BYU—where ninety-five percent of the students and virtually all of the faculty are Mormons, and mostly church-going orthodox Mormons—there are few people who hold such views, and fewer still who might want to express them publicly, and no one at all who does. The student newspaper, which reports on the demonstrations and has devoted a lot of space to the university's protestations of innocence, has been instructed to print no discussion of the Church doctrine that is presumably causing all the trouble, and most students agree that there is no reason to argue about something they have no control over. Although the man-on-the-street interviews in the student paper's special issue on the Stanford decision included one or two with students who thought there might be some prejudice at BYU, the rest of the issue was virtually identical to a special issue of the alumni paper on the same subject—a collection of official statements about the absence of discrimination at BYU and a series of answers to such commonly asked questions as why there are only three or four Negroes among the university's twenty-five thousand students ("their decision, not our policy"). BYU faculty members have always had difficulty distinguishing the positions of the university administration from the positions of the Church—the Church's General Authorities also serve as BYU's board of trustees—and normally express no disagreement with either. At BYU, no one on the faculty has tenure.

Although the young men who serve tours as missionaries for the Church are known for wearing ties and neat white shirts, a Mormon with long hair and a beard could be married in the Salt Lake City temple unless, of course, one of his great-grandfathers was a Negro. At BYU, someone with long hair and a beard would not be allowed to register for classes. Although Mormons undoubtedly tend to be politically conservative, there are liberals as well as conservatives in the Church leadership. At BYU, Wilkinson regularly lectures student assemblies on the federal government having become a socialistic monster, and a few years ago, it was revealed that there was a network of student spies reporting to the administration on what was said in the classroom by a few professors suspected of holding liberal political views. At BYU, peaceful picketing is not permitted, the Young Democrats are the most left-wing political group allowed on campus, and the two political bumper stickers available at the bookstore of the Ernest L. Wilkinson Student Center say I'M PROUD TO BE AN AMERICAN and I'M A MEMBER OF THE SILENT MAJORITY. The strain of political conservatism is sufficiently strong in the Church that, under Wilkinson's emphasis, it becomes practically Church doctrine to BYU students. Among the Mormon religious pamphlets displayed at the bookstore is one called "Civil Rights—Tool of Communist Deception," by Ezra Taft Benson, one of the twelve apostles of the Church. The most politically conservative department at BYU is the religion department, some members of which are said to have quit worrying about the Communist Conspiracy and switched their concern to something called the Illuminati, an ancient cabal that supposedly still looms SMERSH-like above even the Red Menace.

The university does permit a weekly free forum during the lunch hour in one of the lounges of the student union, although there have been some complaints that it amounts to no more than the handful of campus radicals (Young Democrats) talking to each other. The day I saw it, all but a few people in the lounge just happened to be studying or chatting there when the forum started. The radicals were arguing that the Mormon tradition included an intellectual search for the truth and that people should be judged for themselves rather than by the length of their hair; the only applause was for speakers who praised the university or defended its dress regulations. During the discussion of dress, one young man in the audience said that the reason for strict control of student appearance was obviously not religious—the prophets of the Church, after all, wore beards—but economic, the realities of the marketplace having led the university to use the uniquely respectable dress and behavior of its students to raise money. He wasn't objecting; he thought it was obviously worth shaving his beard if shaving helped build a new field house. The largest single gift to the university—a thousand-acre ranch in San Clemente said to be worth several million dollars—was presented in 1967 by Ray Reeves, the inventor of the air-wedge sole, and his wife, Nellie. The university invited the couple to Provo for the official presentation, and students were given THANKS, RAY AND NELLIE lapel stickers to wear for the ceremonies. "Some time ago my wife, Nellie, and I read a syndicated newspaper article describing Brigham Young University as a place where youngsters still had ideals, still cut their hair, still believed in God," Ray Reeves said. "We had to see it, so we drove to Provo, Utah. The young people at BYU were all clean-cut, good-looking. We didn't see any miniskirts. There was no beatnik atmosphere. Those students had their feet on the ground. Instead of finding fault, they were accepting leadership. In short, we liked the way the university was being run. Our association with the people at BYU has been marvelous. To show our support, we've given the university our ranch."

The reaction of BYU to the continuing demonstrations is not likely to diminish the reputation it has acquired among those who are pleased to find one university that stands up to Minority Pressure Groups. The football coach has recruited BYU's first black football player, after making it clear to him that interracial dating is not allowed. But according to the Provo paper, the coach recently told a local Chamber of Commerce breakfast, "A lot of people are mad at me right now because they feel we are giving in." There are a few people at BYU who are considering suggesting to the administration that the university prove the sincerity of its statements about the civil category by recruiting Negro students for the same kind of special-help program that BYU runs for American Indians, but Wilkinson says that limitations on the university's space preclude recruiting of any kind. At the strong urging of the administration, students who organized a nighttime noncredit student academy at BYU this semester reduced their proposed courses in Afro-American history and literature to one composite course; until the planned curriculum was made public, the faculty members involved were under pressure from the administration to teach no course at all on the subject.

INTELLECTUALS WHO TRY TO REMAIN within the Church have always had to face the tension between their faith and their intellectual curiosity, and the few students at BYU who have such problems find them more acute these days. Wilkinson talks of the priesthood restriction on Negroes as if it were some isolated religious practice like total immersion among the Baptists; he often says that Stanford's decision was the equivalent of BYU refusing to play Notre Dame because of different ideas on divorce. But the BYU students who tend to approach official statements questioningly know that those students who have been on missions in the South proselyte only among white people, that the traditional attempts by Mormons to explain the restriction on Negroes all contain some implication of inferiority, that the Church is noted for giving its official support to right-to-work laws rather than civil rights legislation, that the elderly men who preside over Mormonism sometimes have made remarks that would cause the least conspiratorial Negro to shout at BYU basketball players. (The current president of the Church, who completed his college education in the nineteenth century, was quoted a few years ago as saying that "darkies are wonderful people.") A Mormon social scientist has done an attitude study in which he concludes that Mormons in California are no more prejudiced against Negroes than other whites are, but neither side of the argument is heard at BYU.

The vast majority of BYU students accept the official statements of the university administration as unquestioningly as they accept official statements of the Church authorities. It has never occurred to most of them to compare the statement of the university that black athletes are recruited "under exactly the same terms as any other athletes" and the public acknowledgment by coaches that they have warned Negro prospects that a black athlete may not be happy at BYU because of the lack of "social life." BYU has never appeared to place the stimulation of intellectual curiosity high on its list of priorities. The lack of tenure and of a faculty senate have meant some problems with accreditation and the loss of the kind of professors who obviously wouldn't teach in a university that didn't take these institutions for granted, but there has been an accompanying absence of faculty dissent. In the tension between faith and intellect, the university has been a strong supporter of faith. Although the Mormons—people who have placed great value on education—have created what they often call the largest privately operated university in the United States, it is not really the intellectual center of the Church. The center of serious discussions about the race situation and the Church is the state-supported University of Utah. The principal forum for Mormon intellectuals— a fascinating quarterly called *Dialogue*—is published in California rather than Provo, and it includes hardly anyone from BYU on its board of editors. BYU has presumably chosen to make its reputation on instilling its students with religious faith and patriotism and high standards of personal morality. As far as "building character" is concerned, Wilkinson said in a speech not long ago that universities such as Harvard and Yale and, of course, Stanford have "passed their zenith." In its own terms, BYU has assumed leadership in the field.

• • •

In 1978, citing a revelation that had been reached through intense prayer, the First Presidency of the Church ruled that "all worthy male members of the Church may be ordained to the priesthood without regard for race or color." The boycott and demonstrations ended. In the ensuing years, BYU experienced some difficulty in recruiting and retaining black athletes. There have been accusations of racism in the enforcement of the honor code, which at BYU prohibits, among other things, alcoholic beverages, coffee, beards, tattoos, and premarital sex.

G. T. MILLER'S PLAN

Luverne, Alabama
1970

SOME TIME AGO, A FRIEND OF MINE WHO LIVES IN ALABAMA
told me that G. T. Miller, the proprietor of the G. T. Miller
Feed & Grist Mill, in Luverne, had a plan to help Crenshaw County and the entire country. I've run into a lot of
people at one time or another who have plans for helping
the entire country—the plans usually have to do with something like going on the silver standard or signing up for
Moral Re-Armament—but plans for Crenshaw County are
rare. The problem is not that no one cares about Crenshaw
County; it's that most people consider Crenshaw County
beyond help. The one plan that most people who actually
live in Crenshaw County have is a plan to get out. It's a rural county, about an hour south of Montgomery, and it has
been notable in recent years almost entirely for its amazing
rate of shrinkage. I figured that anybody who had a plan
for Crenshaw County must be worth meeting. My friend
admitted he didn't quite understand Miller's plan, but that

didn't disturb me. I don't quite understand the silver standard or Moral Re-Armament.

According to my friend, G. T. Miller was a white man of about seventy who had done pretty well in business around Crenshaw County despite having had only three or four years of schooling. "He's not a racist," my friend said, "and he had some trouble with the Klan a few years ago. But he's not exactly a liberal, either. I'm not sure he'd know what you were talking about if you used that word. He might be more of a populist, in a way, although he believes in business. And he's got a fallout shelter—a huge fallout shelter."

In rural Alabama, people who belong to organizations like the Ku Klux Klan often have a strong notion of general philosophy but get mixed up on details. It wouldn't surprise me to hear that someone in Crenshaw County might get in trouble with the Klan for, say, having a fallout shelter, or for not having one. But my friend said that the Klan had been pretty much on target when it threatened G. T. Miller and organized a boycott of his businesses. Miller had apparently refused to fire a Negro who had somehow interpreted the county's freedom-of-choice school-desegregation plan to mean that his son was free to choose the white school. Miller had even employed the son part-time. Eventually, Miller had explained the issue on CBS television news. "I couldn't see where I'd want to fire him because his young 'un was going to school," Miller said during the interview. "His young 'un's got a life to live, and he just as well have an education as my boy." After the program, a couple of thousand people from all over the country wrote to Miller that they thought he was a hero. Some of them even sent money to help offset the losses he was suffering because of the boycott. A few of them said they thought it might be nicer if a man of Miller's courage and principles didn't use the word "nigger" quite so freely.

"WE WAS DOIN' *EXTRA* GOOD till the Ku Klux got on us," G. T. Miller told me. He was showing me around his feed and grist mill—a roomy, remarkably neat place that smells slightly of the molasses that some farmers like to mix with corn when they grind their cattle feed. Miller is a husky man who doesn't look his age. He was wearing his usual outfit of bib overalls, a sports shirt, and a small felt hat. Before the boycott, Miller's mill was part of what amounted to a kind of one-man, rural, just-folks conglomerate. Only the feed mill remains open, but spread out along the highway, just inside the Luverne city limits, are buildings that once held a supermarket, a cotton gin, a trucking company, and a recreation center that included a dance hall, a bowling alley, and a skating rink. Once, when Miller found himself with some time and space that weren't being exploited properly, he started raising worms and crickets for fish bait. Miller is proud that the Miller enterprises were built by a poor, un-educated country boy—the businesses built up from scratch, the buildings put together with cheap lumber from structures being torn down elsewhere—and he is quick to tell visitors of the kind of youth that most respectable businessmen would not choose to remember. He says that when he was a young man trying to accumulate capital by barbering, a conviction for moonshining gave him the opportunity to practice his trade for a while at the federal penitentiary in Atlanta. He was a Klansman himself for a time as a young man, and he acknowledges that his arguments in those days with the Klan and others included some beatings and some shootings—a couple of which he lost painfully. "In them times," he says, "a man fightin' the Klan around here had about as much chance as a one-legged man at a tail-kickin'."

Having once been poor himself, Miller has always believed in helping people by giving them jobs, but he believes he is helping himself at the same time; it is obvious to him that businessmen get back all the money they spend. "The workin' man don't keep his money but three hours to three days," he told me. "Some of 'em spends it in three hours; some keep it as long as three days. I did me a survey on that once. Those folks on Wall Street oughtn't to be scared to turn loose of that money, 'cause it'll be right back down there in a little while anyhow."

A couple of hours after I met G. T. Miller, I began to sympathize with my friend's difficulty in trying to explain Miller's views. Most of the people my friend and I come across—or at least the people we talk to about plans to help the country—have a set pattern of beliefs. When people tell me what they think about disarmament, I have a pretty good idea of what they are likely to think about school integration. Not G. T. Miller. He believes in school integration ("The niggers need an education, too; you can get along with a fella when he's got a good education"), but he also believes in his fallout shelter—the community's fallout shelter, really, since he built it to hold sixty-four beds. As I understand his views on the war in Vietnam, he's a hawk, but I'm not sure I understand his views on the war in Vietnam. I know he's concerned about the country being torn apart by hatred and dissent, although I don't know whether he holds hatred or dissent to blame. "If we go on like we're goin', we're auto-matically whupped," he told me as we sat in his bomb shelter. "Russia's doin' nothin' but waitin'—like a buzzard on a tree a-waitin' for a mule to die."

Miller believes landowners have dealt unfairly with share-croppers. He also believes that landowners are serving their country and helping to feed their fellow human beings when they figure out methods of more profitable hog production. When he approves of something, he often says, "Every time a man betters himself, he betters his country." When he disapproves, he often says, "That's no way to help your fellow man or your country, either one." He has given a lot of people no-interest loans for down payments on houses, partly because he thinks they have a right to own something and partly because it's a Christian act and partly because he believes that people who own something themselves aren't likely to burn down other people's property. "Let it be *his'n!*" Miller says about housing for the poor man. "Have him pay a small down payment. If he gets in too tight and can't pay it, wait on him till he catches up. When they get out demonstratin', he's not going to stick fire to that house."

Not being burdened with any notion of how he *should* feel about various issues, Miller arrives at some views that have a distinguished simplicity. He is opposed to foundations not paying taxes, for instance, because foundations use the public roads just the way everybody else does. Being a practical man, he is not embarrassed when his Christian ventures and his business ventures overlap. He would be the last man to turn his neighbors away from his fallout shelter; he would be the first man to take his fallout shelter off his taxes. He lends people hospital beds, which he happened to get at a good price under civil-defense regulations, because he wants to be a good neighbor. He used to lend wagons to farmers, partly so they could haul their cotton to his gin, but he thought of that as a neighborly act, too. The plan he has for Crenshaw County seems to entail giving away his business.

A LOT OF MILLER'S IDEAS about Crenshaw County were formed from having spent ten years or so making a film on the area. It's actually split into two films—*What We Have* and *What We Need*. Miller showed them to me one day in the living room of the modern house he and his wife live in—up the road from the feed mill, on top of the fallout shelter. He also got out his charts and his pointer and his American flags, so that I could see precisely what it had been like when he presented the films to church groups and service clubs in the area, before the trouble with the Klan started. "When we learn to love one another as the good Lord is trying to teach us to, we'll find out that our nation will move forward in a record speed," he said by way of introduction. "And at the same time we can help get poor people out of the gully, and help our nation, and accumulate a better world for all races of people." The charts—all hand-drawn—covered a great variety of subjects. One of them said, "We Need a Public Price Commission." One of them indicated the economic impact that one hundred new jobs had on a community. One of them said, "Slums Are Costly to All" and showed a kind of keyhole-shaped representation of an urban area, the round part of the keyhole being very crowded with tiny squares. "Down in the slums," Miller said, pointing to that part of the drawing, "a man becomes a kind of fanatic, due to the fact that he can't accumulate nothin'.'" The charts also had drawings of the recreation centers that Miller would like to see built. Not recreation centers like the one he used to run before the boycott. These recreation centers would be part of the plan to help Crenshaw County and the entire country. Miller has faith in the efficacy of training—he says, "I could take me a boy who don't know nothin' in the world except how to hitch up a mule, and wouldn't know that except the head's on one side and the tail's on another, and teach him to be a carpenter"—and his faith extends to the belief that people could be trained to get along with each other. "You'd have a hundred- or two-hundred-acre lot, and a good, nice tabernacle," he says. "You'd have different talks, twice a day." One architectural rendering—the one of the recreation center's dining hall—looked familiar to me. After a while, I realized that it was exactly the same as the keyhole-shaped representation of an urban area. The tiny squares that had been crowding the slums had become dining-hall tables.

As I watched the films, it occurred to me that white people in Crenshaw County had probably been more receptive to *What We Have* than to *What We Need*—although, the entertainment opportunities being what they are in Crenshaw County, I can't imagine that there would be a very large attrition rate in an audience even if a film turned out to be a laudatory biography of H. Rap Brown. The first film shows a lot of the modern farming methods in the area, but the second shows some slums and some decrepit Negro schools, and even some of the Negro sharecroppers near Selma who were thrown off land for registering to vote and had to live in tents. ("It throwed a hard burden on these people; at the same time, it throwed a hard burden on our federal government that had to give 'em welfare and support 'em.") Miller traces most of the deficiencies shown in the film to one overwhelming problem: that sharecroppers and small farmers and farmhands have had to move to city slums because of mechanization or because a landowner has found it more profitable to put the land into the federal soil bank than to farm it. His plan is to get a lot of the area's small farmers—black and white—to pool their resources and their energies and G. T. Miller's enterprise and run an operation that will allow all of them to remain.

There have never been many white people in Crenshaw County who share Miller's views; there may be nobody anywhere who shares Miller's views. But he was tolerated—and permitted to use the courtroom of the county courthouse for his film lecture—until he refused to fire the Negroes who had offended the Klan. At about the same time, it was rumored around town—correctly—that he had been guilty of overt kindness to some American Friends Service Committee volunteers who were in Luverne to work with the community's Negroes. After one of the ghetto disturbances in the North, someone circulated a paper saying that Miller's most recent lecture had been sponsored by the American Friends Service Committee and that Miller had said he didn't blame slum dwellers for rioting. The county commissioners decided that Miller could no longer give his speech in the courthouse. The Klan, with the support of local businessmen, started a boycott of Miller's businesses that was, by all accounts, pretty effective. Miller countered with a broadsheet arguing that if he were forced out of business, which seemed quite possible, the county would suffer economically. Eventually, the federal judge who had ordered the freedom-of-choice plan into effect enjoined the Klan from harassing Miller and some other citizens. Gradually, some of the farmers who had formerly brought their feed to grind at Miller's started showing up again at the mill; Miller now estimates his mill business at about a third of what it was before the boycott. Through it all, Miller says, if he saw a boycotter across the street, he made it a point to cross over and say hello. The subjects of forgiveness and reconciliation are particularly moving to Miller; his eyes often fill with tears when he recalls his overtures to his enemies. "If a man is a Ku Kluxer and I know he hates me and I find out some of his folks are sick and need help, I call him or I go to see him, either one," he told me one day. "I tell him I got a good hospital bed he can keep as long as he wants, and it won't cost him a penny in the world. You have to learn to forgive if you're askin' the good Lord to forgive *you*. So I never go to bed hating nobody. And that's the only way to win over enemies, too. You can fight 'em, but all you do is make 'em mad and worser. Our federal government needs to have a school for trainin' people on something on this same idea."

With business off, Miller spent a lot of time perfecting his plan for small farmers. He and Mrs. Miller gathered a lot of charts and documents and tables and had them run off in blueprint form, so they could make a set of scrapbooks on the plan. Tom Law, who works for an agency in Montgomery that gives technical assistance to projects applying for federal grants, sees Miller's plan as basically a marketing-and-production cooperative in poultry raising, differing from the normal co-op in that Miller's business would be included in the operation. But as described by Miller or the scrapbooks, it doesn't sound that simple. The scrapbooks include Miller's ideas of what the country has and what it needs, prayers used by various denominations, and photographic layouts featuring pictures of cows with captions like "You take good care of me and I will produce you some good calves." The scrapbooks also contain detailed figures showing precisely how the co-op would work. The Office of Economic Opportunity has shown some interest in the project, and some people in Luverne—being in a position to welcome any kind of investment, even poverty-program investment—have decided that Miller is entitled to his ideas. One of the letters of recommendation in the scrapbooks is from the commissioners of Crenshaw County.

Law is convinced of Miller's sincerity, but he has had some problems explaining to Miller exactly how things are done in the world of government grants—how meetings would have to be held and minutes recorded, how "checkpoint-procedure coordination forms" would have to be filed. Law told Miller that the blueprinted scrapbooks with talking cows were fine for internal distribution but might not be the best way to present the plan to Washington. Miller has some ideas of his own about how the bureaucracy of poverty ought to work. He believes, among other things, that poverty workers ought to be paid on a commission basis.

WHEN I LEFT LUVERNE, MILLER loaded me down with blueprints and broadsheets and letters and files. While looking through the material in New York, I happened to come across the carbons of some letters Miller had written in 1967, a year before he appeared on CBS to say why he couldn't fire the Negroes he had been ordered to fire. "Dear Sir," the letters said, "I finally had to do what you asked me to do. Stop helping the colored people and the poor people out in any way. Also had to lay off the ones you mentioned in our conversation. Yours truly, G. T. Miller. P.S. We appreciate your business in the past and hope to serve you in the future." The letters were addressed to some of the people who were later named in the injunction against the Klan. I telephoned Miller in Luverne.

"Well, we was finally forced to lay 'em off, being our business was off seventy-five percent," he said. "We didn't lay 'em off 'cause we wanted to or 'cause they told us to."

"You mean as long as you had to lay them off anyway, you figured you might as well tell the boycotters about it?" I asked.

"Yeah. To see if the people boycottin' us would come back," he said, sounding pleased that I seemed to have caught on to the simple logic of it. "You understand how it works now?"

I told him I thought I did.

• • •

For her book The Klan, *Patsy Sims interviewed G. T. Miller in 1976, at which time his situation appeared to be as complicated as it had been in 1970. She later confronted him with some old court testimony in which he seemed to have admitted killing "a couple" of black people during his time in the Klan. Miller denied to her that such killings had occurred. "Was he senile?" Sims wrote. "Was he lying? Or had the Klan orchestrated rumors that distorted fact with fiction?" She wasn't certain. According to* The Klan's *second edition, "G. T. Miller died on May 18, 1988, at the age of eighty-eight, taking the full story of his ins and outs with the Klan to his grave."*

NOT SUPER-OUTRAGEOUS

Houston, Texas
1970

IN AUGUST OF 1968, LEE OTIS JOHNSON, THE NOISIEST black militant in Houston, was convicted of giving away one marijuana cigarette and was sentenced to thirty years in the penitentiary. There are people in Houston who believe Johnson was treated unjustly, but nobody of any prominence has ever said so publicly. Even among people who are doing whatever they can to get Johnson out of prison, a sense of outrage about the case is considered a bit naïve. "We make a big thing of it," one of them said recently. "But in Texas it's not really so super-outrageous." In Texas, a jury or judge can give a defendant ninety-nine years for sale or possession of marijuana, and some of them have. Any marijuana sentence sounds mild compared to the sentences handed out for violent crime lately in Dallas, where some juries, in an effort to counter a parole system considered ruinously enlightened, have sent people to jail for several hundred years for rape or a thousand for armed robbery. Last summer, a man convicted in Dallas of selling three caps of heroin was sentenced to fifteen hundred years in the penitentiary. It is said that one Fort Worth man who was given five hundred years or so stopped on his way out of the courtroom and said to the judge, "Judge, I'm not sure I can serve that sentence."

"Well, you do the best you can," the judge replied.

The backers of Lee Otis Johnson maintain that, unlike someone caught with a hundred pounds of marijuana or convicted of armed robbery, Johnson was punished for activities that had nothing to do with the charge in court. But not many people in Houston would find that outrageous or even surprising. When the Houston district attorney, Carol Vance, is asked why he chose to try Johnson's one-marijuana-cigarette case personally, after having left virtually all other cases to his fifty or so assistants, he replies that Johnson was a dangerous man. "Everyone's got a right to criticize," the district attorney has explained. "But when you start trying to encourage people to burn the city, that's a different matter." Johnson was never arrested for inciting to riot or for conspiracy to commit arson, but it is now customary in many parts of the country to use the marijuana laws for imprisoning people considered dangerous by district attorneys, whether whatever makes them dangerous is against the law or not. John Sinclair, the leader of an organization called the White Panthers, was convicted in Detroit of possession of two marijuana cigarettes and is now serving a prison sentence of nine and a half to ten years. *The Texas Observer,* a durable liberal biweekly published in Austin, recently carried an account by Dave Beckwith of the trial of four black students from the University of California at Santa Barbara who were charged with possession of marijuana while traveling through Dallas and were presented to the town as captured black militants. Not long after sentencing two of them to three years in the penitentiary, the judge was quoted by *The Dallas Morning News* as saying, "We had pretty good reason to believe that they were members of the Black Panther organization, dedicated to the overthrow of the government by revolution, but we couldn't prove that."

The *Observer* piece pointed out that the judge's own son had been arrested on a marijuana charge and given two years' probation, which is the customary penalty for non-political whites who fail to have the charges dropped or the case indefinitely continued—the alternative sentence being a minimum of two years in prison for possession and five years for selling. (A Houston lawyer who specializes in such cases has handled thirty or forty of them successfully without yet having had to face a jury, and has come to believe that one reason the law making marijuana a felony is not changed is that "for lawyers, it is the single most lucrative crime.") In Texas, except in cases in which the defendant is thought to be an important pusher, someone who is sent to jail for possession or sale of a small amount of marijuana is likely to be black or Mexican-American, and someone who is sent to jail for a long time is likely to be the kind of man district attorneys consider dangerous, and someone who is sent to jail for thirty years is, it follows as a matter of course, the noisiest black militant in Houston. When Texans interested in such matters hear about a long sentence for marijuana, their natural question is not how much marijuana the defendant had but who he is. "He was Mexican and political and in the Panhandle," a man active in the Houston American

Civil Liberties Union said recently about one such defendant. "And that's a bad combination."

The ACLU man did not sound outraged. In Houston, it has been routine to use all sorts of laws in any way they can serve to maintain the climate of order—a climate that is considered necessary to the hyper-modern, hyper-expanding kind of prosperity the city prides itself on. In Houston, a professor and his teenage daughter were arrested for passing out anti-war handbills, a Rice student who engaged in some guerrilla theater during an anti-war demonstration was sentenced to six months for wearing the distinctive parts of an army uniform, and a group of Mexican-Americans who knocked over some furniture during a demonstration at the school board this fall were indicted not only for disorderly conduct but also for "felony malicious mischief," which carries a penalty of up to twenty years. After a federal court ordered Houston's mayor and city council to grant a parade permit to a peaceful anti-war group, they passed an ordinance requiring an insurance fee from any group wanting to parade in the future, and then openly discussed ways of getting around the law so that the American Legion, which claimed poverty, could have its parade anyway. There are a lot of people who would consider using the law in this way a threat to civil liberties, but not many of them live in Houston. The district attorney asked only that Lee Otis Johnson be sent to jail for twenty years; it was a jury of twelve white citizens who decided on thirty. The Houston police chief has expressed views on civil liberties considerably less sympathetic than those of the district attorney—whose definition of dangerous men does distinguish between "revolutionaries" and people who are "just raising hell"—and the chief seems to have been given an award by just about every organization in Houston with the resources to hold a luncheon and have a plaque made up. When the chief was given the Sons of the American Revolution good-citizenship award this fall, the *Houston Chronicle* account of his acceptance speech began, "Police Chief Herman Short has chastized a society that will allow an organization such as the American Civil Liberties Union to fight prayer in the school on one hand and defend dissenters and revolutionaries on the other."

In this atmosphere, Houston, now the sixth largest city in the country, still has the kind of endemic right-wing violence that used to be associated with small, mean towns in the more backward areas of Alabama. Night riders who fire shotgun blasts at the home of an anti-war leader or the office of an underground paper are routine. The Family Hand, a restaurant that caters to Houston's longhair community, has been fire-bombed twice. A local television newscaster may be threatened for showing pictures of the My Lai massacre, and a local theater may be stink-bombed for showing *Guess Who's Coming to Dinner.* The listener-sponsored radio station that the Pacifica Foundation opened in Houston in March—a station that regularly aired the kind of news and opinions that Houston citizens can count on their newspapers to avoid mentioning—had its transmitter blown up in May, got back on the air in June, and was bombed off again in October. (The station's manager, Larry Lee, who has attempted to keep some rough record of terrorist incidents in Houston, was recently accused by a man from the *Chronicle* of becoming paranoid. "You may be right," Lee said. "I

keep imagining somebody is blowing up my transmitter.")
The Ku Klux Klan is often mentioned as being behind the
night-riding, but nobody has ever been charged, and the
most noted comment of the police chief about the Klan was
less than threatening. "I am not a Klansman, and I know of
no police officer who is a Klansman," he said after the Grand
Dragon had announced that a lot of police officers were in
the Klan—a statement unlikely to be challenged by anyone
in the black community. "You can't fault a man, however,
for praising God, country, and obedience to law and order.
That's what we all stand for." Black people in Houston assume that Lee Otis Johnson was jailed for his political activities; a lot of them assume that he was framed. But then
a lot of them assume that Carl Hampton, who succeeded
Johnson as the noisiest black militant in Houston and died in
a gun battle, was murdered by the police. So in a way, thirty
years in jail for giving away a marijuana cigarette is not really super-outrageous.

"YOU'VE GOT TO REMEMBER THAT in most people's minds,
Lee Otis Johnson was a loudmouthed nigger who called a lot
of names and seemed to go out of his way to irritate everybody," a local man who has followed the Johnson case said
recently. Many white people in Houston thought that thirty
years was just what a man like Lee Otis Johnson deserved;
many other white people thought that thirty years was what
a man like Lee Otis Johnson might have expected from
twelve white people in Houston. In terms of accepting the
decision as non-outrageous, the two views amounted to the

same thing. After the conviction, an organization of social workers expressed doubt as to whether Johnson could have received a fair trial in Houston, and a grand jury, in calling for reform of the marijuana laws, contrasted the thirty-year sentence (without mentioning Johnson's name) with a sentence of two years' probation that had been given a convicted murderer at about the same time. That seems to have been the extent of public outcry. Not many white people in Houston wanted to be involved in any way with Lee Otis Johnson. A kind of freelance militant who had first come to attention as a SNCC leader at Texas Southern University, he provided headlines like LOCAL SNCC LOOKS TO REVOLUTION. (Although when an opportunity for widespread violence came, on the night when Martin Luther King, Jr., died, he helped maintain calm in the city.) Black leaders tend to agree that Johnson presented some danger to the white people who run Houston—not because he was likely to organize a revolution but because he had a peculiar ability to communicate with ordinary black people and a peculiar ability to infuriate white people like the mayor and the chief of police.

By the standards of the Houston Police Department, Johnson certainly qualified as a dangerous man: At about the time of his trial, a member of the department's intelligence unit who specialized in spying on civil rights and anti-war groups told David Brand, of *The Wall Street Journal,* that the tip-off on Communist influence was when someone "talks about social change." The Houston police picked up Johnson so often that it became a kind of routine. The drug charge almost seemed another in a series of arrests that normally resulted in his being fined or in the charges being dropped. It came six weeks after Johnson had allegedly given a marijuana cigarette to a police undercover man (the delay, the police later said, was necessary to protect the agent), and some of Johnson's supporters spoke of it as an obvious manifestation of the mayor's pique, since it came only a couple of days after a memorial rally for King where Johnson had been wildly cheered and the mayor had been booed. The trial was short. Johnson's lawyer asked for a continuance until the mayor and the police chief were available to testify; it was his contention that they had conspired to harass and eventually entrap Johnson in order to prevent "his further exercise of his rights of free speech and assembly." When the motion was denied, he presented no other witnesses. The prosecution called the undercover man and a couple of policemen who testified that the cigarette had been given to them to check and was indeed marijuana. Within a few hours, Johnson was in jail, starting his thirty years, and he has been in jail ever since.

JOHNSON'S APPEAL HAS NOW BEEN through the state courts, and it will soon be taken to federal district court. Among lawyers who have read the transcript, there is agreement that it contains nothing legally outrageous. The hope of some Johnson supporters is that some court—if not the district court or the court of appeals, then the Supreme Court—will decide that it is wrong to sentence a "dangerous man" to thirty years for giving away one marijuana cigarette and will then use something like the judge's refusal to grant a change of venue as a way to order a new trial. Johnson's name is still brought up occasionally—when someone is given a probated sentence for murder or when there is a discussion of the marijuana laws or when people talk about the death of Carl Hampton. There is a Lee Otis Johnson Defense Committee in Houston. A petition was gathered for an appeal to the parole board, and during the recent election campaign, a group of University of Houston students stopped a speech by the Governor, Preston Smith, with shouts of "Free Lee Otis!" (The Governor, seizing a rare opportunity to ridicule two minority groups with one statement, told a group of businessmen that he thought the students were shouting "*frijoles,*' just like 'beans' in South Texas.") Some advertisements and stories have appeared in Eastern papers and in the underground press, but these days any group wanting to focus attention on someone it considers a political prisoner has a lot of competition.

People in Houston who have followed the case still talk occasionally of why the jurors gave Johnson ten years more than the district attorney asked for. The summer after King's death was, of course, a fearful time in American cities, and according to the theory of one Houston lawyer, "they were probably just more scared of him than the DA was." The district attorney believes that the jury may have been affected by the presence in court of several Johnson followers dressed in dashikis and African robes; among costumes commonly worn in Houston to symbolize reverence for a cultural heritage, the dashiki is looked upon as considerably more threatening than the cowboy outfit. There is also a theory—considered rather abstruse in Houston—that the jury may have actually been alarmed at the exchange of a marijuana cigarette as well as being alarmed at Johnson; marijuana was less common among white teenagers in Houston two years ago than it is today, and more people considered it the most dangerous weapon in Satan's arsenal. "If a girl wants to have a career as a syphilitic prostitute or if a boy wants to end in the electric chair because he has killed a grocer in a hijacking, there is no more practical beginning than this cigarette contained in this envelope," the prosecution said before the sentencing. "Any amount of marijuana, any amount of dope, is a shame and disgrace to this community, and its use and effects would be so evil that should I speak to you for a hundred years, I couldn't describe it properly." District Attorney Vance says that he was surprised to hear a harsher sentence than he had asked for, but he has also said that Johnson may have been given less than he deserved. Before the sentencing, Vance introduced into the record a previous conviction for auto theft, and the head of the police intelligence unit— a man who was later quoted in the *Wall Street Journal* piece as calling black demonstrators "arrogant bastards looking for an issue"—testified that he had found Johnson to be a man of bad character. In a documentary that the Pacifica station put on between bombings, Vance was asked about the sentence and replied, "Here was a person who was furnishing marijuana, he was a troublemaker, he tried to stir up a riot, he was a person who'd been to the penitentiary twice before. And yet even though he could have gotten ninety-nine years or life imprisonment—and the minimum being five years—he ended up with a thirty-year sentence. I don't see that this is a very unusual verdict."

. . .

After Lee Otis Johnson had served four years of his sentence, a federal judge vacated the conviction on the ground that a change of venue from Houston should have been granted. The district attorney's office decided not to retry the case. Johnson did not return to activism. In his after-prison life, according to Texas Monthly, *"he could not escape his personal demons, and from then on was in and out of trouble." He died in 2002, at the age of sixty-two.*

VICTORIA DELEE—IN HER OWN WORDS

Dorchester County, South Carolina
1971

GROWING UP IN DORCHESTER COUNTY

"This thing start when I was born. I was born from a family of four of us girls. And I was born from an unwed mother. And this was the first strike against me. So that's why I'm saying it started when I was born: When I was a little girl, we was slighted. We was always treated awful bad, even from our own people. First thing this did to me—it made me hate people. I mostly hated everybody. I loved my grandmama. My grandmama really raised us. And we had a hard time. We was born and raised up on white people's farms. We had to work for the white folks. We was pickin' peas and cotton and this sort of thing. I always wanted to do somethin'. I said when I get grown, I was goin' to be a businesswoman. I didn't know what kind of businesswoman. People said, 'You'll never become nothin'—because you didn't come from nothin'.' But I meant to be somebody. And all along I said, 'When I get growed, I'm going to fix it for my people.' Always in my mind, I always wanted to change things in Dorchester County. And the first thing I had in my mind: I meant to kill up some white people.

"The white people did us so bad. Knowing all the black people that was getting killed, it just worried me 'most to death. One white man one time knocked me out because I was hoeing cotton and he said I left some grass behind the cotton. So he took and knocked me upside the head. And when I come to, my grandmama had to beat me till he was satisfied. Till *he* was satisfied. And this was one that was the first white man I meant to kill. I said, 'I'm goin' to kill him to start off with.' And I didn't know no better. I just hated white folks so bad. And I kept saying I was going to kill women, children, mens, and all. I knew they was going to kill me as soon as I killed up enough of them. But that didn't make me no difference.

"I got married very young. I still had it in my mind to kill the white folks. But after my first little boy was born, we went to church one Sunday and the preacher preached a sermon—'You can get by, but you can't get away.' It was the first time in my life that anything had really got next to me. He said the white folks was killing us, but God had their number and they was going to reap whatever seeds they sowed. He said if they didn't, their children's children's children would reap. He said the same thing went for us: If we hated them and we did to them what they did to us, our children's children would reap our seeds. And I looked at my baby in my arms that Sunday, and I said, 'Lord, I'm glad I haven't killed nobody yet.' And the preacher said you can't even hate 'em. So I went to prayin'. I asked the Lord to help me. I asked Him to help me stop hating people. I wanted Him to make me love my enemies. I really went to goin' to church. I wanted to be converted. I went to my grandmama, and she said that before God would convert my soul, I would have to love the white people. She said, 'You got to *mean* it.' And sure enough, the Lord answered my prayer and I started to love white folks. But I stand up all right. I let 'em know that they wasn't goin' to run over me."

REGISTERING TO VOTE

"I got registered when it was real tough back there. I *made* 'em register me. The same girl who is magistrater of Ridgeville now, I was pregnant with her—Vicki. Now she's twenty-three, and that was before she was born. The power structure had an undertaker who would pick up the blacks they wanted to register. (They wanted certain blacks so that they could say 'Vote for such-and-such one' and the blacks would go and do it. Was nobody registered except them kind of people.) So I went there and I just waited till the door opened and some-body comed out that it was time for somebody else. I stepped in. So I got in there with this guy—he was an old white man. His hair was white. He asked me what I wanted. I told him. I said, 'I want my registration certificate.'

"He said, 'You can't get registered.'

"I said, 'Oh yes I am.' I was real heavy with this baby. Well, I looked like a barrel. I said, 'I'm not going anywhere. I want my registration certificate. Don't you put your hands on me—and nobody else.' I said, 'I want my registration certificate.'

"And he said, 'Why, you can't—'

"And I said, 'Oh yes I can.'

"And he said, 'You got to read this here—the Constitution.' So he gave me a book. It wasn't no Constitution. It was somethin' else he give me to read—a whole big thing there. I read it. He say, 'You read, but you can't read with understanding.'

"I said, 'Who's the person who's supposed to understand it—me or you? I read and I understand what I read, and give me my registration certificate.' I said, 'If you don't'—I says—'Mister, it's goin' to be trouble.'

"So he got scared. This white man got scared. He said, 'You know who you're talking to?'

"I said, 'You know who *you're* talking to?' I said, 'This happen to not be one of your niggers.' I said, 'I want my registration certificate.'

"After a while, he says, 'Okay. Now, you ain't makin' me do this,' he says, 'but I'm goin' to give you this registration certificate. But don't you go there and tell nobodys else I give you this registration certificate.'

"I says, 'You ain't *givin'* me my registration certificate.' I says, 'I applied and I am eligible for it. That's your Constitution—I done read it. That's all that's required.' I said, 'I'm going out here and tell everybody.' And I walked out of the office and I told everybody how I got mine. My husband went in there, but he sent my husband right back out. So I was the only black person in my community who had a registration certificate—except the blacks they wanted to register. That was when I was carrying my third child—Vicki. The one who's magistrater now. Everybody says that's why Vicki is so pushy, like I am."

RAISING CHILDREN

"I had one baby behind the next. I'm the mother of seven. I had to spend quite a lot of time with my family, because I never believed in leaving my children with anybody. Because I had a way I wanted to teach my kids a little different. I taught my kids to stand up and be counted. And I learned them to don't be afraid of nobody. And because a man's skin was white, he wasn't a bit better than they was. But then I told them they weren't any better than anybody else. And I told them that you were just what you make yourself. You could be a dog if you wanted to or you could be a man if you wanted to. I said, 'Nobody give respect to you—you're going to have to take it. But you don't have to go 'round here "Yessir, No sir, Mister, Boss" and all this kind of stuff. That wasn't respect. If he call you Jim, you call him Mike. And if he's nice to you, be nice to him. Always smile first at a person to see whether he goin' smile back. But he don't smile back, don't you keep on smilin',' I said, 'because directly he think you Aunt Jane. And wherever you go, don't you go look for no seat amongst black people. You go anyplace that black and white is sittin' there, wherever a seat is vacant, sit down. Because as long as you is a citizen of the United States'—I said not even South Carolina but the United States—'then nobody is entitled to any more than you.'

"And I taught them that from babies on the breast. And all my children today—and I'm not braggin'—they're some of the nicestest kids you ever met. You talk with 'em, you'll want to talk with 'em again. But you'll find out they're not afraid of you a bit. And my little grandbaby—if you go to

ask, 'Is Victoria home?' he'll say, 'Mrs. DeLee is not here.'
That's right. We taught him that. This is what I did. So I
raised up children like that."

SENDING THE CHILDREN TO SCHOOL

"I went to the superintendent to try to make him put the
same education in the black schools as the white schools, and
they wouldn't do it. Then I filed for transfers. That was in
1964. I did it to get equal education, and I knowed that was
the only way. This is when they started harassing me. This is
when they started shooting in the house. The kids got in in
'65. We done got 'em in there. This is when the kids started
being beat up. Sometimes I've seen my boy got off the bus, he
couldn't see how to walk from the bus to the house, he was
beat so bad. The little girl, they'd tear her clothes, and she's
take the pieces of her dress and pull them around her to hide
her nakedness. They used to be beat up till they was bloody
as hogs. First year, there was my kids and two more families.
Then every year we just kept gettin' a little more and a little
more. The last big fightin' scrape was in February of '70. We
pulled our kids out and we said we *demanded* protection of
our children. That's the first time the judge really comed out
and put his foot down.

"Last year, the school was totally integrated. We got no
serious trouble now. Oh, the school officials still trying to
do their little sneaky devilment. The student body, they got
a white and a black president. Things that used to be elected
are appointed—Miss Homecoming and whatnot. It's not a
hundred percent. It's a hundred percent from what it was,
but it's not a hundred percent from what it ought to be."

ENGAGING IN SELF-DEFENSE

"From '64 till '66, it was living hell. We couldn't go out in the daytime or sleep at night. My house, before they burned it down, looked like a polka-dotted dress. Every kind of bullet hole was in that house. Even with all that, I never hate. But when they would shoot at our house, we'd shoot back. I believe God will take care of us, but I believe that part of Scripture that say help yourself and He'll help you. I believe in lettin' these people know that I do have a gun. If I just sit down and you can just curse and 'buse me out, hit me in my head, and I just put my hand on my head, you just keep on pounding on me. But if I stand up and tell you, 'If you hit me, baby, you goin' to get it back,' you ain't goin' to be so hasty to come beatin' on me."

REGISTERING OTHER PEOPLE TO VOTE

"I set up a citizenship school, which I taught black people, uneducated people, how to read and write. And taught them about the government, the little that I had knowed. I taught them a little about the Constitution. I reads a lot. I always did. All my life, any book I got my hands onto, I read. And I love to study about the government.

"Then, in '65, we really put on a registration drive. The registration director, he *refused* to register black people. We had as high as five hundred there in one day. They'd just register one or two and make the other people stand around and stand around. They put their foots on the desk and look out the window and laugh and say 'black niggers' and 'black crows' and all kind of things like that. And I got a group and we went to Washington, and I *demanded* federal registrars here. We come home thinking they was going to send some, but they didn't do it, so I went back to Washington myself.

"I stayed there for a week. And just harassed the Justice Department. The guy who was in charge of registrars for us then was Rosenberg. And, oh boy, I give that poor guy a hard way to go. I refused to leave his office. Even they'd offer me out for dinner, you know, and all this kind of thing, I just stayed right there. I just kept talkin' and goin' on and on. Rosenberg would get so tired, he would laugh—but he weren't tickled. And if he'd get mad, I'd get mad, too. But I learned a lot from him, even in our arguments and whatnot. Because I'd ask questions and they would tell me. And I would say, 'Well, where can I find that?' And he said, 'Such and such a place.'

"After a week, Rosenberg said, 'Mrs. DeLee, go home.'

"I said, 'I'm not going home, not until you tell me you're sending federal registrars into Dorchester County.'

"So he said, 'I can't tell you that. We're not allowed to. But I'll tell you this: Something will be done.'

"I said, 'Okay. I'll go home. And I'll give you three days. If you don't send those federal registrars by the day after tomorrow, I'm going to be right back.'

"But when I got home the next day, the federal registrars was there."

VISITING WASHINGTON

"The federal government does a very little. A *very* little. But that same little bit they do, it helps a whole lot. Why I'm so hard on the federal government is because while they're making one step if they were to make three—why, things would really get done much faster. But they just takes forever to do whatever need to be done. So that's why I just don't like the way they operates. But then anyway I got to take the little they get done. But to get that little! Brother! You got to put pressure on there. You got to show up and raise sand up there. And they knows that. Everybody in Washington knows Victoria DeLee, too. Because when I go up there to get something done—I don't care what I go after—they just don't have nothin' goin' on while I'm there. Because I just talks. And when I go there to see somebody, I just don't take no for an answer. If I go to see the attorney general and they say, 'Well, I'm sorry, he's up on the Hill,' I say, 'Well, that's all right. I'll stay right here till he come down off the Hill.' They say, 'Well, you haven't made an appointment.' I say, 'Appointment the devil! I made the appointment when we put 'em here, and I'm going to keep it.' So whoever I go to see, he will just see me that day—to get rid of me.

"If I'm going to Washington—like I'm going to HEW for a school problem—I go check on something else while I'm there. Welfare or food stamps or whatnot. I found out one thing: Writin' letters and phone calls don't get action. Best way to get action: Go there. They can't *stand* to see you comin' there. They'll act like they're glad to see you, but it's not. And when you come there, they will do things for you to get rid of you. And I knows that. And that's why always if it's a problem that really need to be solved right away, I just gets busy and go up there."

SETTING UP A DAY-CARE CENTER

"What they call the Four Hole School used to be a school for the Indians. They're a mixture. The white folks treat us bad enough as blacks, but they treated them worser than they did us, because they knowed these people was ignorant. The whites always kept 'em dumb. They always afraid. They's a scary set of people. They didn't even know what their rights was. The school was just pitiful. I went talkin' to the Indian people. We showed them the difference in the books their children was readin' out of. We kept on and on, and finally, they went to seein' it. It was a hard fight gettin' the Indians into the white school. The sheriff and his mens would arrest the Indians, and we'd get bond, and then they'd arrest them again. The Indian children boycotted the Four Hole School, and we taught the Indian children in a Freedom School. And we went to demonstrating and picketing. It's a long story, but now everybody's in the same school.

"Then this building was empty. This guy was runnin' for South Carolina House of Representative from Dorchester County. And he wanted to be elected. We had meetings with him to find out what he was goin' to do and to tell him what we was expectin' we wanted him to do. And one of the things was I wanted this school so we could open up a daycare center. So he promised us if he was elected he would get it. After he was elected, sure enough, he got with the school board and he got the keys and we got the school."

RUNNING FOR CONGRESS

"The idea of the United Citizens Party come out from the way black people was being excluded from the Democrat Party. We is supposed to be black Democrats, but we have never been accepted as Democrats. I've had a harsh struggle with the Democrat Party. I fought the Democrats from the precinct to the county, from the county to the state. One year, I had a hearing before the credentials committee at the state convention. I said, 'It look like the Democrats want our votes, but none of us.' (It seemed real jokey, because this was the first time the Democrats ever had anybody to challenge them, and they looked like they was all scared to death themselves.) One club meeting they had in Ridgeville, we got more blacks to come out and we outvoted them. But we didn't treat them like they did us—we just took the executive committee. That's the only important thing there. They got so sick they like to die. But then we thought in place of fighting the committee all the time, we'd just start our own United Citizens Party. When Mr. Rivers died, we got among ourselves and tried to find the best black to run—the one who was known, you know, throughout the First Congressional District. And everybody come to the conclusion it would have to be me. Because of my work in the past, everybody knowed me and the things that I've been doin'. I'm looking *forwards* to winning."

THINKING ABOUT BEING IN CONGRESS

"To me, it would be just like being here. You know you got a job to do and you're going there to do it. It don't make me any difference, because my way of life is gettin' something done. One thing about it: I don't care where you go, some people thinks just like you do. I'm not the only one thinkin' of doing things right. Some people got better thoughts than I have. But I find that a lot of people which have better thoughts than I've got, sometimes they are so slow with puttin' those thoughts into action. But me, when I thinks about a thing, I believe in just pushin' forward with it. I know that if I was to get to be elected to Congress, everybody would know I was there."

. . .

Victoria DeLee lost her race for Congress, but she remained active in community affairs and civil rights for the rest of her life. She died in 2010, at the age of eighty-five.

KAWAIDA

Newark, New Jersey
1972

THE CONTROVERSY OVER THE CONSTRUCTION OF AN APART-
ment building called Kawaida Towers in the North Ward of
Newark would have been easier to resolve if the important
question about it were really "How will it affect the school
population?" or even "How many black people will it bring
into the neighborhood?" rather than "What does it stand
for?" Symbolic arguments are particularly bitter, because
they leave practically no room for compromise, and after a
few days in Newark, I found myself drawn to a local theory
that all of the nastiest confrontations between Italians and
blacks in the city are over symbols. When the blacks, who
now constitute a majority in Newark, finally gained control
of the school board and began to make some changes, the
changes the Italians found most memorable and most offen-
sive had nothing to do with instruction but with whether
classrooms should be permitted to display black-nationalist
flags or whether a school should be named after Malcolm X.

(According to Imamu Amiri Baraka, the Newark black nationalist whose Temple of Kawaida is sponsoring Kawaida
Towers, one Italian political figure who objected to the name
of Malcolm X High School explained that color was not the
reason, since he had no objection to naming a predominantly
black school after, say, Louis Armstrong. Baraka replied that
he would have no objection to having a predominantly Italian school named after Jimmy Durante. In Newark, both
sides like to choose their own symbols.) City Councilman
Michael Bontempo, one of the Italian politicians who have
usually appeared at the construction site on mornings when
whites picket against Kawaida Towers, likes to explain why
the community would be ruined by any apartment building
under the control of Imamu Baraka—who, when he was
known as the poet and playwright LeRoi Jones, wrote a few
anti-white lines that even some Newark whites who are ordinarily not poetically inclined can quote verbatim—and the
climax of Bontempo's presentation is always the accusation
that Baraka's people refuse to stand at City Council meetings
during the pledge of allegiance to the flag.

Anyone who comes to think of Kawaida Towers as a
symbol rather than an apartment building can listen to its
supporters talk about alleviating Newark's dreadful housing
problems without troubling them with the fact that by far
the most serious housing shortage in Newark—housing for
large families—will not be affected by Kawaida Towers in the
least, since it will have nothing larger than a two-bedroom
apartment. If the controversy over Kawaida Towers were
based on reality rather than on symbols, one would expect
its opponents to denounce it at every opportunity for not
being a genuine attempt to solve the city's most serious hous-

ing shortage—not having the true interests of black people at heart is one of the accusations white Americans have traditionally been most fond of making about black leaders—but I listened to the orations of Italian politicians against Kawaida Towers for a week without hearing that particular denunciation made once. Symbolically, the situation is supposed to involve a tight neighborhood of Italian homeowners threatened by a huge public-housing project that will bulge with apartments holding welfare mothers and their eight teenage sons—all of them living on some government dole that amounts to Aid to Dependent Muggers. That vision would, of course, suffer if anyone dwelled on the fact that the neighborhood in which the apartment house is being built—part of what is commonly referred to as "the predominantly white North Ward"—happens to be at least a quarter black and Puerto Rican already, and consists mostly of rental property rather than the carefully maintained family-owned bungalows that always serve as symbols for the hardworking white ethnics threatened by black expansion. The vision would also suffer from accusations that Baraka's black nationalists, in their first independent attack on the Newark housing problem, are constructing a two-hundred-and-ten-unit centrally air-conditioned apartment building that will consist partly of efficiency apartments for middle-income bachelors. Low-income black families are what decent, hardworking white ethnics are supposed to fear, and New Jersey State Assemblyman Anthony Imperiale, the leader of the demonstrations against Kawaida Towers, has told television interviewers, "My main objection is that it's low-income." A low-interest, long-term mortgage has been furnished by the state, and some tax abatement has been granted by the City

Council, but even if the developers manage to stay within their projections, a two-bedroom apartment in Kawaida Towers will cost close to two hundred dollars a month. Although a certain percentage of the tenants will be eligible for rent subsidies, by far the majority will have to pay their own way. In the 1970 census, the median income of the families in the neighborhood was sixty-five hundred dollars a year. In other words, following the rule that families ordinarily do not spend more than a quarter of their income for housing, most of the people who are supposedly going to be driven to the suburbs by the arrival of a low-cost housing project in their midst couldn't afford to live in it.

Fifteen months ago, Councilman Bontempo had the good fortune to be absent from the City Council meeting at which the tax abatement for Kawaida Towers was approved—no one has ever been prouder of being present at a historic event than Councilman Bontempo is of being absent at that one—but the other Italian councilmen are having an uncomfortable time trying to explain how they happened to vote unanimously in favor of a project they now say will bring ruin to their constituents. Some form of tax abatement is necessary in order to construct an apartment building like Kawaida Towers—Newark is known not only for its deteriorating housing but for its extraordinarily high construction costs and its staggering property tax— and the Italians, who still outnumber the blacks on the City Council six to three, could have withheld that necessity by a simple vote. In Newark, where citizens have come to assume that a certain amount of skulduggery could be found behind even a vote to approve the minutes as read, there is no shortage of imaginative theories to account for five pro-Kawaida votes from five Italian councilmen. The councilmen themselves now say that they were deceived—that important information about who was behind Kawaida Towers was withheld from them. Until the official groundbreaking ceremony on October 12, no Italian politician had said a word against Kawaida Towers, although work on the foundation had been going on for weeks and the Newark *Star-Ledger,* in a prominent piece several days before the ceremony, reported in the second paragraph that the apartment building was "sponsored by Temple Kawaida, which is led by black nationalist Imamu Amiri Baraka." (It also reported that "Kawaida" means "tradition and reason" in Swahili, bringing up to date any councilman who had been laboring under the impression that it was an Italian word.) It appears that the most important piece of information withheld from the councilmen and the other Italian politicians in the North Ward was the information that Kawaida Towers would qualify as a symbol. The one Italian politician who seemed to realize that was Stephen Adubato, the Democratic chairman for the North Ward, who was once thought of by outside liberals (there being virtually no inside liberals) as potentially a nonracist alternative to Anthony Imperiale as leader of North Ward Italians—a Third Force of the kind the CIA man was looking for in *The Quiet American.* (Adubato's office has, instead of a statue of an Italian saint or an autographed picture of an Italian congressman, a poster of Sacco and Vanzetti.) Adubato, alone among Italian politicians, appeared at the groundbreaking ceremony to object to the construction and, displaying a clear understanding of what kind of occasion it could be, suggested to a television newsman present that any apartment house built in that neighborhood ought to be called Garibaldi Towers.

IMAMU BARAKA SAYS HE KNOWS what the Italian politicians are up to, and the Italian politicians say they know what Imamu Baraka is up to, and none of it has much to do with housing. Baraka sees the Kawaida Towers controversy as the result of maneuvering for power among North Ward politicians. "Steve Adubato figured he would establish himself as Defender of the Italians," Baraka told me. "But he didn't realize that he would have to out-fatmouth Imperiale." It has long been Baraka's contention that nobody can out-fatmouth Imperiale. Since 1967, when Imperiale organized some of his neighbors into what some of his critics considered a white-vigilante gang, he has been the most visible spokesman for North Ward Italians—a voluble, rotund, energetic man who is never at a loss for enough words to soak up the questions of television reporters at the construction site or to hold the attention of the hundreds of Italians who crowd into Thomm's Restaurant for anti–Kawaida Towers rallies. Once Adubato had raised the issue and Imperiale had turned it into a movement, Baraka says, every Italian politician in the North Ward had no choice but to spend a lot of time "feverishly trying to out-bigot the others."

In the analysis of Italian political leaders in Newark, Kawaida Towers is not an apartment house for black people but a power base for Imamu Baraka—a power base that will come outfitted with community rooms for organizing, a theater for propagandizing, and a board of directors composed solely of loyal Temple of Kawaida members. It is true, as Baraka says publicly, that the vacant lots in the all-black Central Ward give a false impression of how much land is available there—a lot of land that appears to have nothing on it is actually buried in red tape—but it is also true that the planners of Kawaida Towers looked specifically for land in the North Ward. Even the calmest Newark view of Baraka's motives would interpret Kawaida Towers as an attempt at a symbolic triumph—a demonstration that even in a supposedly Italian area, it is black people who now have the political savvy and organizational ability to erect a flashy, tax-supported apartment building—but, of course, it is not easy to find a calm view of Baraka in the North Ward. For years, Italians in Newark have seen Baraka not as a black leader but as an anti-white racist—a hatemonger who will not be satisfied until Newark is an all-black city.

"Baraka never did a black-white thing in his life," Adubato says. "They're talking about forming *black* institutions and asking *black* questions to get *black* answers. Why the hell should I sit still for that?" Adubato is the political figure most closely identified with the concept that Italians are now "white niggers" in Newark—the minority that gets bullied in the schools and shut out of the federal programs and rejected by universities looking for blacks and bypassed by the people downtown who decide which apartment building will be built where. "Black racism in America is unimportant, because blacks are a minority, but black racism is important in Newark, because they're in control," Adubato has said. "In this country, even a WASP caught in the wrong place is a nigger." The Italians, Adubato says, were just beginning to have their turn at the American Success Story when the rules were changed. (Kenneth A. Gibson became the first black mayor of Newark by defeating the first Italian mayor of Newark.) The most articulate leaders in Newark are black. Watching one of them explain calmly on television that the Italians picketing at the construction site are going through "a predictable fear reaction," an Italian can feel not only outvoted but patronized.

Baraka, as might be expected, is not a subscriber to the white-nigger theory. "They haven't paid their dues to call themselves niggers," he has said. "First they have to have someone steal them out of their homes and sell them into slavery." In the view of George Sternlieb, the director of the Center for Urban Policy Research at Rutgers, Newark has deteriorated to the point where the only important competition for power is not between racial groups but between the people who control agencies that can attract federal funds—the Italians who control the Housing Authority, say, versus the blacks who control Model Cities or some other blacks who control the Poverty Program. "They're like warring baronial gangs," Sternlieb said recently. "The peasants till the fields, barely noticing the horses galloping by."

If Baraka is trying to build Kawaida Towers in order to hasten the movement of a threatened white minority out of the city, the Italian leaders may be helping him along. The construction of one black-owned apartment building in the North Ward, like the installation of a Communist government in South Vietnam, is now more important than it once was merely because of the force that has been committed to prevent it. ("The only thing they're going to do is to frighten part of their political base out of there," Baraka has said.) In his statements to reporters, Imperiale has sounded relatively moderate. "If we lose our battle in court, we have no choice but to live with it and see that the people don't exodus," I heard him tell a black reporter at the site one day. But a protest movement is not kept alive by assuring the participants that the object of their protest is of limited importance. The people in the North Ward have accepted Kawaida Towers as a symbol. They have tacked a sign on the construction-site fence that says R.I.P. NORTH WARD. Their placards imply that Kawaida Towers would mean enough crime and overcrowding to destroy their neighborhood. They do not go to Thomm's in order to hear anyone tell them that they may have no choice but to live with the man they have long been told is committed to destroying them. "The eyes of the world are on this city," Imperiale told them one night at a meeting at Thomm's. "If we lose Kawaida Towers, we not only lose Newark, we may lose every target city." At Thomm's, the domino theory is unquestioned.

Investing Kawaida Towers with great importance will naturally work to Imperiale's advantage if he wins—if the construction is stopped by craft-union refusal to cross the picket lines or by an eventual victory in court. (Imperiale has already announced that he will run against Mayor Gibson in 1974, and that Kawaida Towers is part of his campaign.) A judge who has enjoined both picketing and construction at Kawaida Towers until January 2 has criticized the parties involved and the city administration for not working out some agreement, but the real issues of Kawaida Towers could remain untouched by the kinds of compromises ordinarily made in such disputes—agreeing to make the project smaller, for instance, or agreeing to reserve a certain number of apartments for the elderly. Not long ago, Frank Megaro, the North Ward councilman who introduced the resolution to give tax abatement to Kawaida Towers and later became one of its bitterest critics, suggested on television that a first step toward agreement would be for Imamu Baraka to withdraw from the project. If Kawaida Towers is seen as a confrontation rather than an apartment building, of course, the withdrawal of Imamu Baraka would leave no reason to build it.

• • •

Construction of Kawaida Towers was delayed by demonstrations and picket lines and court challenges—at a time when construction costs were rising steadily. In 1976, the project was abandoned. Anthony Imperiale had run for mayor of Newark in 1974 but lost to Kenneth Gibson, the city's first black mayor. Imperiale died in 1999. Imamu Amiri Baraka, who moved from Black Nationalism to Marxism in his later years, died in 2014. The lengthy obituaries in The New York Times *("one of the major forces in the Black Arts movement") and* The Washington Post *("one of the most influential African American writers of his generation") made no mention of the Kawaida Temple. Later that year, Baraka's son Ras Baraka was elected mayor of Newark.*

CAUSES AND CIRCUMSTANCES

Seattle, Washington
1975

LATE ONE NIGHT IN FEBRUARY, A YOUNG BLACK MAN NAMED
Joseph Hebert was hailed by two uniformed Seattle policemen employing what prosecutors sometimes call a Terry
stop—named for a Supreme Court case that gives law officers the right to frisk someone if they have "reasonable
suspicion" that he might have been involved in a crime. A
Terry stop is what civil libertarians sometimes refer to as
stop-and-frisk. It is what black people often refer to as petty
harassment. Not that many people would deny the reason-
ableness of suspecting Joe Hebert that night. After hearing a
radio report that five armed black men had just fled from a
robbery in a suburb called Woodinville, the two patrolmen
had driven in their unmarked car to the west end of the Mer-
cer Island Floating Bridge, a logical place for anyone driving from Woodinville to enter the section of Seattle usually
known as the Central Area—the home of most of the city's
blacks and virtually all of its black armed robbers. One of

the cars they saw drive off the bridge was a red-and-white Ford in which they had arrested three black men a few weeks before for armed robbery. It was occupied by a single black man. When he parked, on a quiet street in the Central Area, the two patrolmen ordered him to put his hands on the Ford for a search. A few minutes later, the young black man, Joe Hebert, was dead, a single hollow-point bullet from Patrolman Allen Earlywine's revolver in his head.

A black man had been killed by a white policeman. In America, the simple statement of such an incident produces instant conclusions—conclusions that tend to vary according to the race of the person offering them. A white person's instinctive reaction may be to thank the Lord he is white, or to worry about the possibility that such a killing will cause trouble, or even to remark to the white person next to him that the black man probably had it coming. Black people, having a long history of vital interest in such incidents, tend to have a more uniform response: Another black man has been lynched. The naked statement—a black man has been killed by a white policeman—is such a fearsome divider of the races that the people who preside over a city immediately try to cover it with details. There were causes. There were circumstances. It could be said, for instance, that Joe Hebert had often been in trouble with the law; he was identified in the headlines reporting his death not as a black man but as a "robbery suspect." It could be said that Allen J. Earlywine was a young officer of respectable record who, in nearly four years on the force, had never before fired his revolver off the range. The killing of Joe Hebert, in other words, was not the case of a notoriously sadistic policeman shooting down a patently innocent black man. There were a lot of other causes and circumstances, but when they had all been aired, most of the black people in Seattle still seemed to see the death of Joe Hebert in a way that could be expressed in a simple statement: A black man had been killed by a white policeman.

SEATTLE IS OFTEN SPOKEN OF as a city that, as American cities go, "still has a chance"—which is partly a way of saying that it does not have an unmanageable number of poor black people. In the sixties, it did have some scary-talking Black Panthers and a series of several dozen bombings and raucous demonstrations to demand the hiring of more minority workers in the construction industry. The leader of the hiring demonstrations—Tyree Scott, of the United Construction Workers Association—is still put away fairly regularly on various charges, but the bombings stopped long ago, and the Panthers, having turned relentlessly respectable, treat a white visitor to their children's breakfast program or their free medical clinic with a courtesy they must find mildly painful. When the Panthers do stray from the path, a Seattle judge is likely to search for flexibility in the law; Scott manages to make it inside for contempt of court only by flinging at judges remarks that might sound contemptuous to William Kunstler. Aside from their tactical interest in avoiding confrontation, the white people in charge of Seattle institutions tend to strike even black radicals as essentially open and friendly souls. It is a town in which citizens who want to denounce a public official in person usually find his secretary courteous about arranging an appointment, a town in which Tyree Scott, a radical who believes that the police are basically an army of occupation serving the establishment, can refer to the police chief as a "nice old fellow" who tries to be non-racist within the limits of his understanding. It is, these days, the kind of town in which all leading officials would consider it important that all causes and circumstances be aired publicly when a black man was killed by a white policeman.

Not many years ago, the method of airing was for the coroner to form an inquest jury—or, as the process was sometimes described, for the coroner to "go out in the hall and round up six guys." The six guys, magically transformed from a pinochle game into a blue-ribbon panel, would consistently find that the shooting had been justifiable homicide, and the prosecutor would thus be given a convenient reason for not pursuing an irritating and controversial and probably fruitless prosecution of a policeman. When a modern home-rule charter eliminated the coroner's office in 1968, it retained a loosely worded provision requiring that a public inquest be called into "causes and circumstances" whenever a death involved a law-enforcement officer—although the decision whether or not to prosecute anyone for the death remained solely with the county prosecutor. (The state of Washington does not ordinarily employ grand juries.) A couple of years later, a young black man named Larry Ward was killed in a police trap after placing a bomb at the office of a Seattle real estate firm—having been hired for the job by a local hustler whose capital for such enterprises was apparently furnished by the FBI.

It was arranged to include two blacks among the inquest jurors. Even then, the inquest was interrupted by a white radical lawyer who denounced it as a farce and a mockery, and it drew so many angry black people and outraged pamphleteers that it was eventually moved to an auditorium at the site of the Seattle World's Fair. When the jury found, by a vote of three to two, that Larry Ward had met his death by "criminal means," the police and their supporters had a turn denouncing it as a farce and a mockery—a circus that had, in the guise of finding out cause of death, accused a police officer of murder without affording him the due process of a proper trial. There was talk that the inquest-jury system, which had been criticized by some law professors as a community relations device rather than an effective way of establishing cause of death, should be replaced by a simple report from the medical examiner. The anger provoked among white supporters of the police by the jury's decision was, as it turned out, nothing compared to the anger provoked in the black community about two weeks later by an announcement from the prosecutor. Charles O. Carroll, a politician who had filled the office of prosecutor comfortably for twenty-two years, said that he was bringing no charges against the police officer who had killed Larry Ward. As a way of calming the citizenry and smoothing the life of the prosecutor, the inquest-jury process had turned out to contain a rather elemental imperfection: It worked only if it reached a finding of justifiable homicide.

THE MAN WHO SUCCEEDED CARROLL as prosecutor shortly after the Ward inquest, a young attorney named Christopher Bayley, came in as a reformer—an articulate Harvard man who had a reputation as the sort of officeholder who would probably return a bottle-shaped Christmas package without even opening it to check the brand. He had the support of the black community when he ran against Carroll in the Republican primary, and he retained its support for the way he ran his office. The changes he made in the inquest-jury process were the kind that met the criticism of black people who feared a cover-up rather than the criticism of police supporters who feared a kangaroo court; he made it a policy, for instance, to permit lawyers for the deceased's family to cross-examine witnesses and to have access to pertinent police reports. In one case of a black man killed by the police, Bayley even prosecuted a policeman for manslaughter—although the jury returned a not-guilty verdict with a dispatch that bordered on the instantaneous.

The inquest jury looking into the death of Joe Hebert, six citizens selected from the regular jury pool, included two blacks and received its instructions from a black judge. Patrolman Earlywine testified that he had shot Joe Hebert in self-defense—that Hebert, during a foot chase, had suddenly wheeled to face him from thirty feet away with what appeared to be a gun and turned out to be a knife—and attorneys for Hebert's family implied, through demonstrations of bullet trajectory and accusation of conflict in police testimony, that Earlywine's story was a concoction. The Panthers had done a lot of investigating of their own through a Justice for Joe Committee, and the inquest, held in the County Council chambers, was packed with Justice for Joe partisans, many of whom scribbled notes to the attorneys whenever a hole seemed to appear in a policeman's testimony. Although the inquest jury voted, four to two, that Patrolman Earlywine had been in fear for his life—the classic test of self-defense— it also voted, five to one, that the death of Joe Hebert was not justifiable. Two days later, Bayley announced that there would be no charges brought against Officer Earlywine.

As if to make the replay of the Ward case more precise, the inquest was denounced as a carnival by just about anybody having anything to do with the police department. Just after Bayley announced that Earlywine would not be prosecuted, the police chief of Seattle, Robert Hanson, called a press conference in which he stated that Joe Hebert was wanted for another armed robbery at the time of his death, that he was carrying two watches stolen in the Woodinville robbery, and that he had "an extensive criminal-arrest history for such crimes as robbery, larceny, rape, auto theft, and resisting arrest." As a matter of standing up for the reputation of his men, Hanson said, he believed it necessary to demonstrate that Hebert "was not the angel he was portrayed to be at the inquest." He said he also wanted to reassure black people that the real reason for Hebert's death was that he was a criminal who had good reason to flee from the police. There may have been some black people who were privately reassured. It is natural, after all, for anyone to be comforted by the discovery of ways in which the situation of someone who got shot to death does not match his own. But the public response was widespread denunciation of Hanson for using unproved charges to slander a man who could not defend himself, and perpetuating the notion of black criminality while doing it.

Christopher Bayley was criticized not just by the Black Panthers but by the NAACP and the Urban League and an association of black attorneys and a rather conservative black businessman who had served as foreman of the inquest jury. In response to Bayley's remarks that the jury's findings had been contradictory, the foreman said that he took the votes of those who believed Earlywine to have been in fear for his life to mean that any white man would be afraid in a black neighborhood at night. ("Sure he feared for his life," the organizer of the Justice for Joe Committee told a protest meeting. "They teach them to fear for their lives. They teach them that we're animals.") Bayley and Hanson became illustrations for those who argue that in the final issue between the races—the issue of whether a black life has the value of a white life—openly repressive white authority and seemingly sympathetic white authority are, in Tyree Scott's words, "functionally the same." There was talk that Hanson and Bayley may have been motivated by the same kind of pressures that would motivate any officeholders—Hanson trying to solidify his leadership in a department that has had serious morale problems in recent years, Bayley trying to avoid antagonizing the police department or the white electorate. Not long after the inquest, Jerome W. Page, the executive director of the Seattle Urban League, said, "We want to believe that the mayor is better than average, and I know Bayley is better than average. I even have hope in the police chief, because the police chief wants to do good. And what this says to me is that the system must protect itself. In this case, the system is built for failure."

Bayley now says that the universality of the denunciation from the black community surprised him. He did not expect a plaque from the Black Panthers, but he did think that, having established some credentials for fairness in four years, he should have been able to convince people like Page that the decision not to charge Earlywine was correct, or at least objective. Bayley says that inquests were leaned on for so long by prosecutors looking for an excuse not to prosecute that the public began to view them as some form of binding grand jury. Looked at objectively by a prosecutor, Bayley maintains, the Hebert case rests on the credibility of Allen J. Earlywine, the only witness, and it is a credibility that Bayley accepts. Looked at objectively by a prosecutor, of course, the Hebert case has nothing to do with the Larry Ward case or any historical incidence of black men being killed by whites in authority. "People in the minority community view all this in a cumulative sense," Bayley said recently. "To them, it can't be viewed out of context. But that can't be my view as a prosecutor. I can't make a charging decision on the basis of anything except for the person or persons involved."

What seems to have surprised both Bayley and Hanson was the way in which the shooting of a man like Joe Hebert touched respectable, law-abiding black people who theoretically have nothing to fear from the police—although, Bayley has found, "almost every black person has one story to tell about being stopped by the police." What many of the people who trooped into the City Council a few months ago to argue against the police using hollow-point bullets had in common was not that they were potential "fleeing felons" but that they were blacks—blacks from the Urban League as well as blacks from the Panthers. After all this time, black people—law-abiding black bourgeois as well as black street toughs, and particularly law-abiding black bourgeois who fear that their sons may be difficult for a frightened white policeman to distinguish from black street toughs—do not need arguments based on bullet trajectory or statistics about the percentage of blacks among people shot by policemen to feel that a white policeman confronted by a black man may leave a few of the alternatives to shooting unexplored. Chief Hanson tried to make the black people of Seattle see Joe Hebert as a criminal, but they insisted on looking at him as a black man.

THE JUSTICE FOR JOE COMMITTEE is still functioning. The Panthers are expected to try to use it as part of their campaign for community control of the police, a campaign that white radicals tend to look on as futile or irrelevant, and the Justice for Joe Committee is already feeling some of the tension between blacks and white radicals that would be present even if their goals were the same. There is wide agreement in Seattle that the police department should have more black patrolmen—it now has twenty-two in a force of more than a thousand—and Chief Hanson has promised that a police-academy class scheduled to be formed in a couple of months, the first since a hiring freeze was applied to the department three years ago, will be one-third black. Hanson still believes that there is some value in a public airing of the causes and circumstances of a death brought about by a peace officer, but he has suggested to the county executive that the inquest be limited to just that, with the peace officer clearly in the role of a witness rather than a defendant. County Prosecutor Bayley also believes that the inquest-jury process should be changed, at least to the extent of not stating its findings in language that sounds like advice on whether or not to prosecute, but he is concerned that a change so soon after the Hebert case would have the appearance of an attempt to choke off the one channel of independent public inquiry. As it happens, both Bayley and Hanson have been making some hard-line public statements about crime and punishment lately, each in his own way—Hanson criticizing soft judges who let criminals back out on the street, Bayley saying that he has become impressed with the arguments now being made by some social scientists for a "certainty-of-punishment model" rather than a "treatment model" of criminal justice—and both find themselves with a lot of supportive mail that links those views to the Hebert case. A lot of black people in Seattle still seem to believe that the causes of Joe Hebert's death had to do with racism, and that the circumstances amounted to the deadly combination of a white policeman with a gun confronting a black man. "We'll look back and this will just be one of those cases," Jerome Page, of the Urban League, said recently. "You can't take the Hebert case alone, because it is built on so much."

• • •

In 2011, the Department of Justice issued a report that found the Seattle Police Department was engaged in a pattern of unnecessary or excessive force. Over fifty percent of the instances of such force involved minorities. After several months of negotiations aimed at avoiding a civil rights suit by the department, a settlement was reached, resulting in reforms that included more-restrictive rules for the use of force and for making a Terry stop.

The inquest-jury system remained essentially unchanged. In 2014, The Seattle Times analyzed 213 fatal police encounters since 2005 and found that only one police officer had been criminally charged. Dan Satterberg, the prosecuting attorney of King County—where African Americans, who represent 6.3 percent of the population, accounted for over 20 percent of the deaths by police officers—was quoted as saying that the major hurdle to bringing charges was a state law, passed in 1986, that the Times *called "the nation's most restrictive law on holding officers accountable for the unjustified use of deadly force." Under its provisions, the prosecution must prove that the police officer acted out of malice.*

THE UNPLEASANTNESS AT WHIMSEY'S

Boston, Massachusetts
1976

THE UNPLEASANTNESS AT WHIMSEY'S, LIKE A LOT OF EVENTS in American cities these days, both pleasant and unpleasant, followed naturally from an attempt to solve a simple real estate problem. The problem was what to do with a room that seemed too large to sustain a restaurant. The room had been created as the ground floor of an eight-floor parking garage built just off Copley Square to serve the new John Hancock Tower—a dramatic skyscraper that is the tallest structure in New England but is best known for its former tendency to pop off windowpanes from great heights, like a dinosaur shedding scales toward the normal-sized animals grazing below. Mamma Leone's—a branch of the tourist-stuffing operation that has long been a fixture of the Manhattan theater district—was the first tenant of the garage's ground floor. For a number of years, Mamma Leone's has been owned by Restaurant Associates, a food merchandiser once widely admired in the trade for its innovative slickness and more recently known as an operation that is shrinking at the rate of a dime candy bar. Restaurant Associates establishing an out-of-town branch these days is more or less the equivalent of Great Britain establishing a new colony. One lunch at the Boston version of Mamma Leone's was enough to inspire the late essayist L. E. Sissman to write, in his *Atlantic Monthly* column, a critique of American restaurant standards that began, "This kind of nonsense has got to stop." Within a year or so, Mamma Leone's had packed up its manicotti and retreated to the West Forties.

The management of the enormous room fell to the Copley Plaza, just across the street—a stately old hotel that Bostonians might have described a few years ago as lying "just out of range of the Hancock Tower," although it had turned out to be vulnerable from below to the ripples induced by the excavation of the Hancock's awesome foundation. During the skyscraper's construction, the John Hancock Company bought the Copley Plaza, and those Bostonians who savor tales of the Hancock Tower's destructive force the way people in other parts of New England exchange memories of the great hurricane of 1938 have always preferred to believe that the purchase was the result of some cost-effectiveness specialist's realization that fighting Copley Plaza damage claims in court would be more expensive than buying the hotel. According to the new proprietors, the true reason for the purchase was merely "protection." By the normal laws of real estate, the Copley Plaza was as likely to remain unaffected by a neighboring project the size of the John Hancock Tower as Finland is likely to remain uninfluenced by a neighboring country the size of the Soviet Union.

The president of the company formed to operate the Copley Plaza—Hotels of Distinction—is Alan Tremain, a richly mustachioed Englishman who managed to restore the hotel to something approximating its original elegance. Tremain, who likes to do business with the sort of flair identified with the early Restaurant Associates entrepreneurs, established a huge restaurant called Whimsey's in the parking garage. But the room—which is twenty-five thousand square feet, large enough for a restaurant that seats seven hundred and fifty people—resisted his every effort. Tremain attacked the problem with market research and heavy advertising. He tried a dinner theater, and he tried renting out part of the restaurant to the Press Club of Boston. He could not make the room pay. The heat, light, and power bill alone ran a hundred and fifty thousand dollars a year. Tremain had to attract double the number of patrons that would support an ordinary-sized restaurant and, as he later summed up his difficulties, "to bring people to a garage in the middle of a city is tough." He began to consider another approach—turning Whimsey's into a discotheque. "Before we opened, people used to say to me, 'I can't picture you with a disco,'" Tremain said recently. "And I'd say, 'Well, I can't picture myself with a dud restaurant.'"

In Boston, the most recent incarnation of discotheques began a few years ago in the form of places where homosexuals could go to dance. By the time Tremain began to look into the matter, cities like Boston and New York had a variety of discos—gay and straight, chic and seedy. What they had in common was some system of flashing lights and recorded music played with a beat that could often be felt as well as heard by the dancers, like the concussion of a series of minor explosions. Enthroned above the dance floor of almost any disco is the disc jockey—a rhythmically bobbing figure, often in earphones, who is too electronically oriented to speak words but so skilled in manipulating dancers with his selection and blending of music that he is likely to have a following of his own. Although some discos have the reputation of being run by the sort of businessmen with whom people on parole would do well not to be seen, Tremain found that established corporations were beginning to move into the field. The subhead of a *Forbes* article he was particularly struck by said, "The kids are storming the discos, and the owners are swinging all the way to the bank. Big business is getting interested. Very interested." The *Forbes* piece reported, among other success stories, that in Washington, a singles-bar operator and a restaurant proprietor had, with an investment of a hundred thousand dollars, turned a little-used banquet room into a disco that earned four hundred thousand dollars a year. Tremain set out to create a tony, professionally run disco that, as he says, would "make a real effort to really make some magic for them." He visited twenty or thirty discos in New York. He went to places that amounted to nothing more than a large unkempt room with a scratchy hi-fi. He dropped three hundred and eighty-five dollars for a dinner for five at Regine's, an East Side place apparently founded on the sound Manhattan marketing principle that telling a Wall Street conglomerateur or a midtown real estate shark that he is among those privileged to pay an enormous price at The Place to Be Seen is the equivalent of telling a farm boy that he is among those who need pay only one thin quarter to enter the tent that contains both a hermaphrodite and a three-headed goat.

Tremain was aiming for a market somewhere in between—a sort of singles-bar crowd of youngish people who might be intimidated by a pretentious restaurant but could spend the equivalent amount of money at the bar between dances. Whimsey's would have to be the sort of place where conventioneers staying at the hotel could mingle with the younger set without feeling like polka fans at a rock concert. It would be listed among the attractions of the hotel, along with rooms like the Café Plaza ("Boston's Bastion of Dining Elegance") and the Merry-Go-Round ("Boston's Posh Night Club"). Tremain spent what he estimates as five hundred thousand dollars to transform Whimsey's into a disco. He invested in the most sophisticated quadraphonic sound system available and a light system that can produce what appears to be an approximation of the lighting that detained members of the IRA might accuse the British Army of using in attempting to force them to betray their comrades. A dress code was established, requiring that gentlemen wear suits or sport coats, and proscribing even those jeans that cost more than a suit or a sport coat. For Whimsey's opening this fall, Tremain, who says he spent up to fifteen thousand dollars a month in advertising trying to attract people to the enormous room when it was a restaurant, merely gave a stack of invitations to a number of people known to be close to the Boston disco scene. The place was jammed—an obvious smash success. Two nights later—a Saturday night—there was some unpleasantness at Whimsey's. Eventually, ten people filed complaints with one government agency or another in Boston claiming that they had been kept out of Whimsey's because of discrimination. All of the complainants were black.

* * *

Nobody familiar with Boston discos was particularly surprised. Although the Whimsey's case caused the first large splash of publicity about racial discrimination in Boston discos, blacks have always had reason to approach the door of a disco warily. Reporters working on the Whimsey's incident found that the files of the Massachusetts Commission Against Discrimination contained more than thirty complaints from blacks about being barred from nightspots—including complaints against practically every disco in town. The most common method of keeping people out of a disco is having the man at the door "card" them—a request for identification cards that goes well beyond establishing that a customer is of legal drinking age. When disco managers are asked why identification is required at the door, they tend to answer the way Whimsey's manager did at a hearing held on the unpleasantness: "We like to get to know the people. . . . It's more of a get-to-know-you type of thing." If a doorman wants to get to know a prospective customer who is black, it is not unusual for him to ask for three photo IDs—three cards that, like the Massachusetts driver's license and some industrial identifications, include a picture.

"Does anyone actually *have* three photo IDs?" someone who once worked as a disco doorman was asked recently.

"It's funny," he said. "I carded this black lady once, and she spread three photo IDs right out in front of me. I said, 'Well, you called my bluff, lady. Go right in.'" It has been common for a disco to answer a discrimination complaint by saying that the person in question was being raucous, and it often turns out that what he was being raucous about was being asked for three photo IDs after watching half a dozen people in front of him enter without being asked for anything.

Blacks are not the only people who are particularly likely to be carded by disco doormen. Discos in Boston started as a sort of refuge for homosexuals, and as gay discos became increasingly invaded by straight couples, homosexuals began to feel that keeping out straight voyeurs was a matter of protection rather than discrimination. It has been argued that as long as gay men dancing together in a straight disco would subject themselves to ridicule or even ejection, they should be able to enjoy themselves somewhere without being gawked at by a gaggle of suburbanites looking for kicks. The proprietor of a gay disco, of course, is likely to want to keep it gay not because of a deep commitment to gay liberation but because he wants to preserve what he has found to be a reliable clientele—the same reasoning that proprietors of basically white discos (including white gay discos) have apparently used in trying to keep them white. It all turns out to be a matter of market selection. The custom has not been to bar all blacks but merely to hold the number well below the level that could cause the place to be thought of as a black disco. Discos, like any other business, decide which market they are after, and they are no more likely to welcome people who threaten that market than magazines interested in presenting advertisers with statistics of reader affluence are likely to direct their subscription solicitations to the slums. In denying that Whimsey's has ever had a policy of discriminating against blacks or any other group, Alan Tremain has based his argument partly on what amounts to a market assessment: He says that Whimsey's is so enormous that any sort of minority could safely be let in without fear of having it "take over."

* * *

THE MASSACHUSETTS COMMISSION AGAINST DISCRIMINA-
TION is understaffed and underfunded and overburdened
with complicated mandatory procedures. Although disco
complaints have been on file since 1973, the MCAD made
its first settlement of a disco discrimination case just a few
weeks after the Whimsey's incident—a consolidation of nine
complaints against a place called Zelda's. (It was agreed that
Zelda's, without acknowledging guilt, would pay one hundred dollars to each complainant, send each complainant a
letter of apology, and post a sign of nondiscrimination at its
door.) Some of the people who believed they had been ill-
treated by Whimsey's decided to take their case to the Boston
Licensing Board, which has the power to suspend or revoke
the licenses that permit Whimsey's to operate. Organized by
a lawyer from the city's Office of Human Rights who happened to be at Whimsey's that night—the only black member
of his party was one of the complainants—they showed up
at a Licensing Board hearing looking like black versions of
just the sort of people Tremain had been hoping to attract
to Whimsey's. Nobody who testified would have had any
trouble at all with Whimsey's dress code.

A variety of black people—a Boston State College professor, an FBI secretary, an elementary school teacher—testified
that they had faced a variety of problems at the door of
Whimsey's that Saturday night. Some of them said that after
having been told on the telephone that proper dress was the
only requirement for admittance, they arrived to be told that
they could enter only after going through a two-week admissions procedure to join a club. Others testified that they

were told they could not enter unless they were on a special guest list. All of them said they believed the real reason they were stopped at the door of Whimsey's was that they were black. They had apparently been angry with the doormen at the time ("Like, I had a lot to say," one of the women testified), and at the hearing they still seemed exasperated—exasperated at the triviality of it all, in the way that middle-class black college students in the South seemed exasperated, upon reflection, at the effort necessary to win something as trivial as the right to have a lunch-counter hamburger. "There shouldn't have to be all this hassle just to get into a disco," one of them told the licensing commissioners.

Tremain defended Whimsey's aggressively. He strongly denied any policy or practice of racial discrimination. He reminded the commissioners that licensees had the common-law right—indeed, the obligation—to keep undesirables such as pimps and prostitutes and drunks from the premises. He reminded the commissioners that he was no fly-by-night operator but someone who paid a million dollars a year in real estate taxes. He seemed constantly just on the edge of saying, "See here, my good man!"

The manager of Whimsey's said that the people whose complaints the hearing officially dealt with were kept out of Whimsey's because one of them had used foul language at the door. Faced with the consistency of complaints by a number of witnesses who had not previously known each other, though, Whimsey's attorney seemed almost apologetic in his closing argument. He reminded the commissioners that controlling the door was a difficult task in what even the complainants acknowledged was a crowded and harried situation. "They did not have a policy to discriminate against people because of their race or color," he said. "If they made a mistake, then I think that we would only hope that they would learn from their mistake. This is a serious problem. Mr. Tremain has got an expensive investment."

During the weeks the commissioners spent in deliberation, Whimsey's business was what Tremain describes as "fantastic, just unbelievable." A month after the hearing, the commissioners announced that, having found Whimsey's guilty of racial discrimination, they were ordering a four-day suspension of its licenses. The verdict was unprecedented— the Licensing Board had never before suspended a license for discrimination—but the punishment fell well short of cruel and unusual. The state Alcoholic Beverages Control Commission normally orders a longer suspension for a bar found guilty for the first time of serving a minor. The Licensing Board ordered that Whimsey's suspension need not be implemented until the second week in January—the post-holiday lull, during which the proprietors of some nightspots would welcome an opportunity to close for a few days. Tremain expressed irritation at the verdict and continued optimism about Whimsey's as a disco. "We've proved to ourselves that there is in fact a market," he said recently. "And it's going to be there for at least a couple of years." In a couple of years, Tremain figures, he will have to devise some other way to fill the enormous room.

* * *

Whimsey's closed in 1978. In The Boston Globe, *Alan Tremain cited competition from the recently opened Quincy Market ("People who patronize discotheques are very fick-*

le"). In 1981, *when the management finally secured a new tenant, the Liberty Mutual Medical Services Center, a column in the* Globe *began, "That spacious ground floor retail space in the massive John Hancock Garage . . . hasn't thus far proved to be the most successful retail space in the city."*

REMEMBRANCE OF MODERATES PAST

1977

"I KEEP HEARING ABOUT WHITE PEOPLE WHO SAY THEY'VE been working behind the scenes," a black lawyer in New Orleans told me during the desegregation of the public schools there, in 1960—a time when the business and professional leadership of New Orleans stood silent while the city seemed to be taken over by a bunch of women in hair curlers screaming obscenities at six-year-olds. "Yes, sir," he said. "It must be getting mighty crowded back there, behind the scenes." From then on, and whenever somebody mentioned working behind the scenes during a time of racial turmoil in the South, a picture planted by that black lawyer came into my mind: Onstage, little of interest is going on—just the usual succession of Southern pols, often in chorus, doing their "never-never" number and dancing off into the wings to great applause from the cheap seats. Every so often, that routine is broken by the appearance onstage of a solitary figure who presents a declamation about obeying the law of the land and is, predictably, pelted with rotten tomatoes or worse.

Behind the scenes, hordes of community leaders—prominent businessmen and pillars of the local bar and charity-drive chairmen and country-club presidents—are silently moving scenery around and around and around.

After many years, the picture was conjured up for me once again by the testimony of Griffin Bell, the new Attorney General, at his confirmation hearings before the Senate Judiciary Committee. Bell, he and his supporters emphasized, was one of the people working behind the scenes in those days when Georgia would finally have to decide how to respond to a court ordering a black child into a white school. Hearing those days recalled, I could again remember the politicians shouting, "Never!"—or, in the rhythmic variation of Ernest Vandiver, then Governor of Georgia, "Not one, no, not one"—and I could remember that occasional speech about obeying the law made by a housewife or a newspaper editor, or even, on exceptionally rare occasions, a lawyer. Those were, as Bell testified again and again, tumultuous times. Looking back, he told the senators, he was proud to have been there and to have been "in the middle of it." Some of the people who testified in opposition to Bell's confirmation seemed astounded that someone who had worked behind the scenes instead of going onstage—going onstage with the knowledge that it might result in a brick through the window or calls in the night threatening the children—could think of himself as having been in the middle of it. But thanks to what that black lawyer in New Orleans told me, I think I could appreciate what Bell meant. I know it was mighty crowded back there.

* * *

ONE OF THE SENATORS APOLOGIZED for bringing up the matter of political categorizing by saying that he, naturally, hated labels. Bell doesn't seem to mind labels. He is an out-and-out moderate and not afraid to tell you so to your face. In those tumultuous times, those of us who found ourselves with slack time at a scene of tumult sometimes tried to figure out what a moderate was. According to Harold Fleming, for instance, who was then director of the Southern Regional Council, a small Atlanta hotbed of what he now calls "premature integrationists," a moderate was "a white man without sidearms." The precision of any definition was limited, of course, by the fact that most moderates could not be closely observed in action, being behind the scenes.

Civil rights activists in the North tended to label white people in positions of power in the South not as "moderates" or "segregationists" but as "smart segs" or "dumb segs." By the late fifties, for instance, smart segs, realizing that the courts had gradually rendered massive resistance useless as a strategy for avoiding desegregation, concentrated instead on delaying tactics in the courts and the sort of anti-integration laws that usually avoided the words "Negro" and "race." In the early sixties, Laurie Pritchett, the police chief who easily smothered Martin Luther King's desegregation campaign in Albany, Georgia, by being very polite about putting everyone involved in jail, was considered a smart seg compared to Eugene "Bull" Connor, the public safety commissioner of Birmingham, who reacted to a similar King campaign by turning police dogs on children and thus managed to inspire the Civil Rights Act of 1964. In 1961, a smart seg was someone who counseled that the best way to keep his city's bus station segregated was to permit the Freedom Riders to integrate to their hearts' content until, their rest stop being over, the bus carried them off to the next town, and the station returned to normal. The Freedom Riders, having traveled all the way from Virginia through the Carolinas and Georgia more or less in peace, were not attacked until they reached Alabama, which, it was generally agreed, was the world headquarters for dumb segs.

Some of the people who testified against Griffin Bell's confirmation were claiming, basically, that he was not a moderate but just a smart seg. As a counsel for Governor Vandiver in the late fifties, after all, he had helped draw up what were universally referred to at the time as "anti-integration laws," which would constitute Georgia's last-ditch defense against school desegregation—laws that established age limits for university applicants (black applicants often being over the customary age for college students, at least by the time the state's lawyers had stalled them in court for a few years) and provided for private-school tax credits and gave the Governor power to close any school in order to preserve "good order." Bell testified that the laws were more moderate than the old massive-resistance laws, since they permitted the Governor to close only one school instead of the entire system—the school to be closed, of course, being the one that had been ordered integrated.

Bell's real reputation for moderation, though, rested on what he had done behind the scenes. He had, it was testified, organized the Sibley Commission, whose hearings around the state began educating politicians to the reality that many white people in Georgia preferred integrated schools to no schools at all. He had kept in secret contact with Warren Cochrane, then a leader of the Atlanta black community, to whom he freely gave advice about not pressing desegregation suits until a more moderate climate of opinion could be arranged. When the desegregation order finally did come—unexpectedly, at the University of Georgia, which no governor would have dared close, instead of at the Atlanta public schools—Bell was among those counseling Vandiver to abandon the anti-integration laws and capitulate with a series of laws that Vandiver called, with the felicity of phrase common to the times, "the child-protection freedom-of-association defense package."

It could be argued that Bell was merely stalling Cochrane in those meetings. It could be pointed out that the anti-integration laws that he, as a moderate, suggested abandoning were those that he himself had helped devise. Still, I think that most of us who traveled the South in those days would have agreed that Bell was, as he claimed to have been, a moderate within the context of the times. A moderate, according to one of our definitions, was someone who valued something more than segregation, and the people Bell was identified with in Georgia did value something more than segregation—business.

IT WAS CUSTOMARY IN THE South for outside observers to interpret events in terms of ideology (usually racial ideology) and for local observers to interpret the same events in terms of money (usually graft). When Governor Orval Faubus, of Arkansas, was the symbol of Southern resistance to desegregation, a huge bond issue that his administration had put together was considered by many to be a key to whether Faubus would attempt a Senate race against William Fulbright. Outside observers tended to think that passage of the bond-issue referendum would provide the confirmation of Faubus race politics that the Governor needed to challenge Fulbright, who, despite his signing of the Southern Manifesto against the Supreme Court decision, was always suspected of being too worldly to be an authentic bigot. Local reporters assumed that if the bond issue passed, Fulbright was safe, since it would generate so much money that Faubus would not be able to afford to leave the Governor's office. When Faubus finally did leave office some years later, reporters asked him how he managed to build a two-hundred-thousand-dollar house after so many years of earning an annual salary of only ten thousand dollars, and he said he owed it all to thrift.

As the time for a start on school desegregation in Georgia approached, in the late fifties, moderation became a position favored by businessmen—although, being unaccustomed to public speaking on matters more controversial than the United Fund, they tended to promote the position from well behind the scenes. The propaganda for peaceful compliance presented to leaders in Atlanta by such organizations as the Southern Regional Council did not emphasize racial justice or even lawful obedience; it emphasized "the specter of Little Rock," the fearful blow that defiance and chaos had dealt Arkansas's industrial development. When it seemed that the first desegregation would come in the Atlanta public schools, businessmen feared that the state legislature, then controlled by rural types who could campaign almost as well on hating Atlanta as on loving segregation, would find great entertainment in the closing of the schools and the filling of the streets with troops. The definition of a moderate that became most important was the one that described a moderate as someone who had something to lose.

The people in Georgia who had the most to lose from economic disaster controlled institutions like Coca-Cola and the Trust Company of Georgia. Their law firm was King & Spalding, one of whose partners was Griffin Bell. There are firms like King & Spalding in every state—firms that provide the contact between government and the large corporate interests that have certain needs government must fill. King & Spalding represents not just many of the largest corporations in Georgia but also many of the municipalities that want to float bond issues. The firm's primary mission from the start may have been to keep the world safe for Coca-Cola, but methods have changed over the years. It used to be said of one of King & Spalding's founders—and not in an unkindly way—"The history of Georgia politics for the past twenty years is written in the stubs of his checkbook."

The sort of people King & Spalding represented were not averse to having desegregation stalled as long as possible—through devices like the package of laws that Bell and his colleagues concocted for Vandiver. (In an early example of public-interest law, Bell's services were donated by the firm to the Governor.) It could be argued, in fact, that if Bell and Warren Cochrane had been left to themselves—if the federal court had not finally decided that the time had come, if Cochrane had not been edged aside by some younger men—they would today be discussing when an opportune moment for a start on desegregation might arrive. But a little delay is quite different from economic chaos. The state's most powerful businessmen wanted as little integration as possible, but they also wanted as little trouble as possible accompanying the integration that had to come. It was assumed at the time that the Sibley Commission—organized by Bell, headed by a former senior partner of King & Spalding who was also chairman of the board of the Trust Company of Georgia—was, for all of the rhetoric in its report that may have seemed segregationist in the North, an attempt by the moneyed interests in Georgia to feel around for some accommodation. To those who tend to interpret the goings-on in the South according to money rather than ideology, what ties together Bell's roles in the Atlanta school case—holding secret conversations with Warren Cochrane as an adviser to Vandiver in the late fifties, proposing an out-of-court settlement as a federal judge in the early seventies—is not moderation or smartseg manipulation but simply the fact that both represented the wishes of the most powerful businessmen in the state.

I have always suspected interpretations of public events that imply an understanding of personal motives. In Bell's situation, for instance, who is to say what part friendship or ambition or political commitment or chance played in his connection with Vandiver and the Sibley Commission? The economic interpretation of Southern events has always been tempting, especially in Atlanta, a city whose atmosphere has usually had more in common with Houston than with Savannah. I admit that when I saw those campaign commercials last fall of Jimmy Carter dressed in beautifully cut neopopulist blue jeans, walking through the fields toward his farmhouse, it often occurred to me that when he got there, he would pick up the telephone and call Charles Kirbo, who happened to be all dressed up in a suit himself, sitting in his office at King & Spalding. I admit also that I found some significance in the fact that the proprietors of *The Atlanta Constitution,* having been forbearing for so many years while Ralph McGill and Eugene Patterson stood right out onstage to make unpopular arguments for racial justice, finally drew the line in a way that prompted Patterson's resignation when he defended a column criticizing the Georgia Power Company—or when, as the Georgia saying goes, "he quit preachin' and got to meddlin'."

THE NAME OF FRANK JOHNSON, a federal district judge in Montgomery, was often mentioned in the confirmation hearings as an example of what a federal judge in the South could be, as opposed to what Griffin Bell was. Julian Bond, who seems to have emerged as the only resident of Greater Atlanta, black or white, willing to say anything that might limit access to the executive branch, asked the senators with a straight face, "Why not the best?" Johnson, like the other Southern judges often mentioned as most resolute about dismantling the South's system of legal white supremacy, is a Republican—appointed by Dwight Eisenhower, who, with the advantage of having no Southern senators of his own party to assist him, named the old sort of Southern Republicans whose party affiliation might have signified nothing more ideological than having been born in a hill county that had been unenthusiastic about secession in the first place. In the early sixties, in fact, it used to occur to me that a foreign traveler who knew nothing about the Republican Party except what he gathered from observing federal judges in the South could easily mistake it for the party of Lincoln.

I once saw Frank Johnson on the bench. The details of the legal matter that brought me to his courtroom, some government motion against the Klan during the Freedom Rides, long ago faded from my mind, but I can still picture Johnson himself—a stern-looking man pacing up and down on the dais, dressed in a dark suit but no robe, stopping now and then to point an accusing finger at a Klan witness or a government lawyer and demand the truth. He seemed to be a judge from the Old Testament; the first impression I got from watching him was that one form of justice might consist of being equally terrifying to both sides. During the Bell confirmation hearings, I could sometimes picture Frank Johnson striding up and down behind the members of the Judiciary Committee, frowning impatiently as one of the liberal Democratic senators who had been so vigilant in searching out a racist remark made by Harrold Carswell in 1948 sympathized at length with Bell about how difficult it must have been for a man in the middle of it down there in Georgia in 1960, then pausing in his stride to point a finger at the senator and say, "I don't want to hear any more about the 'temper of the times,' Counselor." When I read in the late sixties that, the outrage of the local gentry over some of Johnson's decisions having turned the country club into a hostile camp, Johnson was forced to play golf at a nearby air base, it occurred to me that an Old Testament judge must consider the location of his golf course a trifling matter indeed.

What brought Judge Johnson's golfing problems to mind was a discussion during the hearings of Bell's membership in the Piedmont Driving Club, an Atlanta country club that excludes Jews and, it almost goes without saying, blacks. One witness before the committee turned a good phrase by saying that Bell's initial notion of suspending his club membership while he was Attorney General revealed him to be a man willing to "put his conscience in blind trust," but most white Protestant Americans, including most federal judges and most people who have been Attorney General of the United States, consider clubs to be within the large category of activities that are not subject to inspection for racial or religious discrimination. Although Jimmy Carter's complaint that the matter had been raised only because of Bell being a Southerner was, in its echo of similar complaints during the primaries, a reminder of how easily public debate can turn the drawl into a whine, I thought Bell's old friends and clients at the Piedmont Driving Club did have a point in saying that he was being asked to adhere to standards of purity that had not been applied to others. In light of Frank Johnson's experience, it seemed to me, the question to ask of someone about to become what was often called during the hearings the people's lawyer was not whether he belonged to a restricted country club but whether, as a lawyer or as a judge, he had ever done anything that might make him feel even remotely uncomfortable as he walked through the front door.

JUST BEFORE THE CONFIRMATION HEARINGS on Griffin Bell's nomination, I read a column by Phil Gailey in *The Miami Herald* that raised the question of how Jimmy Carter would have fared under similar senatorial examination. Carter was, after all, a member of the Sumter County Board of Education when, as Murray Kempton has pointed out, a liberal was someone who didn't object to putting a coat of paint on the colored school. In fact, Sumter County, now visited by tourists interested in observing their President's idyllic small-town roots, had a reputation among reporters as the nastiest county in the state—partly because the presence of Koinonia Farm, an interracial Christian community, had constituted what its founder once called a "divine irritant." In Americus, the county seat, a federal court order was required in 1960 to admit *white* children from Koinonia into the white high school. (A few years later, another federal court order was required to free four civil rights workers held in Americus under a state insurrection law that carried the death penalty.) There is no record of Jimmy Carter, a prominent businessman in the county, stepping forward (as some local ministers did) to remind his neighbors that firing shotguns at people's houses and burning down their barns constituted unchristian behavior. As late as 1970, Carter ran a campaign against Carl Sanders that included a promise to invite George Wallace to speak in Georgia, an appearance just before the election at one of the new private schools known as Seg Academies, and a charge that Sanders had revealed himself to be a captive of "the ultra-liberal wing of the Democratic Party" by sharing a platform and some platform courtesies with Hubert Humphrey. Would any of this be considered disabling to a man who wanted to be, say, Attorney General of the United States? Does Jimmy Carter have in his past what the senators on the Judiciary Committee like to refer to as a smoking gun? Clarence Mitchell, the Washington representative of the NAACP, was widely criticized for characterizing Bell as what amounted to a Good German, but a confirmation hearing on a white Southerner of Bell's age does carry some atmosphere of a de-Nazification court.

It is true, as Bell's defenders said during the hearings, that white people in the South in the fifties and sixties were tested in a way that white people in the rest of the country were not. The time had not yet come when white parents in the North would have to decide if principle required them to expose their child to the sort of mob that encircled the desegregated schools of New Orleans. It is also true that there were white people in the South, some of them believers in segregation, who drew the line at what they would do in its name. Pretending that "there was no choice in Georgia 1960 but silence, segregation, and subversion of the law," according to Julian Bond, "would dishonor the memory of those who bravely fought for what was right." There were lawyers in the South whose view of the law would not have permitted them to defend school segregation "by all legal means" in court once Supreme Court decisions had reduced the means available to little more than evasion and perjury. (The state's defense in the University of Georgia desegregation case consisted partly of hauling to the witness stand university administrators who swore they knew of no policy to exclude Negroes.)

When the Sibley Commission held its first public hearing, in Americus, several dozen politicians and educators and civic leaders appeared before it to say that an end to public education would be preferable to any integration at all, but a few people—a housewife, a priest, a labor leader—stood up publicly to say the opposite. There were white people in the South in those days like William Tate, the dean of men at the University of Georgia, who did not seem to consider the possibility of looking the other way if a student placed under his charge, black or white, was being harassed. As I look back at those people who did stand up onstage, though, it occurs to me that a lot of them did not survive the period well. Some of them were driven from their hometowns. Some of them found their personal lives unraveling under the tension. Whatever their views on segregation, they were, for all practical pur-

poses, "premature integrationists." Jimmy Carter had an opportunity to testify before the Sibley Commission at Americus
that, as a member of the Sumter County Board of Education,
he was unwilling to preside over the abandonment of public
education in the name of segregation, but if he had he would
probably not now be the President of the United States.

Some of the Southern politicians who were prominently
featured onstage in those days shouting "Never!" survived
remarkably well, considering the fact that the rather sudden
appearance of a huge black vote required some of them to
make a well-timed leap to the other side as the drawbridge
was going up. Herman Talmadge escorted to confirmation
hearings not merely Griffin Bell but Andrew Young. During
his remarks about how fortunate Georgia was in having had
people like Griffin Bell "to pour oil on troubled waters . . .
during a tumultuous and even inflammatory era," it was difficult to keep in mind that Senator Talmadge spoke as someone who had himself caused a good deal of the tumult. It
was hard for someone hearing him refer to Ralph McGill
as "the highly respected, internationally renowned human
rights advocate" to realize that he was talking about old
Rastus McGill the Race-Mixer—the man who could make
any Georgia governor's day if caught drinking tea with black
people by a photographer kept on the state payroll for just
such game. Those events are best forgotten now by black
Georgians who have an interest in sharing power, as well as
by whites. Birch Bayh, who, in defending Bell's nomination
on the Senate floor, argued that no man with racism in his
past would have received an honorary degree from Morris
Brown College, a predominantly black school in Atlanta,

had apparently been absent from the hearing room when Julian Bond remarked that another recent recipient of a Morris Brown honorary degree was Senator Herman Talmadge.

Carter, perhaps alone among Southern politicians of his age, made the transition adroitly enough to run for national as well as statewide office—stating at his gubernatorial inauguration, four months after he stood inside the Seg Academy door, that the time for racial discrimination was over, hanging a portrait of Martin Luther King, Jr., in the state capitol, and conducting himself ever since in a way that has caused many blacks and white liberals to give him the benefit of believing that his actions in the Sanders campaign constituted merely a deceitful attempt to get elected. If the hearings on Bell are an indication, whether or not Carter would have any trouble being confirmed by a Senate committee would depend on the party affiliation of the President who appointed him. With the Democrats in control of the Senate, more smoke is required of a Democratic gun than of a Republican gun. When one anti-Bell witness testified, apparently mistakenly, that Bell had once promised the Georgia legislature to delay desegregation by every legal means, Senator Bayh said that such a statement would constitute a smoking gun. But no unearthed statement was necessary to prove that Bell had attempted to delay desegregation by every legal means. He testified to that himself; it was, after all, what he regarded as the moderate position. Under questioning from Senator Charles Mathias, he acknowledged that such delay was carried out with the knowledge that the Supreme Court had said, in *Cooper v. Aaron,* "that delay in any guise in order to deny the constitutional rights of Negro children could not be countenanced, and that only a prompt start, diligently and earnestly pursued, to eliminate racial segregation from the public schools could constitute good faith compliance." The liberal Democrats on the committee talked about redemption and how a man could change over the years; Bell testified that his maneuvering for Vandiver constituted one of the best pieces of legal work of his career.

IF GRIFFIN BELL WAS GUILTY of racism during those tumultuous days, his supporters asked, how can it be explained that John F. Kennedy appointed him to the Fifth Circuit Court of Appeals in 1961? The cruelest explanation would be an examination of the other federal judges the Kennedy administration appointed in the South—Kennedy having been the President who entrusted the legal rights of the black people of Mississippi to Senator James Eastland's college friend W. Harold Cox, a man who has referred to blacks as "niggers" and "chimpanzees" from the bench. Bell was certainly a moderate compared to the Kennedy judge who said the 1954 Supreme Court desegregation decision was "one of the truly regrettable decisions of all time"—although no one seemed to care much one way or another in 1961. The chairman of the American Bar Association committee charged with checking Bell's credentials in 1961 happened to be Leon Jaworski, who, according to his testimony in the recent hearings, seems to have cleared Bell from any suspicion of racism largely by consulting his predecessor as committee chairman, Charles Bloch, of Macon, Georgia—an attorney best known in Georgia, it was later pointed out, as an architect of the state's massive-resistance laws.

Until Bull Connor committed the final dumb-seg folly in

Birmingham in 1963, the Kennedy administration's policy on civil rights could best be described as moderate. At a time when virtually no blacks were allowed to vote in Alabama or Mississippi, the administration had made it clear that no attempt to pass voting-rights legislation would be made. A suggestion by the Commission on Civil Rights in 1963 that federal funds be withheld from the state of Mississippi for "direct defiance of the Constitution" was considered the fantasy of impractical zealots, and the administration treated it as hardly worthy a reply. The Kennedy administration, like past administrations, dealt with civil rights as one item of business, not a national commitment that was allowed to interfere with other items of business. In the early sixties, the notion that racism was not acceptable even in certain regions or certain clubs or certain circumstances—the notion that it could not be treated with moderation—was a notion largely confined to black people. A lot of laws have been passed and a lot of marches have been marched and a lot of changes have been made since the early sixties, but as I listened to the witnesses who testified at the Bell hearings, I realized that it still may be a notion largely confined to black people. "Every time you say that this is something that happened a long time ago, it convinces me that your assessment of this set of circumstances is different from mine," Clarence Mitchell, of the NAACP, told Senator Bayh during a discussion of Bell's legal work for Ernest Vandiver. "I have been the victim. I know the victims." Identifying with the victims is required in order to testify, as Mitchell testified, that Bell's maneuvering did not constitute some understandable tactical stalling of school desegregation but "the stealing of the precious constitutional rights of thousands of black children." When it comes to race, I think, most white Americans are still, like Griffin Bell, moderates.

. . .

Griffin Bell served as Attorney General until 1979, when he returned to King & Spalding. He died in 2009 at the age of ninety. Referring to his service as an appeals court judge, the headline of his obituary in The Washington Post *identified him as "a voice of moderation."*

BLACK OR WHITE

Louisiana
1986

Susie Guillory Phipps thinks this all started in 1977, when she wanted to apply for a passport. Jack Westholz thinks it started long before that. In 1977, Susie Phipps was forty-three years old, but, as it happened, she had never before found herself in need of a passport. She had grown up in Acadia Parish, Louisiana, in a poor French-speaking farm family that found a trip to Eunice or Crowley an occasion. After a brief teenage marriage to one of her cousins, she went to Lake Charles, in the southwest corner of the state, where she worked mainly as a waitress, and where, eventually, she met a pipe fitter from South Texas named Andy Phipps. Phipps was a rough-cut man who, like so many of the people who came to that stretch of the Gulf Coast to build ships or work in the oil industry, had grown up poor himself. When he wasn't on his construction job, he was often butterflying for shrimp in an inlet of the Gulf of Mexico called Calcasieu Lake. Andy Phipps did well at that. Eventually, he turned to shrimping full-time, and then he established a wholesale operation. By 1977, when his wife drove from their home on the outskirts of Sulphur, a town ten miles west of Lake Charles, to New Orleans to pick up her birth certificate for the passport application, Phipps was well-off—a man who wore diamond rings and drove expensive cars and lived in a large brick house and could take a vacation in South America if he felt like it. In New Orleans, the clerk at the Division of Vital Records apparently said there was a problem, and she took Mrs. Phipps into an office to show her what it was. The birth certificate for Susie Guillory, duly recorded in Acadia Parish in 1934, showed the race of both parents as "Col."—colored. Mrs. Phipps has said many times what her response to learning that was: "It shocked me. I was sick for three days."

The state official to consult about how to have a birth certificate changed was—and still is—H. M. (Jack) Westholz, Jr., chief of the New Orleans section of the Office of the General Counsel of the Louisiana Department of Health and Human Resources. For some changes, Westholz can refer people to a statute or a regulation that lists precisely which documents have to be provided. Some changes, like the spelling of a name, are relatively simple to make. The most complicated of all has always been race. Louisiana has a rich history of court cases brought by people who maintain that the racial designation on their birth certificates is incorrect. From its earliest days as a French and Spanish colony, it has had a substantial number of residents who are not easily categorized racially by their appearance, and the question of what constitutes blackness or whiteness has been a matter of almost constant contention. At the time Susie Guillory's birth certificate was recorded, the definition of a black person was a matter of court precedent: A black person was anyone who had "any traceable amount" of black ancestry. In Louisiana courts, the burden of proof for anyone who wanted to change, say, "Col." to "white" on a birth certificate was evidence that left "no doubt at all."

Of course, the vital-records office has always had the discretion to permit the correction of obvious errors, and Susie Guillory Phipps said that the racial designation on her birth certificate was just that. The designation had originally been provided, after all, by a rural midwife, who was hardly likely to have arrived at it through a diligent examination of genealogical records; a lot of people in that part of Acadia Parish, including Susie Guillory's parents, could neither read nor write. "I was brought up white, I married white twice," she has often said. Her assumption has always been that the information on her birth certificate about the race of her parents flies in the face of what anyone can see with his own eyes: In the words of Jack Westholz himself, "Susie looks like a white person."

After Mrs. Phipps returned to Sulphur, she got in touch with Westholz about her problem, and he asked her to furnish certain information—the complete names of her parents, for instance, and the names and place of birth of her brothers and sisters. Eventually, he informed Mrs. Phipps that, having checked the records, he had concluded that no error had been made. The racial designations on her birth certificate were consistent with the information on the birth certificates of her brothers and sisters. None showed signs of having been tampered with. As far as the state of Louisiana was concerned, Westholz said, Susie Guillory seemed to have been correctly identified on her birth certificate as the child of two colored people.

IT MIGHT HAVE ENDED THERE. Whatever Mrs. Phipps's views on race, there was a lot to be said for simply forgetting about her encounter with the vital-records office. If the racial designations on her birth certificate had not affected her life for forty-three years, why pursue the issue? The system of legal separation of the races had been dismantled years before; nobody was trying to take away her right to vote or trying to force her to sit in the back of the bus. Susie Guillory Phipps lived as a white woman. Virtually nobody even knew what her birth certificate said. She was recorded as white on her own children's birth certificates. When her parents died, she had identified them as white on their death certificates. She had brothers and sisters and nieces and nephews who lived as white people. Nobody had challenged any of that. There was nothing to prevent her from using the birth certificate to obtain a passport—passports do not designate race—and then never using it again. She could have left well enough alone.

But she would not accept a copy of a birth certificate that identified her as black. She insisted that the designation be changed. Undoubtedly, she didn't realize how difficult and, in time, how public attempting to change it would turn out to be. When she began—she retained a legal clinic whose advertisement she saw in the New Orleans Yellow Pages— the process was so private that she didn't feel the need to tell her husband what had happened at the vital-records of-

fice. Even when she and a number of her relatives filed suit—
by that time, the legal clinic had been dissolved, and one of its
partners had handed the case over to a New Orleans lawyer
named Brian Bégué as part payment for a fee—she was listed
as Jane Doe. But when it became apparent that continuing
her efforts would involve considerable publicity, not to speak
of considerable expense, Susie Phipps decided to go ahead.
In the view of Jack Westholz, "She was very insistent—to the
point of obsession—that she wanted to get judicial blessing
of her color." Why? Not, she has always maintained, because
she has anything against black people. At times, she has said
that if her birth certificate did not get corrected, her descendants might come across it and think she was somebody she
wasn't. At times, she has said that she had to stand up for
what she believed in. From the start, she made it clear precisely what it was that she believed in: "I am white."

It could also be said, of course, that Jack Westholz might
have easily allowed Susie Phipps to change her birth certificate to say whatever she wanted it to say about her race.
Nobody would have cared. Louisiana is no longer the sort
of place where politicians are waiting to pounce on some
bureaucrat who has failed to enforce rigid standards of racial purity. Westholz acknowledges that he could have ful-
filled the obligations of his office by advising Mrs. Phipps
to seek a court order and then opposing the order only in a
token manner. Instead, he marshaled an elaborate defense of
Susie Guillory's birth certificate. Before he was finished, he
had accumulated two large cardboard boxes full of exhibits—
dozens of pages of depositions, a genealogy that went back
to the eighteenth century, and a chart that depicted the race

of the Guillory family according to something called the Robertson Fontenot System of Visual Percentage Analysis.

Why? Understandably, some have suggested that Jack Westholz was simply reflecting the zeal with which so many Louisiana officials in the bad old days used to search out any hint of what was known as "a touch of the tarbrush." It's a suggestion that Westholz bitterly and vocally resents. He has said that he acted partly out of a belief that he was being presented with a rare opportunity for a test case that might give his department some guidelines for settling disputed racial designations without litigation, or might even get rid of a strange law passed quietly, in 1970, mandating that a person "having one thirty-second or less of Negro blood" could not be designated non-white. The department considered that law at least unworkable and almost certainly unconstitutional. He also saw himself as defending the integrity of the records that his department was charged with gathering and preserving. Jack Westholz is a voluble man in his fifties with a somewhat anxious manner—a man accustomed to dealing with the demands of people who don't understand the limitations imposed by the rules as well as he does. He has worked for the state Health Department for eleven years, and he gives the impression that he would simply find it galling if someone were allowed to get away with pretending that the records said something they plainly did not say. "It's a historical record," he said recently of Susie Guillory's birth certificate. "Let it be. We can't go back and change history." Whatever his original interest in the case, Westholz acknowledges, any lawyer who is involved in protracted litigation becomes overtaken by an additional motivation: He wants to win.

* * *

"WHAT CREATED THE PROBLEM IS the overlapping of Anglo-Saxon and Latin views of the nature of descent," Munro Edmonson, an anthropologist at Tulane, said not long ago while discussing the constant wrestling with racial classification that has gone on in Louisiana. During the time Louisiana was a French or a Spanish colony—a time when liaisons between white men and black women were widespread and, in some cases, nearly formalized—the offspring were treated according to a Latin view of race that left room for a spectrum of colors between black and white. The French had eight terms to calibrate the spectrum. The Spanish managed to come up with sixty-four terms. Then, in 1803, Louisiana was taken over by the Americans, who imposed what Edmonson refers to as a Germanic view of descent, common to northern Europe and England: "When it comes to mixing between in-group and out-group, the offspring is flawed, and becomes a member of the out-group." It is a view that ultimately leaves room for only two categories: black and white.

There were a lot of people of mixed ancestry who didn't fit easily into either category. Many of them were people who had been given their freedom, and they were not eager to be lumped with people subject to the laws governing slaves. Despite decades of pressure to eliminate ambiguities in what became a system of separating two races, people of mixed race in Louisiana—light-complexioned, Catholic people, often with French names—managed well into this century to maintain themselves as nearly a third race in between. They are often called Creoles—a usage that can cause ferocious arguments in Louisiana, since the word is used by some people to mean only the white descendants of French or Spanish colonists. They are sometimes called Creoles of Color or Colored Creoles or, lately, Black Creoles. In the rural parishes of southern Louisiana, where some of them settled generations ago and continued until recent years to speak what is sometimes called Creole French, they are often known as mulattoes, or *mulatres*. In the section of New Orleans that is downriver from Canal Street, they used to be known as Downtown Negroes. When it came to nomenclature, what most interested people of mixed ancestry in Louisiana was not being called black—the category that segregationist authorities were constantly trying to force them into.

For generations, Creoles of Color were nearly obsessed with physical appearance—they admired "fine" hair and "fair" skin—and with separating themselves from black people. In New Orleans, a lot of Downtown Negroes were artisans of one sort or another, and it used to be said that black schoolteachers in New Orleans tended to be very dark-complexioned, because their choice of career had been dictated by their being too dark to get into the plasterers' union. There were always some Creoles of Color who could pass for Creoles of no color at all, and, particularly in the days when Louisiana operated a two-caste society based on race, it would not have been difficult to convince some of them of the advantage of simply marrying a white person and melting into the privileged caste. Traditionally, the way for light-skinned Creoles of Color to change races has been to change addresses. After World War II, a lot of servicemen from Downtown settled in other parts of the country—particularly Southern California. (It used to be said in New Orleans that half the white bricklayers in Los Angeles were from below Canal Street.) For some of the people who have changed races over the years, the changed address has been simply a different town or a different neighborhood. In southern Louisiana, it is taken for granted that a lot of white families have at least one ancestor who became white about the time he joined the family. Huey Long apparently used to say that if you had a loaf of sliced bread and handed it out only to pure-white people in Louisiana, it would last a year.

That was not the attitude found in the vital-records office. At Vital Records, it was taken for granted that certain families were white and certain families had a traceable amount of black blood, and that it was up to the vital-records office to tell them apart. When it came to tracing traceable amounts, nobody ever accused the vital-records office of bureaucratic lethargy. Vital Records saw itself as upholding the law. For decades, after all, the statutes of Louisiana made it illegal for a white person and a person with a traceable amount of black blood to get married; in fact, people of different races would have been breaking state law by competing against each other in a tennis tournament. The vital-records office has always been in New Orleans rather than Baton Rouge, and there is hardly a lawyer in town of a certain age who doesn't have a story to tell about a battle—almost always an unsuccessful battle—he fought to obtain a marriage license or a birth certificate for an ostensibly white client whose family the vital-records office considered partly black. Years after laws like the anti-miscegenation statute were taken off the books, Vital Records employees known informally as race clerks continued to flag the records of any family they considered genealogically suspect. In 1978, a woman who had been fired from her job as an assistant secretary of the

Department of Health and Human Resources revealed that, until the previous year, when she discovered the practice and put a stop to it, race clerks had maintained a list of two hundred and fifty families living as white but suspected of having black ancestry. "If you've got a good Louisiana French name, it's probably on the list," she said.

It appears that the zeal of the race clerks led to the 1970 law that, in a reverse sort of way, defined a black person as someone who had at least one-thirty-second black ancestry. The 1970 law has customarily been interpreted as a change in the state's policy on race—an attempt to moderate the "any traceable amount" standard or, in the other view, a piece of latter-day racism that seemed to be a throwback to the Nuremberg Laws. But there is a lawyer in New Orleans—he can be called Baxter—who says that he managed to have the law passed to serve the needs of a client. According to Baxter, he was approached in the late sixties by a blond, blue-eyed young man from Tangipahoa Parish, across Lake Pontchartrain from New Orleans. The man and his wife were both identified on their birth certificates as white, but apparently, his family name had since been flagged. A child had just been born to the couple, and the vital-records office was refusing to accept the man's designation as white on the child's birth certificate. Baxter says that he looked into the records and found that Vital Records had the law on its side: His client was, according to Baxter's calculations, one-one-hundred-and-twenty-eighth black. "I thought that was a hell of a note," Baxter said recently. "There wasn't anything for me to do except to try to change the law." As it happened, Baxter had been, by family tradition and by inclination, strongly associated with the segregationist forces during the civil rights struggle. He had continued to consider himself a believer in separation of the races, but, he says, the notion that someone with one black ancestor out of a hundred and twenty-eight was black struck him as silly—particularly when the man in question happened to be his client. Baxter says that, working with a politically influential member of another prominent segregationist family, he lobbied the relevant members of the legislature about a change in defining what a black person was. He figured that his credentials as a segregationist would reassure even those unreconstructed souls from rural districts of northern Louisiana that the proposed change did not represent a plot by the race-mixers. How was the magic fraction of one-thirty-second reached? Simple, Baxter says. He knew he might have to compromise, so he originally proposed one-sixteenth as the cutoff—leaving plenty of room between the opening offer and his client. There was some support for one-sixty-fourth. Baxter settled for one-thirty-second.

WESTHOLZ'S GENEALOGIST TRACED SUSIE GUILLORY Phipps's forebears to her great-great-great-great-grandmother, a slave named Margarita who was owned by a planter in Mobile named Gregoire Guillory. Around the time Guillory's wife died, he moved to what is now Acadia Parish and had four children with Margarita. One of their sons married a free person of color named Eloisa Meuillen, and thus began one of many Guillory family trees in Louisiana. This one was studded with people described in various documents with words like "quadroon" and *"marabout,"* and it led straight to the birth, in 1934, of Susie Guillory.

In looking for further evidence that the state's records

were correct, Jack Westholz spent a lot of time in the countryside where Gregoire Guillory had settled over a hundred
and fifty years before. It's in the flat farm-and-cattle country sometimes known as the Cajun prairies, to distinguish
it from the Cajun bayous, the swampy trapping-and-fishing
territory that French Acadians also settled in the middle of
the eighteenth century, after they were forced out of Nova
Scotia by the English. Frey Community, where Susie Guillory grew up, hasn't survived. It now seems less a town than
just a few farmhouses that might be a bit closer to one another than is customary. The church burned down years
ago. So did the one-room school where Susie Guillory, in
the company of a couple of dozen cousins, got her formal
education, which ended after the third grade. Susie Guillory's
parents died some years ago; her surviving brothers and sisters live elsewhere. Still, it wasn't difficult for Westholz to
find people who knew the Guillory family. He also found
school records and census field reports. The documents and
the interviews were consistent. The Guillorys were among
the families in the area known as mulattoes. They got along
well with their neighbors, but at the church in Frey Community, where whites sat on the left side of the aisle and blacks
on the right, there was no doubt that the Guillorys were on
the right. When the school that the Guillory kids and their
cousins went to was closed, the school they were bused to in
Iota, the nearest town, was the Negro school.

The people Westholz interviewed and deposed said they
were "raised for colored" or "went for colored" or "followed
the colored" or, in the case of an older woman who had to
be questioned through an interpreter, *"J'ai été élevé couleur."*
They were certain that being raised for colored was not the

same as being raised for black. One of them, an eighty-nine-year-old woman named Eve Denise Orebo, recalled recently that when a dark man showed up at a *bal* being held by her family, her father said in French the equivalent of "Get that nigger out of my house!" But when they moved from the countryside into town they found themselves on the black side of a black-and-white society. Mrs. Orebo lives in what amounts to Iota's black neighborhood. One of her sons, a retired army sergeant major, is considered Iota's first black councilman. The people who have traditionally been known as mulattoes in Acadia Parish have followed the usual pattern: Those who live as whites tend to be those who live somewhere else. There are light-complexioned people in Acadia Parish who would be recognized by an outsider as Creoles of Color rather than white only if the outsider happened to have an ear for the difference between Creole French and Cajun French, but for those who have always lived in the parish, there is no mystery about who is who.

WESTHOLZ SAYS THAT WHEN HE showed Brian Bégué the evidence he had amassed, at a time when not even Andy Phipps knew about the efforts to change the Guillory birth certificates, he expected Bégué to drop the suit. By that time, the Department of Health and Human Resources had promulgated some new regulations that would have made it simple for Susie Phipps to acquire a copy of her birth certificate in a short form that included nothing about race. The alternative was a major court challenge of state law. Some of the relatives who had joined Susie Guillory Phipps as plaintiffs had dropped out. Their children had white birth certificates, and they decided to leave well enough alone. But Susie Guillory Phipps continued. In a way, the information collected by Jack Westholz never seemed to have had much effect on her belief that the racial information on her birth certificate was a mistake. The testimony Westholz gathered concerning which side of the church the Guillorys sat on or how her cousins were raised did not seem to alter her insistence that she was raised white. She did not stop saying "I married white twice" simply because Westholz's research indicated that her first husband, who was also named Guillory, was also a Creole of Color.

Is it possible that Susie Guillory Phipps, who left Acadia Parish when she was fifteen, could have reached that age under the impression that there was no difference between her family and Frey Community families like the Daigles and the Kleins and the Zaunbrechers and the Burtons? There is no question that Frey Community lacked the constant reminders of racial separation that would have existed in a less remote Louisiana environment in the forties. It had no established section for black people in buses, because there were no buses. Although the little country school that Susie Guillory went to was considered the Negro school by parish school authorities, local people referred to it simply as the Guillory school. Still, people in Acadia Parish of either color tend not to take seriously the proposition that someone growing up there in a Colored Creole family could have been under the impression that she was being raised white.

Of course, some families commonly identified as Creoles of Color in rural Louisiana had legends that explained the identification without exactly acknowledging black ancestry—the legend, for instance, that an ancestor might have had to identify himself as colored in order to marry an Indian. Nobody doubts that Mrs. Phipps was genuinely surprised to hear about Margarita. Her claim, though, has not been that she was incorrectly regarded as a Creole of Color but that she was regarded as white and that she is, in fact, white. (She eventually came to believe, she said in a 1983 interview with Dawn Ruth of the New Orleans *Times-Picayune*, that Margarita had been dark rather than black.) Only rarely has she even acknowledged the existence of the sort of triracial society portrayed by Jack Westholz—most notably when, after many delays, her case finally came to trial in a New Orleans district court, five years after that disturbing day in the Division of Vital Records. Mrs. Phipps, the only plaintiff to testify, was asked in direct examination by Brian Bégué if she had always thought of herself as white.

"Sure have," Mrs. Phipps replied.

Then Bégué asked when she first found out that she might not be considered white—presumably expecting her to answer with the story about needing a passport in 1977. Instead, she spoke of an incident at her First Communion, when a black mother shoved her child ahead of Susie, only to be told by the catechism teacher to return the child to the back of the line. At the time of her confirmation, Mrs. Phipps said, it was still clear to all where her proper place in line was: "always in the back of the white but ahead of the black."

BECAUSE OF THE TRIAL, SUSIE Guillory Phipps became famous for a while. So did what reporters liked to call "Louisiana's black-blood law"—the only law in the country that attempted a mathematical definition of race. There were a lot of pictures on the wire of Brian Bégué leaving the courthouse with Mrs. Phipps. There were interviews with Andy Phipps, who flashed what were usually described as "walnut-size" diamond rings and said that his wife had gone through two Lincoln Continentals driving back and forth from Sulphur to New Orleans. (According to one reporter present, Julia Cass of *The Philadelphia Inquirer*, Phipps underlined his support of his wife by saying, "Hell, she ain't a nigger." He later told another reporter that he never used that epithet, "although I might if I got mad.") Susie Guillory Phipps tended to answer reporters' questions about her race by asking a question in return: "Let me ask you this: Do I look colored?"

A lot of the trial coverage irritated Jack Westholz. He implied that Brian Bégué—a self-assured man with a breezy manner and an office in a French Quarter courtyard and a wife in advertising—was manipulating the press. Although Bégué might avoid the word "manipulating," he now says that he was indeed conscious of the value of publicity. "Going public was the only way," he said recently. "If it's secret, we lose. The law was against us, and the facts were against us. We had to try it in the newspapers. We had to educate the judiciary with the voice of the people." For whatever reason, the newspaper articles tended to leave the impression that the state was trying to call an ostensibly white person black by means of a bizarre law that defined a black person as anyone with more than one-thirty-second "black blood."

From the testimony, it appeared that once the race-clerk system was finally abandoned, Louisiana had adopted the policy that other states follow in determining racial designations on birth certificates: The race of a newborn baby's parents is whatever they say it is. Scientists testified, from the witness stand and by deposition, that modern science didn't offer any better way than that of determining race. They stressed that the concept of race was legal or political or cultural, not scientific. They all seemed to agree that race could be spoken of in terms of entire populations—you could, Munro Edmonson testified, calculate "differing frequencies of certain genes in definable populations"—but not in terms of individuals. Edmonson also testified that the notion of calculating someone's race by genealogical fractions contradicts basic genetics: Since genes are randomly distributed, someone who has, say, an African great-grandfather might not have inherited any genes from him at all.

Westholz made no attempt to refute such testimony. "I know you can't scientifically ascertain race," he said recently. "I knew that before the trial." In his view, though, that was not the question at issue. What the judge had to decide, Westholz insisted, was whether Susie Guillory Phipps could prove, beyond any doubt at all, that the information on her birth certificate was incorrect. To that end, he brought in his boxes of documents and his charts and his genealogical experts. Bégué tried to demonstrate that, partly because of imprecise use of the terms inherited from colonial days, genealogical records could not reflect racial ancestry with mathematical certainty. He also said that the one-thirty-second law gave the state the burden of proving that it could legally classify Susie Guillory Phipps as black. (Westholz had, in fact, come prepared to demonstrate that Mrs. Phipps was more than one-thirty-second black; the figure he had reached, through some complicated computations, was five-thirty-seconds.) But Bégué did not make a strenuous attempt to refute the state's mountain of genealogical evidence. Instead, he argued that if any racial classification had to be done it should be based on "the self-image of the classified." In a post-trial memorandum, he argued that the entire system of classifying people by race was an unconstitutional hangover from Jim Crow for which the state had demonstrated no compelling need. It simply made no sense, Bégué maintained, for people who think of themselves as white and are thought of by their neighbors as white to have to prove in court that they are indeed white.

The judge did not agree. In May of 1983, finding that the state Vital Statistics Law "clearly places the burden of proving the propriety of an alteration on the person seeking to have it made," he ruled that the plaintiffs' contention that "because they appear to be 'white,' the State must prove otherwise" was "without legal foundation." In his decision, the judge said it was clear that the plaintiffs "have the appearance of 'white' people. They have fair skins and, in some cases, blue eyes and blond hair. It is also entirely clear that they are of mixed white and Negro blood." Jack Westholz called the decision a "bittersweet victory," since it did not alter the burden of proof and did not offer Vital Records any guidelines for the future. He told reporters that he hoped Mrs. Phipps would appeal, and she did.

The one-thirty-second law had not figured prominently in the testimony. Still, most of the headlines reporting the decision said something like LAW DEFINING "BLACK BLOOD" IN LA. UPHELD. In Baton Rouge, it was taken for granted that the days of the one-thirty-second law were numbered the moment it made the national news wires. "Louisiana was made the laughingstock of the nation," said a New Orleans legislator who introduced a repeal measure. In June 1983, only a month after the decision in the Susie Guillory Phipps case was announced, the legislature repealed the one-thirty-second law and, at the same time, established "a preponderance of the evidence" as the burden of proof borne by someone who wanted to argue that information on a vital record should be changed.

SUSIE GUILLORY PHIPPS CALCULATED THAT by the time the case was argued before the Fourth Circuit Court of Appeals she had spent over forty thousand dollars attempting to change her birth certificate. There were more delays to come. When the decision was finally handed down last fall, it upheld the District Court decision. Pointing out that it was her parents' racial designations that Susie Phipps would have had to change, the court said, "We do not believe that an individual may change the racial designation of another person, whether his parent or anyone else." In holding for the state, the appeals court managed to agree with both sides: "Individual racial designations are purely social and cultural perceptions, and the evidence conclusively proves those subjective perceptions were correctly recorded at the time appellants' birth certificates were issued." Bégué applied for a hearing before the Louisiana Supreme Court, but last week, by a vote of five to two, the Supreme Court denied the application.

What Brian Bégué had been arguing is that when it comes to racial designation, Susie Guillory Phipps should be bound not by the obviously racist notions of 1934 but by the same policy that is in effect for someone filling out a birth-certificate application in a New Orleans hospital today: You're whatever race you think you are. What Jack Westholz had been arguing is that history is history; he doesn't quarrel with Mrs. Phipps calling her children white, but he doesn't think there is anything she can do about her parents being colored. Bégué has said that if the Louisiana Supreme Court will not reconsider its decision, he will ask the Supreme Court of the United States to hear Susie Phipps's case. The central federal issue, he says, is denial of equal protection: "If you're a little bit black, you're black. If you're a little bit white, you're still black." Even Bégué would acknowledge that he is working against exceedingly long odds. Jack Westholz tends to believe that, for all intents and purposes, the legal battle over changing Susie Phipps's birth certificate is at an end. If so, he has his victory. The case has provoked the legislature into making two of the reforms he wanted. If Jack Westholz has won, Brian Bégué has not exactly lost. Even assuming that the Supreme Court refuses to hear his appeal, he has already enjoyed the benefits that come to a lawyer with a juicy, highly public case. It's difficult, though, to imagine what Susie Guillory Phipps could come away with that would satisfy her. Even if the Supreme Court were to take the case and strike down the racial classification system, that wouldn't obliterate the documents that identify Margarita as a "free Negress." Margarita, as Jack Westholz might say, is history. In a way, no court can make Susie Guillory Phipps white—or whiter than she has already made herself. Still, she has said that she will keep on trying. In her interview with Dawn Ruth after the original court decision, she said that if she lost in Louisiana, she would go to the Supreme Court of the United States. If she lost there, she said, she would go to the President. She would ask him if he thought she looked colored.

. . .

In 1986, the Supreme Court of the United States let the decision on the Phipps case stand "for want of a substantial federal question." Susie Guillory Phipps did not go to the President and ask him if she looked colored.

THE COLOR OF BLOOD

Long Island, New York
2008

WHAT HAPPENED AT THE FOOT OF THE DRIVEWAY AT 40 Independence Way that hot August night in 2006 took less than three minutes. The police later managed to time it precisely, using a surveillance camera that points directly at the street from a house a couple of doors to the north. The readout on the surveillance tape said that it was 23:06:11 when two cars whizzed by going south, toward the cul-de-sac at the end of the street. At 23:09:06, the first car passed back in front of the camera, going north. A minute later, a second car passed in the same direction. In the backseat of that second car—a black Mustang Cobra convertible—was a seventeen-year-old boy named Daniel Cicciaro, Jr., known to his friends as Dano. He was unconscious and bleeding profusely. He had been shot through the cheek. A .32-caliber bullet was lodged in his head.

Normally, at that time of night, not many cars are seen on Independence Way, a quiet street in a town called Miller

Place. Just east of Port Jefferson, on the North Shore of Long Island, Miller Place is in the part of Suffolk County where the commuters have begun to thin out. To the east is a large swatch of the county that doesn't seem strongly connected to the huge city in one direction or to the high-priced summer resorts and North Fork wineries in the other. The house at 40 Independence Way is part of a development, Talmadge Woods, that five or six years ago was a peach orchard; it's now a collection of substantial two-story, four-bedroom houses that the developer started offering in 2003 for about half a million dollars each. The houses vary in design, but they all have an arched front door topped by the arched glass transom known in the trade as a Palladian window—a way to bring light into the double-height entry hall. When people are asked to describe the neighborhood, they tend to say "upper-middle-class." The homeowner with the surveillance system is an orthodontist.

Miller Place could also be described as overwhelmingly white. According to a study released a few years ago, Long Island is the single most segregated suburban area in the United States. The residents of 40 Independence Way—John and Sonia White and their youngest son, Aaron—are African American and so are their next-door neighbors, but the black population of Miller Place is less than one half of one percent. The Whites, who began married life in Brooklyn in the early seventies, had moved to Miller Place after ten years in North Babylon, which is forty minutes or so closer to the city. "You want to raise your family in a safe environment," John White, a tall, very thin man in his early fifties, has said, explaining why he was willing to spend three hours a day in his car commuting. "The educational standards are higher.

You want to live a comfortable life, which is the American dream." One of the Whites' sons is married with children of his own, and a second is in college in the South. But Aaron was able to spend his senior year at Miller Place High School, which takes pride in such statistics as how many of its students are in Advanced Placement history courses. Aaron, an erect young man who is likely to say "sir" when addressing one of his elders, graduated in June of 2005. He was one of four black students in the class.

In an area where home maintenance is a priority, 40 Independence Way could hold its own. John White is a serious gardener—a nurturer of daylilies and clematis, a planter of peel-bark birch trees—and someone who had always been proud, maybe even touchy, about his property. People who have been neighbors of the Whites tend to use the word "meticulous" in describing John White; so do people who have worked with him. He has described himself as "a doer"—someone too restless to sit around reading a book or watching television. He says that he's fished from Nova Scotia to the Bahamas. He's done a lot of hunting—a pastime he was taught by his grandfather Napoleon White, whose family's migration from Alabama apparently took place after a murderous attack by the Ku Klux Klan. At the Faith Baptist Church, in Coram, Long Island, John White sang in both the men's choir and the mixed Celebration Choir. A couple of polished wood tables in the Whites' house were made by him. He's a broadly accomplished man and proud of it. His wife, who was born in Panama, works as a manager in a department store and has that Caribbean accent which, maybe because it's close to the accent of West Indian nurses, conveys both competence and the firm intention to brook no nonsense. The Whites' furniture tastes lean toward Stickley, Audi. Their sons dress in a style that's preppy. Sitting in his well-appointed family room, John White could be taken for middle management.

But he doesn't have the sort of education or occupation that would seem to go along with the house he lives in. After graduating from a technical program at Samuel Gompers High School, he worked as an electrician for seven or eight years and then, during a slow time for electricians, he began working in the paving industry. For the past twenty-five years, he has worked for an asphalt company in Queens, patching the potholes left by utility repair crews. He is often described as a foreman, which he once was, but he says that, partly because of an aversion to paperwork, he didn't try to reclaim that job after it evaporated during a reduction in the workforce. ("I'm actually a laborer.") On August 9, 2006, a Wednesday, he had, as usual, awakened at three-thirty in the morning for the drive to Queens, spent the day at work, and, after a stop to pick up some bargain peony plants, returned to what he calls his "dream house" or his "castle." He retired early, so that he could do the same thing the next day. A couple of hours later, according to his testimony, he was awakened by Aaron, who, with a level of terror John White had never heard in his son's voice, shouted, "Dad, these guys are coming here to kill me!" Instead, as it turned out, John White killed Daniel Cicciaro, Jr.

THERE HAD BEEN A BIRTHDAY party that evening for Craig Martin, Jr., a recent Miller Place High School graduate. Craig lives with his parents and his younger sister, Jennifer, in Sound Beach—a town just to the east that grew into a year-round neighborhood from what had begun as beach lots purchased in the twenties as part of a *Daily Mirror* circulation-promotion scheme. The party was mostly in the Martins' backyard, where there was an aboveground pool, a lot of cold beer, and a succession of beer-pong games. This was not the AP-history crowd. Craig was connected to a number of the boys at the party through an interest in cars. Some of them were members of the Blackout car club, a loose organization of teenagers who, in good weather, gather in the parking lot of the Stop & Shop mall in Miller Place on Thursday nights for an informal car show—displaying cars whose lights and windows are likely to have been tinted in pursuit of sleekness. Dano Cicciaro (pronounced Danno Cicero) was a regular at Stop & Shop, driving a white Mustang Mach 1 with two black stripes. Dano had grown up in Selden, a blue-collar town to the south, and finished at Newfield High School there after his family moved in his senior year to one of a half-dozen houses clustered around a cul-de-sac called Old Town Estates, in Port Jefferson Station.

His father, Daniel Cicciaro, Sr., runs an automobile-repair shop in Port Jeff Station called Dano's Auto Clinic—a two-bay operation that also has some used cars parked in its lot, their prices marked on the windshields. Dano's Auto Clinic is where Dano Jr. spent a lot of his spare time. As a boy, he had the usual range of interests, his father has recalled, but "as he turned into a teenager, it was all cars." Even as a teenager, he ran a car-detailing business out of the shop, and he'd planned to keep that up when he started at Suffolk County Community College in the fall. Dano Jr.'s long-term plan was to take over Dano's Auto Clinic someday and expand its services. "He did exactly as I did, in that he set goals for himself and conquered them, never sitting idle," a *Newsday* reporter was told by Daniel Cicciaro, Sr., a father who'd felt the validation of having a son who was eager to follow his calling and work by his side.

Aaron White, who had finished his first year at Suffolk County Community College, was having dinner that evening in Port Jefferson with Michael Longo, his best friend from Miller Place High School. From having attended a few of the Stop & Shop gatherings, Aaron knew some of the car crowd, and, while phoning around for something to do, he learned about the birthday party at the Martins'. Craig greeted Aaron cheerfully enough, but a few minutes later Jennifer, who was then fifteen, told her brother that, because of a past incident, she felt frightened in Aaron's presence. Dano Cicciaro was assigned to ask Aaron to leave. It isn't clear why he was given that task. It couldn't have been his size: Dano was five feet four and weighed a hundred and twenty-nine pounds. It certainly wasn't his sobriety. Dano was drunk. When his blood-alcohol content was checked later at the hospital, it was almost twice the level required to prove intoxication. Still, Dano, who thought of himself as a protective older brother to Jennifer, handled the situation smoothly, saying to Aaron something like "It's nothing personal, but you'll have to leave." Aaron later said that he was puzzled ("I never get kicked out of parties"), but he got into his car and drove back to Miller Place.

When Dano learned exactly why Jennifer felt uncomfortable around Aaron, she later testified, "he freaked out." While in an Internet chat room with a couple of other boys, Jennifer told Dano, Aaron had posted a message saying that he wanted to rape her. Obtaining Aaron's cell-phone number from Michael Longo, Dano touched off what became a series of heated calls involving several people at the party. Dano wanted to confront Aaron immediately. It didn't matter that Aaron denied having posted the message. It didn't matter that the posting had taken place nine months before and that Jennifer's real older brother, Craig, had actually forgotten about it. In court many months later, Jennifer Martin was asked if she'd eventually learned that the offending message had not, in fact, been sent by Aaron—it had grown out of something said on a MySpace account set up in Aaron's name as a prank—and she answered in the affirmative. That didn't matter, either, because by then it was much too late. On the evening of August 9, when Jennifer told Dano about the rape posting, there were other elements involved. A lot of beer had been consumed. It was late in the evening, a time when the teenage penchant for melodrama tends to be in full flower. Dano was filled with what Paul Gianelli, one of John White's defense attorneys, called "a warped sense of chivalry" and Dano's godfather, Gregg Sarra, preferred to characterize as "valor, protecting a woman, honor." For whatever reason, Dano Cicciaro and four of his friends were soon heading toward the Whites' house in two beautifully painted and carefully polished cars that passed the orthodontist's surveillance camera when its readout said 23:06:11.

What happened when they got there remains a matter of sharp dispute. There is no doubt that the boys were displaying no weapons when they got out of their cars, although one of them, Joseph Serrano, had brought along a baseball bat that remained in the backseat of the Mustang. There is no doubt that John White emerged from his garage carrying a pre–World War II Beretta pistol that he kept there—part of an inheritance from his grandfather that had also included, White later said, "rifles and shotguns and a lot of advice." Aaron was a few steps behind him, carrying a 20-gauge shotgun. There is no doubt that Dano "slapped" or "whacked" or "grabbed" the Beretta. There is no doubt that, before the shot was fired, there had been shouting and foul language from both sides. The tenor of the conversation, the defense team eventually maintained, could be surmised from the tape of a 911 line that the boys did not realize was open as they rushed their friend to a Port Jefferson hospital in the black Mustang Cobra. The 911 operator can be heard saying, "Sir . . . hello . . . hello . . . sir, pick up the phone." The boys, their muffled voices almost hysterical, can be heard shouting directions to one another and giving assurances that Dano is still breathing. The operator keeps saying, "Hello . . . sir." Then the voice of Joseph Serrano, sitting in the backseat with his bleeding friend and his baseball bat, comes through clearly: "Fucking niggers! Dano, I'll get 'em for you, Dano."

Back at 40 Independence Way, John White and his son were sitting in front of their house, hugging. Sonia White was screaming, "What happened? What happened?" In the trial testimony and police reports and newspaper accounts and grand-jury minutes dealing with what occurred in the meticulous front yard of 40 Independence Way after the cars had sped away, three statements attributed to John White stand out. One was in the testimony of Officer David Murray, the first Suffolk County policeman to reach the scene, who said that John White approached him with his arms extended, saying, "I did what I had to do. You might as well put the cuffs on me." Another is what Officer Murray said he heard John White say to his son: "I told you those friends of yours would turn on you." The third is what Sonia White testified that her husband said to her as he walked back into their castle: "We lost the house. We lost it all."

A WEEK AFTER THE DEATH of Daniel Cicciaro, Jr., several hundred people turned out for his funeral, held at St. Sylvester's Roman Catholic Church in Medford, Long Island. The gathering was heavy with symbolism. Some of the younger mourners displayed "Dano Jr." tattoos. Dano Jr.'s main car was there—the white Mustang that was familiar from Stop & Shop and had won Best Mach 1 Mustang in a competition at McCarville Ford. Gregg Sarra, a boyhood friend of Daniel Cicciaro, Sr., and a local sports columnist for *Newsday,* gave the eulogy, praising his godson's loyalty and his diligence and his gift for friendship. After the burial, some of Dano Jr.'s car-club friends revved their engines and chanted, "Dan-o, Dan-o, Dan-o." As a tribute to his son, Daniel Cicciaro, Sr., attended the service in a Dano's Auto Clinic tank top. The Stop & Shop car show that Thursday, according to a *Newsday* piece, turned into a sort of vigil for Dano Jr., with Jennifer Martin helping to light a ring of candles—red and white candles, for the colors of Newfield High—around his Mustang and his first car, a Mercedes E55 AMG.

The sadness was accompanied by a good deal of anger. John White found that understandable. "I know how I would feel if someone hurt my kid," he said in a *Times* interview some weeks later. "There wouldn't be a rock left to crawl under." Speaking to one reporter, Daniel Cicciaro, Sr., had referred to White as an "animal." For a while after the shooting, Michael Longo—the friend who had accompanied Aaron White to the birthday party and had, as it turned out, telephoned to warn him that there were plans to jump him if he returned—slept with a baseball bat next to his bed. Sonia White later testified that after some particularly menacing instant messages ("i need ur adreass you dumb nigger"), to which Aaron replied in what sounded like a suburban teenager's notion of gangster talk ("u da bitch tlaking big n bad like u gonna come down to my crib n do sumthin"), the Whites decided that he was no longer safe in the house, and they sent him to live outside the area.

The mourners who talked to reporters after the service rejected the notion, brought up by a lawyer for the White family shortly after the shooting, that Dano Cicciaro and his friends had used racial epithets during the argument in front of 40 Independence Way. Daniel Cicciaro, Sr.—a short man with a shaved head and a Fu Manchu mustache and an assertive manner and a lifelong involvement in martial arts—had called any connection of his son with racism "absurd." But by the time a grand jury met, a month or so after the shooting, even the prosecutor, who would presumably need the boys as witnesses against John White, was saying that racial epithets had indeed been used. The district attorney said, though, that if John White had simply remained in his house and dialed 911, he wouldn't be in any trouble, and Daniel Cicciaro, Jr., would still be alive. The grand jury was asked to indict White for murder. Grand juries ordinarily go along with district attorneys, but this one didn't. When the trial finally began, in Riverhead, fifteen months after the shooting, the charge was second-degree manslaughter.

The grand-jury decision may have reflected public opinion in Suffolk County, where there are strong feelings about a homeowner's right to protect his property and his family. Suffolk County is a place where a good number of residents are active or retired law-enforcement officers, and where even a lot of residents who aren't own guns—a place where it is not surprising to come across a plaque that bears the picture of a pistol and the phrase "We Don't Dial 911." James Chalifoux, the assistant district attorney who was assigned to try the case against John White, apparently had that in mind when, during jury selection, he asked jurors if they would be able to distinguish between what might be considered morally right—what could cause you to say, "I might have done the same thing"—and what was permissible under the law. He asked jurors if they could put aside sympathy when they were considering the case—meaning sympathy for John White. Judging by comments posted online in response to *Newsday* articles, public opinion seemed muddled by the conflict between two underpinnings of life in Suffolk County: a devotion to the sanctity of private property, particularly one's home, and an assumption that the owner of the property is white.

Dano's mother—Joanne Cicciaro, a primary school ESL teacher who had grown up in Suffolk County—said she was extremely disappointed that the grand jury had declined to indict John White for murder. Daniel Cicciaro, Sr., told a reporter, "Here this man points his gun at the boys and says, 'I'm going to shoot.' He says it three times. Then he shoots my son. To me, that's intentional murder." On the other hand, some of White's strongest supporters—people like Lucius Ware, the president of the Eastern Long Island branch of the NAACP, and Marie Michel, a black attorney who joined the defense team—believed that if a white homeowner in Miller Place had been confronted late at night by five hostile black teenagers, there would have been, in Marie Michel's words, "no arrests, no indictment, and no trial." The homeowner would have been judged to have had "a well-founded fear," they thought, and if the justice system dealt with the incident in any way, it would have been to charge the boys with something like breach of the peace or aggravated harassment ("What were they doing in that neighborhood at that time of night?"). For that matter, these supporters would argue, would Dano have "freaked out" if the male accused of wanting to rape Jenny Martin hadn't been black? Wouldn't teenagers spoiling for a fight have dispersed if a white father walked out of the house, with or without a gun, and told them in no uncertain terms to go home? In other words, before a word of testimony had been heard, some people attending the trial of John White believed that in a just world he would have been on trial for murder instead of only manslaughter, and some believed that in a just world he wouldn't have been on trial at all.

THE ARTHUR M. CROMARTY COURT Complex is set apart from Riverhead, the seat of Suffolk County, on a campus that seems to be mostly parking lots—a judicial version of Long Island shopping malls. Those who were there to attend John White's trial, which began just after Thanksgiving, seemed to be roughly separated by race, on opposite sides of the aisle that ran down the center of the courtroom's spectator section. That may have been partly because the room was small, and on many days the prosecution's supporters, mostly Cicciaro relatives and young friends of Dano's, nearly filled half of it. Dano Jr.'s parents did not sit next to each other—they had separated before their son's death—but they came together as a family in hallway huddles of supporters and in speaking to the press. The people who stood out on their side of the courtroom were a couple of friends of Daniel Cicciaro, Sr., who also had shaved heads, but with modifications that included a scalp tattoo saying "Dano Jr." Although they looked menacing, both of them could be described as designers: One is a detailer, specializing in the fancy painting of motorcycles; the other does graphic design, specializing in sports uniforms.

People on the Cicciaro side might have felt some menace emanating from the phalanx of black men, all of them in suits and ties and many of them offensive-tackle-size, who escorted Aaron White (wearing a bulletproof vest) through the courthouse on the first day of his testimony and then took seats across the aisle, near some women from John White's church choir. The escorts were from an organization called 100 Blacks in Law Enforcement Who Care. On that first day, their ranks were augmented by members of the Fruit of Islam, wearing their trademark bow ties, although the black leader called to mind by John White's life would probably be Booker T. Washington rather than Louis Farrakhan. As it turned out, there was no overt hostility between those on either side of the courtroom aisle, and at the end of testimony, the Cicciaros made it clear that they would accept any decision the jury brought in—none of which, Joanne Cicciaro pointed out, would bring their son back. Talking to a *News-*

day reporter after the trial about prejudice, Daniel Cicciaro, Sr., maintained that bias existed toward what some people called skinheads. "Don't judge a book by its cover," he said.

The four boys who accompanied Dano Cicciaro to Aaron White's house that night are all car enthusiasts who now hold jobs that echo their high school hobby. Alex Delgado does maintenance on race cars. Joseph Serrano is a motorcycle mechanic. Tom Maloney, who drove the Mustang Cobra, sells Volkswagens. Anthony Simeone works for his father's auto-salvage business. Among those who testified that they'd tried to prevent Dano from going to the Whites' house were Alex Delgado, who drove him there, and Joseph Serrano, who brought along a baseball bat. ("He's stubborn," Anthony Simeone had explained to the grand jury. "When he wants to do something, he wants to do it.") Although there had been testimony that Dano Cicciaro used the word "nigger" once or twice in the cell-phone exchange with Aaron White, his friends denied using racial slurs at 40 Independence Way. (With the jury out of the courtroom, Paul Gianelli brought up an incident that had been investigated by the police but not included in the notes and reports that they are required to turn over to the defense: According to two or three witnesses, Daniel Cicciaro had gone to Sayville Ford with a complaint a few weeks before he was shot and, when approached by a black salesman, had said, "I don't talk to niggers." The judge wouldn't admit that into evidence, but the headline of the next day's *Newsday* story was ATTORNEY: COPS HID MILLER PLACE VICTIM'S RACISM.) The friends who'd gone with Dano Jr. to the Whites' house that night testified that after John White's gun was slapped away, he raised it again and shot Dano in the face. As they described how Dano Cicciaro fell and how he'd been lifted from the street by Tom Maloney and rushed to the hospital, there were occasional sobs from both Joanne and Daniel Cicciaro.

Dano's friends had said that both of their cars were in the street facing north, but the Whites testified that one was in their driveway, with the lights shining up into the house—a contention that the defense bolstered by analyzing the headlight reflections on the orthodontist's mailbox in the surveillance tape. The boys testified that they'd never set foot on the Whites' property—that contention was bolstered by pictures showing Dano's blood and his cell phone in the street rather than in the driveway—but the Whites claimed that the boys had been advancing toward the house. "They came to my home as if they owned it," Sonia White said on the stand. "What gall!"

John White testified that, believing the young men had come to harm his family, he backed them off his property with Napoleon White's old pistol. In the frenzy that followed his abrupt awakening, he said, he had yelled, "Call the cops!" to his wife as he raced into the garage, but she hadn't heard him. He described Dano Cicciaro and his friends as a lynch mob shouting, among other things, "We could take that skinny nigger motherfucker." Recalling that evening, White said, "In my family history, that's how the Klan comes. They pull up to your house, blind you with their lights, burn your house down. That's how they come." In White's telling, the confrontation had seemed over, and he was turning to go back into the house, when Dano Cicciaro grabbed the gun, causing it to fire. "I didn't mean to shoot this young man," John White said. "This young man was another child of God." This time, it was John White who broke down, and the court had to take a recess. One of the jurors was also wiping away tears.

To CONVICT SOMEONE OF SECOND-DEGREE manslaughter in the state of New York, the prosecution has to prove that he recklessly caused the death of the victim—"recklessly" being defined as creating a risk so substantial that disregarding it constitutes "a gross deviation from the standard of conduct that a reasonable person would observe"—and that he had no justification. In its decision in the case of Bernard Goetz, the white man who, in 1984, shot four young black men who had approached him on the subway demanding money, the New York Court of Appeals, the highest court in the state, ruled that justification could have a subjective as well as an objective component—fears raised by the defendant's past experiences, for instance. By bringing up the history that White's family had with the Klan, the defense team raised a subjective component of justification, along with the objective component of home protection. "We are all products of our past," Paul Gianelli said of his client during one of the breaks in the trial. "He brought to that particular evening who he is." The defense was making a case for, among other things, the power of race memory.

The racial divide is obviously less overt in John White's Long Island than it was in Napoleon White's Alabama. Tom Maloney, who'd also graduated from Miller Place High School, had apparently thought of Aaron White as a friend. Alex Delgado, who drove Dano Cicciaro to Aaron's house on

August 9, had been there before as a guest. In John White's testimony, Delgado was described as Hispanic. Joanne Cicciaro, who, by name and appearance and accent, might be assumed to have come from one of the many Italian-American families that moved to Suffolk County in recent decades from the boroughs, is actually Puerto Rican—a fact brought up to reporters by the Cicciaros in countering any implications of racism in Dano's upbringing. ("Our family is multicultural.") Even without those complications, the case for race memory would be harder to make to white people than to black people. White people are likely to say that times have changed: These days, after all, a real estate agent who tried to steer John White away from buying a house in an overwhelmingly white Long Island neighborhood would be risking her license.

If times have changed, black people might ask in response, how come Long Island is still so segregated? In his summation, the prosecutor asked a series of questions as a way to illustrate how White's behavior had deviated from the behavior of a reasonable person. Two of the huge black men who had been part of Aaron White's escort were sitting in the courtroom at the time, and when the DA asked whether a reasonable person would really be guided partly by the memory of a Ku Klux Klan attack that happened years before he was born, they both began to nod their heads.

In that closing statement, James Chalifoux said that it wasn't until the trial began that John White started talking about a lynch mob. (It's true that in a newspaper interview in September of 2006 White seemed to downplay race, but it's also true that in his grand-jury testimony, less than a month after the shooting, he spoke about a "lynch mob.") Race,

Chalifoux said, was being used to distract the jurors from the simple fact that by walking down the driveway with a loaded pistol, John White, a man intimately familiar with firearms, had engaged in conduct that had recklessly caused the death of Dano Cicciaro. Matching up testimony with cell-phone logs, Chalifoux argued that the Whites had more time before the arrival of the cars than their story of a panicky few minutes implied. Chalifoux acknowledged that Dano and his friends were wrong to go to the Whites' that night, that Dano was wrong to use a racial epithet when he phoned Aaron White, and that John White had found himself "in a very bad situation that night and a situation that was not his fault." But how White responded to that situation, Chalifoux said, *was* his fault.

Chalifoux's summation followed that of Frederick K. Brewington, a black attorney, active in black causes on Long Island, who was Paul Gianelli's co-counsel. "Race has so much to do with this case, ladies and gentlemen, that it's painful," Brewington told the jury: Dano Cicciaro and his friends thought they had a right to go to John White's house and "terrorize his family with impunity and arrogance" because of "the false racial privilege they felt empowered by." In Brewington's argument, John White thought, " 'Once they see I have a gun they'll back off' . . . but they did not take 'the skinny old nigger' seriously." While Chalifoux presented Joseph Serrano's slur on the 911 tape as, however deplorable, an indication that the argument at the foot of the driveway didn't include the barrage of insults that the Whites had testified to—if it had, he said, "you would have heard racial epithet after racial epithet after racial epithet"—Brewington saw it as a mirror of the boys' true feelings. "What we do under cover of darkness sometimes comes to light," he said.

Shortly after the beginning of deliberations, ten jurors, including the sole African American, were prepared to convict John White of having recklessly caused Dano Cicciaro's death. Two jurors resisted that verdict for four days. Then they capitulated. They later told reporters that they felt bullied and pressured by jurors who were impatient to be liberated as Christmas approached. In a courtroom crowded with court officers, the jury reported that it had found John White guilty of manslaughter and a weapons charge. The Cicciaros and their supporters were ecstatic. Dano's parents seemed to take John White's conviction principally as proof that the accusations of racism against their son had been shown to be false. "My son is finally vindicated," a tearful Joanne Cicciaro said outside the courtroom. Daniel Cicciaro, Sr., said, "Maybe now they'll stop slinging my son's name and accusing him of all this racism." Outside the courthouse, friends of Dano Jr. honked their horns and revved their engines and chanted, "Dan-o, Dan-o, Dan-o." The next day, Sunday, the celebration continued with a sort of open house at Dano's Auto Clinic, which bore a sign saying, THANK YOU JURORS. THANK GOD. DANO JR. REST IN PEACE. In Miller Place, John White briefly spoke to the reporters who were waiting in front of his house. ("I'm not inhuman," he said. "I have very deep feelings for this young man.") But before that he went to the Faith Baptist Church, in Coram, and sang in the choir.

* * *

"JOHN WHITE IS A HERO," Frederick Brewington said two weeks later, addressing a crowd of several hundred people, almost all of them black, who had gathered on a cold Saturday afternoon in front of the criminal-court building in Riverhead. He repeated, "John White is a hero." The guilty verdict had made White the sort of hero all too familiar in the race memory of African Americans—someone held up as an example of the unjustly treated black man. On the podium were black officeholders, speakers from the spectrum of black organizations on Long Island, and two people who had come from Manhattan—Kevin Muhammad, of Muhammad Mosque No. 7, and Al Sharpton. A lot of NAACP people were in the audience, and so were a lot of people from Faith Baptist Church. Various speakers demanded a retrial, or called for the resignation of the district attorney, or pointed out the difference in how white homeowners in similar situations have been treated, or called for the young white men involved to be indicted. ("We will raise this to a level of national attention until these young men are brought to justice," Sharpton said.) There were chants like "No Justice— No Peace" and, loudest of all, "Free John White."

That chant was not meant literally. For the time being, John White is free—he addressed the rally briefly, mainly to thank his supporters—and his attorneys hope that, while an appeal is pending, he will be allowed to remain free after his sentencing, scheduled for March 19. ("I think he should get as much time as possible," a *Post* reporter was told by Jennifer Martin, whose response to Aaron White's arrival at her house set the events of August 9 in motion. "I really do.") Until the sentencing, White is back to rising at three-thirty every morning to go into the city and patch utility holes.

Everything he was quoted as saying in the aftermath of the shooting that night turned out to be true. The fatalism reflected in his statement to Officer Murray as he held out his hands to be cuffed was well-founded. Aaron White accepted the fact that those friends of his had indeed turned on him. In his testimony, he said, "They have no respect for me or my family or my mother or my father. . . . They have no respect for life whatsoever. They're scum." And John White had understood the situation well when he told his wife that they had lost their dream house—a comment that, as it turned out, particularly incensed Joanne Cicciaro. (His sorrow, she said to reporters after testimony had ended, "was all for themselves—sorrow about losing their house, about their life changing. He never said, 'Oh my God! What did I do to that boy? Oh my God. This kid is bleeding on the driveway. What did I do to him?' He had no sympathy, no sorrow for shooting a child.") Even before the trial, 40 Independence Way was listed with a real estate broker. Its description began, "Stately 2 year young post-modern colonial in prestigious neighborhood."

· · ·

The Whites actually remained at 40 Independence Way for some time. At his sentencing, John White was given two to four years; Daniel Cicciaro, Sr., enraged by the lightness of the sentence, shouted outside the courtroom, "Let's see what happens when Aaron White gets shot." White was permitted to remain out on bail and at work while the conviction was being appealed. Two years later, the appeal having been rejected, he was committed to the Mount McGregor Cor-

rectional Facility in upstate New York. However, after White had served five and a half months, Governor David Paterson, in his final days in office, commuted the sentence. The following Sunday, White appeared at the Faith Baptist Church in Coram to express his thankfulness and read from Psalm 27 ("The Lord is my light and my salvation; what shall I fear?") and sing in the men's choir. In 2015, the Whites finally sold their house on Independence Way and retired in Florida.

STATE SECRETS

Mississippi
1995

WHEN IT COMES TO THE OPERATIONS OF THE MISSISSIPPI State Sovereignty Commission, I have always been partial to the smaller stories. Consider, for example, the Grenada, Mississippi, baby inspection. In the early sixties, a white woman in Grenada, a county seat in the north-central part of the state, gave birth to an out-of-wedlock baby, and there were rumors around town that the baby had been fathered by a black man. The State Sovereignty Commission had been established by the legislature in 1956, in the days when the white South was erecting its defenses against the decision of the United States Supreme Court that segregation in public education is unconstitutional. The Commission was charged to "do and perform any and all acts and things deemed necessary and proper to protect the sovereignty of the State of Mississippi, and her sister states, from encroachment thereon by the federal government." Being an agency that always interpreted that mission broadly, it dispatched one of its investigators, Tom Scarbrough, to see if Grenada had truly been the scene of what Southern politicians of that era tended to call the mongrelization of the races.

After interviewing a number of Grenada residents, Scarbrough accompanied the local sheriff for an inspection of the baby under suspicion. It's easy to envision those two officials of the state of Mississippi trying to edge in close to the crib—large men, as I imagine them, with the sheriff wearing a pistol and further burdened, perhaps, by what people in regular contact with the Southern law-enforcement community come to think of as a sheriff's belly. In Scarbrough's report, which ran four or five thousand words, he wrote, "I was looking at the child's fingernails and the end of its fingers very closely." From this I assume that he believed African ancestry could be detected by the presence of distinctive half-moons at the cuticles—a theory that was an article of faith in my grade school in Missouri, during a period when I was also persuaded for a while that Japanese people had yellow blood. The baby's fingernails might have been too small for a conclusive half-moon search. Scarbrough said in his report, "We both agreed we were not qualified to say it was a part Negro child, but we could say it was not 100 percent Caucasian." Perhaps sensing this indecision, the mother parried shrewdly: The baby's father, she said, was Italian.

Even as a connoisseur of the smaller stories, I acknowledge that the big stories do carry a certain impact. Officially, the files of the State Sovereignty Commission remain sealed until a lawsuit to open them is resolved. But the activity surrounding the suit has already dislodged formerly secret information that has resulted in front-page headlines about stories that made front-page headlines the first time around. It is now known, for instance, that an early black applicant to the University of Southern Mississippi who was convicted of several crimes and thrown into prison was framed; an alternative plan was to murder him. It is known that during the 1964 trial of Byron De La Beckwith for the murder of Medgar Evers, the Sovereignty Commission investigated potential jurors for the defense and furnished such capsule biographies as "He is a contractor and believed to be Jewish." It is known that the Sovereignty Commission got weekly reports from paid spies within the Council of Federated Organizations (COFO), the umbrella organization of the 1964 voter-registration effort known as the Mississippi Summer Project, and that it distributed license-plate numbers of COFO cars, including the one that Michael Schwerner and James Chaney and Andrew Goodman had been riding in before they were murdered in Neshoba County that summer.

In 1990, such stories, based on State Sovereignty Commission documents, ran for eight pages one day in the Jackson *Clarion-Ledger*, which reported not only that a black newspaper editor had been on the Commission's payroll—one of his duties was to run a story, furnished by the Sovereignty Commission, that linked Martin Luther King, Jr., to the Communist Party—but that the *Clarion-Ledger* itself had routinely killed stories that the Sovereignty Commission wanted killed and run stories that the Sovereignty Commission wanted run. According to a memo quoted in the *Clarion-Ledger* in 1990 by Jerry Mitchell, the reporter who revealed many of the Sovereignty Commission documents, the Commission had even prevailed on the Jackson newspapers to drop the honorific "Rev." from the names of ministers who were civil rights activists: "Our friends of the press could drop their titles from news articles and if queried they could say they do not consider them as ministers 'as how can a man profess to serve God when he is actually serving atheistic Communism?' "

For me, practically any document in the secret files of the State Sovereignty Commission has a certain resonance from the beginning of the sixties, when I was in and out of Mississippi as a reporter. I can now place the source, say, of a front-page Jackson *Daily News* item that I've kept all these years—an item that begins, under a four-column headline, "Mississippi authorities have learned that the apparently endless 'freedom' rides into Mississippi and the south were planned in Havana, Cuba, last winter by officials of the Soviet Union." Reading about Tom Scarbrough's fingernail inspection brings back into focus what I came to think of during my time in the South as a regional obsession with yard-sale anthropology. Any number of white people explained to me, for instance, that the brains of black people were capable of processing specific statements but not general or abstract statements. (My response was always "Give me an example.")

But as I go through the State Sovereignty Commission material now available, what I still find most interesting is how small a deviation from the Mississippi way of life was required to attract the attention of Scarbrough or one of his colleagues—a pastor's attendance at an interracial meeting or a professor's choice of a suspect textbook or a student's attendance at the wrong concert. That was the aspect of the Commission that had most fascinated me from the start— from the time in 1961 when I spent a few days in the state to look into revelations that the Sovereignty Commission had tried to smear a senior at the University of Mississippi named Billy Barton, who was running for the editorship of the Ole Miss newspaper, by spreading rumors that he was a protégé of Ralph McGill, the Atlanta newspaperman then widely considered by people outside the South to be the region's most distinguished journalist.

Because Barton's file became public and could easily be shown to be nonsense, the case provoked some weekly newspaper editors in Mississippi into criticizing the Commission as a sort of cornpone Gestapo that had gotten out of hand. But in 1961 the Mississippi State Sovereignty Commission had no reason to fear grumbling from a few county weeklies. It acknowledged, in a speech given around the state, that it kept a file on "persons whose utterances or actions indicate they should be watched with suspicion on future racial attitudes"—an estimated ten thousand people. It openly contributed five thousand dollars of taxpayers' money every month to the Citizens' Council—sometimes referred to as the uptown Klan—which claimed a membership of ninety thousand and was considered the most influential political force in the state. Several members of the Citizens' Council's executive committee also sat on the Sovereignty Commission, and some observers considered the Commission to be basically a device for providing the Citizens' Council with the resources and legitimacy of the state. Except for the smattering of editorials provoked by the Billy Barton case, there was little significant opposition to any of this. Partly through the economic intimidation that was the specialty of the Citizens' Council, most of Mississippi's small store of moderate and liberal whites had been silenced or driven from the state.

One of those who remained, an Ole Miss history professor named James W. Silver, wrote in the early sixties that "Mississippi is the way it is not because of its views on the Negro—here it is simply 'the South exaggerated'—but because of its closed society, its refusal to allow freedom of inquiry or to tolerate 'error of opinion.' " (Even before those words were printed in an influential book by Silver called *Mississippi: The Closed Society,* the director of the State Sovereignty Commission had written to the chairman of the university's board of trustees outlining what a Commission report described as "various reasons why Dr. James Silver could be terminated from his position at the University of Mississippi without any risk of losing the University's accreditation.") Being guilty of an error of opinion did not require a drastic deviation from the Mississippi mainstream: At the time, the Citizens' Council's definition of subversive organizations was broad enough to include both the Methodist Church and the United States Air Force.

Mississippi was the only place where a state agency saw its duty as coordinating all aspects of the effort to maintain white supremacy, including propaganda films, thought control, and baby inspection. A completely closed society in one out of fifty states was not possible, of course, but any effort in that direction had to include the attention to minutiae that I found so fascinating. In Mississippi, everything appeared to be under control. The segregation of the races was complete. Voting was essentially a privilege limited to white people. Until a sit-in at the Jackson public library by students from Tougaloo, a black college on the outskirts of town, the demonstrations then sweeping other Southern cities were not seen in Jackson. Those who ran the state operated as if the Mississippi way of life were invulnerable. The State Sovereignty

Commission was actually sending various prominent Mississippians to Northern service-club luncheons to talk about the tranquillity of Mississippi's race relations. The premise was not that the movement had not yet arrived in Mississippi but that it would never arrive.

In Alabama, the Freedom Riders, who came through a couple of months after the Billy Barton controversy, were attacked in Anniston and Birmingham and Montgomery; in Mississippi, residents lined the road as the bus passed, like an army under orders to stand down, and the Freedom Riders were politely arrested in the Jackson bus station for breach of peace. The next day, the Governor, Ross Barnett, welcomed the reporters who were covering the Freedom Ride, and the mayor of Jackson gave each one an honorary Jackson police badge. I still have mine. (There were three black reporters on the bus, and they had not been arrested. "Professional courtesy," the police chief explained.) Among reporters in the South, Alabama was considered more dangerous then, but Mississippi, where strangers might say hello on the street and ask you how you were enjoying your visit, was somehow more ominous. Sometimes, after working in Mississippi for a few days, I'd drive to Memphis to write my copy and send it out. When I called my office in Atlanta, I'd say, "I've slipped over the border."

BY 1964, WHEN PAUL B. Johnson, Jr., became Governor, the Mississippi monolith was beginning to show cracks. It had taken some serious hits, like the desegregation of Ole Miss, and there was enough activity by the race-mixers to make Johnson's term among the busiest four years in the State

Sovereignty Commission's history. Documents and reports and correspondence that the Commission routinely sent to Governor Johnson's office constitute the largest collection of Commission papers now accessible to the public. They were among the papers that the Johnson family donated to the University of Southern Mississippi, in Hattiesburg, and they were made accessible in 1989 through a state court order obtained by the *Clarion-Ledger*. The picture that emerges from the Paul Johnson papers is of a Sovereignty Commission staff, which was never very large, dashing around the state in an effort to spy on a voter-registration drive here and put an end to a boycott there. Still, as I went through the files in the W. D. McCain Library and Archives of USM one day not long ago, I found that the Commission always seemed to have time for missions of the baby-inspection variety. In 1965, for instance, Governor Johnson received a letter, written in longhand, from a couple in Biloxi. "Dear Governor Johnson," it began. "We regret to say that for the first time in our lives we need your help very badly. We are native Mississippians and are presently living in Biloxi. Our only daughter is a freshman at the University of Southern Miss. She has never before caused us any worry. However, she is in love with a Biloxi boy who looks and is said to be part Negro . . ."

"Your recent letter and your situation fills me with great apprehension," the Governor wrote back at once. "I am having this matter investigated to the fullest." Tom Scarbrough had already been dispatched to the Gulf Coast to investigate the lineage of the suitor—presumably under orders to exercise a level of discretion that would have made a close inspection of fingernails out of the question. In a three-thousand-word report, Scarbrough concluded that the young man was from a group of people in Vancleave, Mississippi, who were sometimes called "red-bones" or "Vancleave Indians"—people who had always gone to white schools and churches but had always been suspected by their neighbors of being part black. The possibility of arranging to have the suitor drafted—a solution hinted at in the letter from his girlfriend's distraught parents—was looked into and dropped when it became apparent that he was too young for the draft. I couldn't find any indication in the McCain Library files that the Sovereignty Commission was able to break up the romance, but in what other state in what other period of American history could parents of no great influence write to the Governor about a suitor they considered inappropriate and have the Governor get right on the case?

At the McCain Library, the people who brought me a library cart full of files and collected documents to be photocopied could not have been more helpful—a fact that I would have found unremarkable except that, not having been in Mississippi on matters concerning race since the summer of 1964, I still remembered the narrowed eyes and suspicious looks that, in those days, made me long for the moment when I could slip over the border. The University of Southern Mississippi is now integrated, of course. There are a thousand black students at Ole Miss, where the admission of one, James Meredith, once caused something close to an insurrection. If the librarians helping me had heard on the radio news that morning about a court ruling against a man who said he had been passed over for the job of Jackson chief of police because of racial bias, they probably hadn't been startled even for a moment by hearing later in the account that the man in question is white and the new police chief and the former police chief are both black.

Some of the people helping me with my copying weren't yet born in 1960, when W. D. McCain, the Southern Mississippi president after whom the library is named, went to Chicago to deliver a State Sovereignty Commission speech that said, among other things, "We maintain that Negroes receive better treatment and more consideration of their welfare in Mississippi than in any state in the nation" and "The Negroes prefer that control of the government remain in the white man's hands." Unless members of the library staff had reason to go through the files themselves, they would have no way of knowing that it was President McCain who received a memorandum from the director of the Sovereignty Commission dated March 2, 1964, with instructions on how to handle a black man who had announced that he was applying to the university. Confirming a conversation, the director wrote that McCain or his registrar should say to the applicant, "We have information that you are a homosexual. We also have sufficient information to prove it if necessary. If you change your mind about enrolling at an all-white university we will say no more about it. If you persist in your application, we will give this information to the press."

WHAT I HAD MISSED IN Mississippi was the transition. That took a while, the pace set partly by the gradual increase in registered black voters. In 1973, a Mississippi governor vetoed the appropriations bill for the State Sovereignty Commission, although his public explanation was not that its activities were wrong or silly but that they overlapped with the activities of other agencies. In 1977, the Commission, by then moribund, was finally abolished. That left the question of what would become of its files. This was only fifteen years after Mississippi university presidents were delivering Sovereignty Commission speeches in the North and bar-association leaders were presiding over Citizens' Council chapters in the Delta and virtually all Mississippi politicians were behaving in ways that black voters would have found distinctly unappealing. By an overwhelming majority, the Mississippi House of Representatives passed a bill that read, in part, "The Secretary of State is hereby directed to destroy the said files in their entirety."

A court injunction prevented that, and the legislature instead voted to seal the files for fifty years. The injunction was part of a suit to open the files, brought by the American Civil Liberties Union of Mississippi, among others, on behalf of all those who had been spied on or smeared or harassed by the Mississippi State Sovereignty Commission. The plaintiff's side was eventually joined by a collection of old comrades from the civil rights movement, including Ken Lawrence, the Mississippi director for an American Friends Service Committee project on government surveillance that had been one of the inspirations for the suit. There were also two white civil rights activists who had been faculty members at Tougaloo—Edwin King, the college chaplain, and John R. Salter, Jr., sometimes known in Jackson as "the mustard man" because of a noted newspaper picture in which he is shown covered with condiments poured on him during a lunch-counter sit-in. The suit has now been going on for eighteen years.

It was first heard by Federal District Court Judge W. Harold Cox, the most openly racist jurist on the federal bench. Judge Cox dismissed it on his own motion. There was a successful appeal to the Fifth Circuit, but in the six years until Cox's retirement little progress was made. In 1984, the judge who inherited the case, William H. Barbour, Jr., granted the plaintiffs the right to discovery, meaning that Ken Lawrence could read every bit of what had survived as the files of the Mississippi State Sovereignty Commission—eight filing cabinets full of documents, locked in a vault at the state archives. Lawrence, a white radical from Chicago who had spent many years in Mississippi, assembled photocopies in a twelve-volume plaintiff's exhibit, organized into nearly a hundred categories. Some of the categories were general, such as "Spying on Elementary School Curricula" and "Interference with and Denial of Voting Rights." Some were specific, such as "Investigating B'nai B'rith" and "Targeting Michael Schwerner" and "Spying on an Italian Filmmaker in Natchez."

In 1989, Judge Barbour decided in favor of the plaintiffs. He said that opening the files "would further the general principle of informed discussion of the actions of government, while to leave the files closed would perpetuate the attempt of the State to escape accountability." Those referred to in the files would have the opportunity to add corrective information, Judge Barbour ruled, and then the public would have the same access to the documents that it had to other papers in the state archives. At the time of Barbour's decision, the Governor and the Attorney General were young, reform-minded men who carried no baggage from the sixties; the Attorney General announced that the state of Mississippi would not appeal.

That would have been that, except that by the time Judge Barbour handed down his decision a split among the plaintiffs had divided them into two subclasses, which the judge called the access class and the privacy class. The access class, which represented those who wanted the public to have virtually unrestricted access to the files, included the ACLU itself and almost everyone else on the plaintiff side. The privacy class consisted of John Salter and Ed King, the two former Tougaloo faculty members. Their view was that unlimited access would be a way of recirculating the Commission's dirt—compounding the damage that the spying and smearing had done to innocent people in the first place. The privacy class appealed Barbour's ruling, and the Fifth Circuit directed Barbour to construct a plan that would protect privacy. The plan that Judge Barbour came up with included mechanisms by which victims of the State Sovereignty Commission—but not informers or people who had been acting for the state—would be given an opportunity to ask that their names be blocked out. Salter, who is now retired in North Dakota, dropped out of the case, but King appealed to the Fifth Circuit again. Because of that appeal, the case continues, and so does the disagreement between Ed King and the rest of the plaintiffs about just how much of the secret past needs to be uncovered.

"I DON'T THINK I'M EITHER insane or a traitor," Ed King said within a few seconds of our meeting. He is aware that people say that he must have something to fear from public access to the files, or that he can't bear to see the case end because he is still living in the sixties, or that he has simply gone over the edge. Ken Lawrence, who believes that opening the files is "a weapon of the struggle," makes no bones about considering King the enemy. "People assume that I couldn't be carrying on this fight on principle," King told me. "I must be covering something up." But among those who disagree with him there are some people who do believe that he is carrying on the fight on principle—that he is, in the words of one of them, "pure of heart." Even those people, though, are tired of looking at documents about the case that King has annotated. Even those people tend to respond to the mention of Ed King's name with a sigh and a rolling of the eyes. King is aware of that, too.

King's bitterest critics would not deny that he was an authentic hero of the civil rights struggle. He was an activist at a time when few white Mississippians would have publicly supported even the theoretical right of black people to demonstrate. King, who grew up in a conventionally segregationist family, tends to credit his apostasy to the Methodists—an indication that the subversion hunters of the Citizens' Council might have been, in their own special way, on the right track. He went to Millsaps, a liberal arts college in Jackson connected to the Methodist Church. The very fact that the Methodists had healed their Civil War split—unlike, say, the American Baptists and the Southern Baptists—meant that even in Mississippi, Methodists were exposed to a national-church point of view on race. Among the Paul Johnson papers at USM, I came across the report of a surprise visit to King's mother made by the State Sovereignty Commission director, who concluded from the conversation that one of two Millsaps sociology professors named in the report must have been the prime influence in transforming Ed King into a race-mixer.

To me, Ed King didn't sound insane—just highly fo-
cused. He has any number of specific problems with the privacy protections proposed by Judge Barbour. He thinks, for
instance, that insufficient distinction is made between "the
dirty spies who each week turned in their neighbors" and
someone who might have made a remark at a party which
found its way into a report after some phrase like "Information was received from . . ." He says that notification in
newspaper advertisements about how to arrange to have your
name blocked out would mean nothing to people who have
no reason to think that their names would be in such files in
the first place. What if, he says, a report on a black minister
who allowed COFO to use his church for mass meetings in
1964 includes the allegation that he had affairs with certain
women in the congregation? Why would those women, who
may have had nothing at all to do with the civil rights movement, think that their names might be in the files of the State
Sovereignty Commission? He says he will not be satisfied unless it is agreed to block out the name of everyone who could
be in any way considered a victim or a bystander rather than
an oppressor. He often repeats the simplest formulation of
his viewpoint: "We need to know what the government did,
but not to whom."

Whatever dangers unrestricted access would bring are,
of course, already present in the several years' worth of Sovereignty Commission documents accessible to anyone willing
to go to the McCain Library at the University of Southern
Mississippi and ask for the Paul Johnson papers. If the ready
availability of the Johnson collection since 1989 has caused
any instances of divorce or mortification or blackmail, they
have not become public knowledge. What I saw in the John-

son documents seemed to confirm what I'd heard from people familiar with the files as a whole: There is relatively little material that people would find personally embarrassing or damaging, particularly thirty years after the fact. One report from someone who spied for the Commission during the summer of 1964 says that the students occupying what the civil rights volunteers called Freedom Houses were especially careful not to engage in any behavior that would give the police an excuse to arrest them. In King's view, though, "if only a dozen people are affected, they have their rights."

I did feel uneasy about reading a few of the documents I saw in the McCain Library—a report that mentioned the treatment of one jailed demonstrator for a social disease, for instance, and a medical report that seemed to be a psychiatric workup of a young man admitted to the state mental hospital. On the other hand, I felt exhilarated by another document. It was the report of a spy in the COFO office that mentioned someone I knew—a woman who had come to the South even before 1964 to work with the Student Nonviolent Coordinating Committee. The spy, who was identified on his reports as "Operator #79," wrote, "The 'strong' females on the permanent office staff have told me earlier of a revolution among females, 'the women's fight for equality with men.' To the students, this is a deeply serious matter. I have watched it gain momentum over the past months. There are many male supporters of this new 'thing.'" My acquaintance was named as one of the new thing's ringleaders. I sent her a copy of the report. I figure that if she ever gets into a dispute with other feminists about who does and who doesn't have bona fides in the movement, the report that Operator #79 filed in July of 1964 will trump anything in the room.

* * *

THE LARGEST CHUNK OF COMMISSION documents to have surfaced during the litigation over access to the files was put into circulation by Erle Johnston, who happens to be the only surviving director of the Mississippi State Sovereignty Commission. In 1989, Johnston borrowed part of Ken Lawrence's plaintiff's exhibit from an unsuspecting legal secretary and headed straight for the copying store. Liberator of the files is an unusual role for a former director of the Sovereignty Commission to play—it might be assumed that the people who actually worked for the Commission would have a strong interest in keeping everything locked tightly in the basement of the state archives—but Johnston was an unusual Sovereignty Commission director. Although he succeeded a former sheriff and preceded a former FBI man, he himself was a former editor and publisher of *The Scott County Times,* in Forest, Mississippi. He has always been a man who tries to get along. A book he wrote on the period, *Mississippi's Defiant Years: 1953–1973,* includes testimonials from both William F. Winter, a relatively liberal governor in the early eighties, and William J. Simmons, the longtime administrator of the Citizens' Council. It also contains a tribute to Aaron Henry and Charles Evers, "the two most visible and aggressive black civil rights leaders in Mississippi during the 'defiant years'"—sort of in the spirit of a trial lawyer lifting a glass to his adversary after a particularly rancorous day in court.

Johnston maintains that he has nothing to fear from public access to the files, since they would portray him as a "practical segregationist" rather than an authentic hater. But he seems half resigned to being considered a villain. "I'm the only one left," he told me when I stopped by Forest to see him. "I'm the one they can point the finger at and say, 'There goes that monster.' " Anyone who wanted to defend or condemn Johnston's behavior at the Sovereignty Commission could find plenty of supporting material for either in the papers of Paul Johnson. This was in a period when thugs were beginning to crawl out of the cracks that had been made in Mississippi's confident defense, and there are reports in the USM papers showing that the Sovereignty Commission under Johnston's leadership quietly settled some confrontations before the dynamite-and-shotgun crowd could take over. There are papers reflecting the attempt of the Citizens' Council and its kookier cousin, Americans for the Preservation of the White Race, to get Johnston fired for suspicion of moderation. On the other hand, the USM files also show that it was Erle Johnston who wrote the University of Mississippi trustees trying to get James Silver fired and Erle Johnston, on a similar errand at Rust College, who sent the trustees a report smearing their president as "a known liar and ladies' man." The memo instructing McCain on how to blackmail an applicant to the University of Southern Mississippi into withdrawing his application was also signed by Erle Johnston.

It isn't likely that the files under court seal hold documents that would drastically affect the reputation of Erle Johnston, and what is true of him is thought to be true of most people who were well-known in what he calls the defiant years. Nobody I talked to in Mississippi believes that what remains secret includes many more front-page stories. Judge Barbour has estimated that three quarters of the papers locked away at the state archives have already been seen in one way or another. Also, it is taken for granted that some of the more explosive material gathered by the State Sovereignty Commission was long ago weeded out. Most of the segregationist politicians of that era are out of politics by now, or dead. The paucity of dramatic stories about prominent black people who were discovered to have been spies is such that one man who seems to have been an operative known as Agent X has been exposed in the media again and again. Among those familiar with the material, there is general agreement that a lot of what's in the files amounts to newspaper clippings and turgid essays ("Comments on 'Yesterday's Constitution Today,' a Textbook Taught at the University of Mississippi") and spying reports so mundane that they have the sound of the "Social Notes" column in a county weekly. Also, the Mississippi State Sovereignty Commission, like any other government agency, generated a lot of paper that had more to do with justifying next year's appropriation than with completing the job at hand. There are pages in the files, for instance, concerning Erle Johnston's efforts to bring about the firing of A. D. Beittel, a Tougaloo president who had been openly supportive of civil rights demonstrations; a week after Johnston flew to New York to put his case before Tougaloo trustees, it was announced that Beittel's contract would not be renewed. But the historian John Dittmer, who has studied the incident in some detail, is convinced that Johnston, finding out from a spy at Tougaloo that Beittel was going to be forced out, staged the campaign so that the State Sovereignty Commission could take credit—a theory that Erle Johnston has been only too happy to embrace. ("I was always looking for something I could do to satisfy the white power structure without doing something terrible.")

At times, the State Sovereignty Commission was indeed capable of forcing people from their jobs, but its predilection for sending large men to examine tiny fingernails can make it seem more ludicrous than ominous. A phrase that keeps popping up in current descriptions of its activities is "Keystone Cops." A passage in a 1964 report reflects the level of sophistication the Commission sometimes demonstrated in the area of Cold War skulduggery: "In order to receive regularly publications of communist front organizations and preferring that the Sovereignty Commission not be on their mailing lists, we made arrangement with John Kochtitzky, Jr., to be the subscriber and deliver the publications to our office each week. We wanted a name which sounded 'Russianish.'" In 1964, when the Commission began dealing with the Mississippi Summer Project volunteers, many of them students from first-rank Northern universities, reports from investigators and spies began to include sentences like "The Kirschenbaum boy said that he did not believe in Jesus Christ."

Of course, what sound like Keystone Cops antics now were probably not funny at all thirty years ago—certainly not to the Kirschenbaum boy if he was being questioned at the side of a lonely country road around dusk by armed officials of the state of Mississippi who wanted to know exactly what he had against the Savior. In those days, being called a Communist was also considerably less amusing than it might be now. It's difficult for anyone sitting in the McCain Library in 1995, several years after the end of the Cold War, to take seriously references to the role of the Red Menace in the events of 1964, when black Americans in Mississippi were routinely denied even the elementary American right to vote, and a number of people went to the state with the goal of helping to remedy that situation. But Communism was serious business at the time. A Mississippi politician who was asked why black people were not allowed to vote in his state might answer that certain people involved in the voter-registration campaign had once been to a meeting of an organization cited by the House Un-American Activities Committee as a Communist front. Case closed.

The civil rights movement itself was seriously split over the question of whether accepting the assistance of organizations that could easily be attacked as subversive was counterproductive, or perhaps even immoral. Association with such organizations could mean the loss of funding in the North, because the concern—some would say obsession— with Communism was national. It was the federal government, in the form of the Attorney General's office and congressional committees, that gathered lists of subversive organizations. In one of the clippings I ran across in Mississippi, Erle Johnston is quoted as saying that the State Sovereignty Commission "operated like a state-level FBI." That characterization seemed grandiose, given the Sovereignty Commission's penchant for bloodline inspections, but then I started thinking about what the FBI was up to at that time—bugging motel rooms in order to embarrass or blackmail Martin Luther King, Jr., gathering information on law-abiding citizens right down to the names of people they had spoken to at the high school reunion or the Hadassah dinner dance. Mississippi was not the only state government to keep secret files on its residents. *The Police Threat to Political Liberty,* the report that came out of the

American Friends Service Committee project on surveillance, has chapters not just on Jackson but also on Seattle and Baltimore and Los Angeles and Philadelphia.

In a way, the code phrases Mississippi used—"state sovereignty" for its system of white supremacy, "federal encroachment" for the national pressure to change—offered an accurate reflection of the situation. The Mississippi way of life was always vulnerable to contact with national institutions—the Methodist Church or the United States Air Force or the United States Court of Appeals for the Fifth Circuit. For many years, though, the pressure from Washington was not much more than nominal. Federal civil rights legislation was bottled up by a powerful bloc of Southern senators. The presidents in office in the decade after the *Brown* decision, when Mississippi was doing its best to run what James Silver called the Closed Society, did not treat the restoration of civil rights to black people in the South as a national priority. Dwight D. Eisenhower was identified with the view that you can't legislate morality. John F. Kennedy seemed to consider segregation a regional situation that was inconvenient mainly because it caused embarrassment overseas. Even Northern politicians who were particularly critical of Mississippi's single-race elections would not challenge their legitimacy, as Ed King and other delegates of the Freedom Democratic Party found out at the Democratic National Convention of 1964 when they tried to get seated in place of the all-white delegation from Mississippi. Reading through State Sovereignty Commission documents did not change my view that Mississippi had been sui generis, but it did remind me that the Closed Society had existed quite comfortably for years within the society of the United States of America. When I was in Mississippi in those days, I may have had thoughts of slipping over the border, but I was in my own country the entire time.

· · ·

The files of the Mississippi State Sovereignty Commission were officially released in 1998 and eventually became available online. As expected, the documents that had not already been seen did not trigger another spate of front-page news stories. Under the mechanism established by Judge Barbour, people who were not "state actors" could request that their files remain private. Forty-two people did that, including Ed King.

My own file was sparse—a single "Letter from the Publisher" feature from Time *that dealt mainly with some uncomfortable minutes I'd spent at the Montgomery bus station when the Freedom Riders arrived from Birmingham. I had to consider the possibility that those strangers on the streets of Jackson who had asked how my visit was going were simply being hospitable to someone who looked like he might be an out-of-towner.*

ABOUT THE AUTHOR

CALVIN TRILLIN has been a staff writer at *The New Yorker*, concentrating on reporting on America, since 1963, when the magazine published his account of the desegregation of the University of Georgia. His nonfiction books include the memoirs *About Alice* and *Remembering Denny*. He has also published comic novels, such as *Tepper Isn't Going Out,* and books of political verse. His humor writing has been collected most recently in *Quite Enough of Calvin Trillin.*

ABOUT THE TYPE

This book was set in Sabon, a typeface designed by the well-known German typographer Jan Tschichold (1902–74). Sabon's design is based upon the original letter forms of sixteenth-century French type designer Claude Garamond and was created specifically to be used for three sources: foundry type for hand composition, Linotype, and Monotype. Tschichold named his typeface for the famous Frankfurt typefounder Jacques Sabon (c. 1520–80).